Praise for *Paul: A Brief History*

C000137189

"*Paul: A Brief History* is a good guide
Paul.' But it is more like Jarosla
Centuries, whose subtitle is 'Jesus' place in the history of culture.
Robert Seesengood provides an accessible narrative of interpretations and manifestations of Paul's intellectual, religious, and
political influence on history. He offers a 'brief' though impressive
survey of the history of scholarship about Paul, and he unmasks
myths, legends, and popular images of Paul. This excellent
resource for undergraduate and seminary students will also be of
interest to non-specialist general readers and to biblical scholars."

David J. Lull
Wartburg Theological Seminary

"This outstanding and accessible book is a welcome and timely
contribution. At a time when writers beyond theologians and
biblical scholars have begun to examine Paul's thought and use
his perceived ideas to discuss contemporary philosophical issues,
this clear-eyed account and critique of the use (and abuse) of Paul
through the centuries opens for students and sharpens for scholars
the worlds of historical method and postmodern cultural critique.
With his skillful and judicious use of the tools of postmodern
historiography, Seesengood goes beyond telling what interpreters
said about Paul in various eras to showing why readers constructed
Paul as they did. This text is a rich addition to the study of Paul
through the ages and a paradigm for how to think about such
matters."

Jerry L. Sumney
Lexington Theological Seminary

Paul

A Brief History

Robert Paul Seesengood

A John Wiley & Sons, Ltd., Publication

Blackwell Publishing was acquired by John Wiley & Sons in February 2007. Blackwell's publishing program has been merged with Wiley's global Scientific, Technical, and Medical business to form Wiley-Blackwell.

Registered Office
John Wiley & Sons Ltd, The Atrium, Southern Gate, Chichester, West Sussex, PO19 8SQ, United Kingdom

Editorial Offices
350 Main Street, Malden, MA 02148-5020, USA
9600 Garsington Road, Oxford, OX4 2DQ, UK
The Atrium, Southern Gate, Chichester, West Sussex, PO19 8SQ, UK

For details of our global editorial offices, for customer services, and for information about how to apply for permission to reuse the copyright material in this book please see our website at www.wiley.com/wiley-blackwell.

Library of Congress Cataloging-in-Publication Data

Seesengood, Robert Paul.
  Paul : a brief history / Robert Paul Seesengood.
    p. cm. – (Blackwell brief histories of religion series)
  Includes bibliographical references (p.   ) and index.
  ISBN 978-1-4051-7891-4 (hardcover : alk. paper) – ISBN 978-1-4051-7890-7 (pbk. : alk. paper) 1. Paul, the Apostle, Saint. 2. Bible. N. T. Epistles of Paul–Criticism, interpretation, etc.–History. I. Title.
  BS2506.3.S44 2010
  225.9′2–dc22

                                        2009030387

A catalogue record for this book is available from the British Library.

Set in 10/12.5pt Meridien by SPi Publisher Services, Pondicherry, India
Printed and bound in Singapore by Ho Printing Singapore Pte Ltd

1   2010

Contents

Acknowledgments

There are certain conventional parts, rhetorical forms, to any book's "acknowledgments" section. Books on Paul seem to have their own sub-genre. I find myself rejecting, adopting, and adapting many of these conventions. For example, biographies of Paul often make a great deal out of how the authors threw themselves into the Greek text of Paul, avoiding other works of scholarship which might infect or corrupt any independent reflection. I have not. Though I have spent more than a few hours going over – again, and again – Paul's sometimes distracted Greek, I have wallowed in secondary scholarship, quaffing down great gulps of it at a time. This book is presented as a general "tourist guide" to that world of scholarship. I have left out much more than I include. It is written for the non-specialist, but I can't help feeling my colleagues' eyes reading over our collective shoulders. I hope that I have been representative and accurate. I hope I have provided a few thoughts that my colleagues will find worthwhile amidst the general introductions. Yet I have written mostly for those eager to learn more. I have not been, in any way, comprehensive. I can hope nothing more than that I have begun more questions than I can answer. I begin my acknowledgments with a deeply felt expression of gratitude to those centuries of scholars who have gone before me and about whom I write. Very few – if any – of my own ideas arose just from my own reflection.

A second convention is for the author to thank his competent midwives at the press, students, and scholarly colleagues. This one

I shall completely concede. Andrew Humphries commissioned this book and saw it through its initial proposal, first peer review, and adoption. When he moved on to other opportunities Rebecca Harkin put a steady hand to the helm; she is a remarkably kind and professional reader. Bridget Jennings and Lucy Potter also tended to the final stages of editing, peer review, and production. In all, everyone at Wiley-Blackwell has been superb. The initial ideas for this book began in a series of conference papers presented at the annual national and international meetings of the Society for Biblical Literature. I thank those conversation partners. In particular, thanks are due to Gail Streete, Dale Martin, and Jerry Sumney, who offered ideas, encouragement, and correction for more than a few errors. Sheila Nicole Woodlief, my undergraduate research assistant at the University of North Carolina-Pembroke, was a valuable aide in the last stages of editing.

Biographies of Paul often turn, in the end, to express thanks to communities of support. Here, I shall adapt. I omit thanks to a particular community of believers or a church and, in its place, would like to thank the faculty of the Department of Philosophy and Religion at the University of North Carolina, Pembroke, who politely listened to some of these early chapters in their regular faculty colloquia and offered their own insights, in turn. In particular, I am grateful to Merrill Miller and Jeff Geller. My current colleagues in the Religious Studies Department at Albright College have been, to a one, highly encouraging and patient. "Thank you," as well, to my students in New Jersey and North Carolina, who attended my various seminars on the Pauline writings. They pushed me to find clear ways to articulate the ideas found in Pauline scholarship; they also pushed against those ideas in ways that helped me see better ways of reading.

Abigail, you are always, indeed, a joy to me. Thank you for asking so often about the book. My wife, Jennifer Koosed, graced me with her legendary patience (particularly during the intensely busy days of the final edits). An extraordinary biblical scholar in her own right, she took time away from writing her own book during her sabbatical to read mine. A teaching scholar can pay no higher compliment or extend a richer gift. She is my first reader, and my last. Jennifer, I am better, in every way, because of your company. I love you.

This book has been written over a couple of tumultuous and busy years in my life. I will forever be grateful to my sister Gina and my aunt Mary for seeing me through and holding things together. (You're right, you know. Sunscreen and saltwater mix together into an epoxy just sticky enough, most days.) This book is what I was sneaking off to work on. Here it is, at last, a gift of thanks to the two of you.

Robert Paul Seesengood
Reading, Pennsylvania

Introduction: Meeting
Paul Again for the First Time

John Dominic Crossan and Jonathan Reed open their recent biography of the apostle Paul with the charming image of a simple, unassuming man walking into the main gates of one of the most bustling cities of the ancient world. They describe at length the grandeur of the city walls and gates, the hum of everyday traffic, the mixture of all sorts of languages and cultures. Passed by carts full of all sorts of commercial goods, surrounded by travelers, peasant and prosperous alike, their opening image is a tight shot of an ordinary, curious man walking into the city, taking in the new sights and sounds as if he were any other new arrival. Around him are conversations of others, whispered complaints about the government or shouted debates about contemporary news. Little did anyone realize, they suggest, how revolutionary this one traveler would prove to be in time. Paul arrives as if his teachings were a strange cultural and intellectual virus into the bustling port city of the early Roman empire, his coming unannounced, his impact only fully realized in time. Paul, almost innocent of his potential, had arrived at Philippi, bringing his message of Jesus Christ to European shores for the first time.

Crossan and Reed's "Paul," as he is presented in their biography, tends to fade into their general picture of the culture and context of the early Roman empire. Crossan and Reed focus far more on Paul's historical setting, noting the stark political changes in the world that surrounded him as well as the general conversation among Jews of Paul's day. They carefully and precisely reconstruct Paul's cultural and intellectual world – a highly valuable and commendable task. Yet Paul himself becomes so ordinary that he vanishes into the crowd. Paul appears for his cameo, the central figure in an establishing shot of the bustling traffic of an ancient Roman city gate; as Crossan and Reed pull back, Paul becomes lost.

In the late nineteenth century the scholar Ferdinand C. Baur wrote a different biography of Paul, in which Paul remained center stage. For Baur, Paul was a bitter, sickly, aggressive prophet of doom. Paul's message to his fellow Jews was a message of bitter recrimination. With the zeal and anger of one who was himself a convert, he called down curses on any Jew who refused to acknowledge Jesus as messiah. His message to non-Jews was only slightly better: the arrival of Jesus as God's messiah offered them hope, but also placed them squarely under the judgment of God. Though non-Jews now had access to God's mercy (the "good news"), they also desperately needed it, being subject to God's wrath as well (the less celebrated "bad news"). Where Jew and non-Jew met was a particular moment of tension. Paul, Baur asserted, taught that Jew and non-Jew alike had access to God via faith in Jesus. Exclusively. Neither Jew nor gentile was subject, any longer, to Jewish law or Torah. Torah had been trumped, made vacuous by an empty Jerusalem tomb.

For Baur, Paul's message of inclusion (and repudiation of Torah) put him squarely at odds with Jesus' earliest followers. Taking Jesus' own assertions that he did not come to "destroy the Law, but to fulfill it," these followers of Jesus, led by apostles such as James and Peter, advocated that non-Jews could come to God via Jesus, but only if they also adopted Jewish ritual practices. The showdown occurred in some of Paul's churches in what is now modern Turkey (then called "Galatia"). Some teachers loyal to James, Baur asserted, had come to visit Paul's churches in Paul's absence. They told the new believers that everyone needed to keep the Jewish ritual law, including food laws and circumcision. On hearing news of this, Paul dashed off an angry letter (what we now have in our New Testaments as "To the Galatians"). "Foolish Galatians," he writes, "who has bewitched you?" (3:1) "If anyone … even an angel from God teaches you another message of 'good news' than the one we first brought to you, may God damn him!

I say it again ... God damn him!" (1:8, 9) What follows is a long, somewhat paranoid tirade where Paul recounts his own commission for ministry, his independence from the apostles in Jerusalem, a report of a shouting match he held with Peter (and, presumably, felt he had won), and a long appeal to "scripture" and pathos to persuade the Galatian Christians to return to Paul's teachings. For Baur, then, Paul was an angry, often troubled, confrontational, self-appointed missionary of apocalyptic doom to the gentiles, squarely at odds with James and Peter.

In between these two pictures of Paul, both chronologically and intellectually, Sir William Ramsay devoted the bulk of his career to a study of Paul and his message in its context. Ramsay was relentless about establishing the intellectual "soil" of Paul's ancient world. Ramsay began his work on Paul as a classical studies scholar, uninterested in Christian theology. Indeed, he began his work with the assumption that the biblical accounts were so theologically motivated they could not provide a reasonable historical account. As he studied the New Testament book, the Acts of the Apostles (closely reading the text in its original Greek and against other ancient historical documents), Ramsay asserts that he became more and more convinced that Acts was reliable history. The book of Acts tells the story of Paul's early career in Judaism, his "conversion" to faith in Jesus, and his missionary career; roughly half the book is dedicated to Paul. In the end, he found himself intellectually compelled to accept Acts' picture of Paul. The rest of Ramsay's scholarly work from that pivotal point forward was either a study of Paul's message and missionary career or occasional surveys of the political and cultural world in which Paul worked.

For Ramsay, Paul was the consummate ancient intellectual, a brilliant and innovative scholar of the Bible. Paul was very much a man of his intellectual era. He had been schooled (Ramsay thought formally) in Greek philosophy and rhetoric. Paul brought these skills into his mission work and assumptions about Jesus. As Ramsay presents him, Paul's passion – arising from a direct encounter with the resurrected Jesus – led him to traverse the major cities of the eastern Mediterranean coast, finding communities of interested Jewish and gentile intellectuals and engaging them in debate about Jesus. Marshalling prodigious skill in Greek philosophical argument and fantastic knowledge of the Jewish scriptures, Paul, Ramsay thought, presented an overwhelming case for the messianic status of Jesus. Any opposition he encountered arose from the insincere (and threatened) minds of his audience. Confronted with a Paul they could not out-debate, Paul's opponents' frustrations turned to violence.

A fourth (and, for now, final) scholar, E. P. Sanders, presented his own work on Paul in the late 1980s and is largely credited (perhaps ambitiously) with sparking a "New Perspective" on Paul and his writings. Sanders was concerned about how contemporary pastors, churchfolk, and clergy were reading Paul. His major concern was how Christian communities were reading and understanding Paul's remarks about Judaism. Sanders argued that, led by the scholarship of the early Protestant theologian Martin Luther, modern Christians had drawn too sharp a separation between Paul's understanding of Jesus and theology of salvation by faith and grace, and Judaism's observance of ritual law (halakhah). Sanders argued that such readings were a distortion of Jewish law, reducing it to a system of legalistic righteousness – where people "earned" God's favor by being good and by keeping all the right rules. These readings diminished any sense of faith or hope in Judaism. Further, they understood Judaism as a crushing burden of impossible laws, producing people overcome with guilt and feelings of inadequacy before God. Luther countered this with a celebration of grace in Paul. God, through the work of Jesus, had overturned the system of law. Salvation now was achieved only through faith. The emphasis shifted to love and the sacrifice of God.

While this position is in part very comforting, Sanders argues first that it is based on a gross misrepresentation of Jewish law as presented in the Hebrew Bible (particularly in the book of Deuteronomy). The Bible never presents a doctrine of salvation of Jews based on their successful achievement of or observance of Jewish law. Indeed, quite the opposite occurs. Jews are "elected" or chosen by God simply because of God's love. As a result of their selection, they are given the law in order to publicly demonstrate their status as God's distinct people. Law is, then, a blessing, not a burden. Of course God would offer forgiveness under the law. The purpose of law was to create a "unique people," distinct from "the Nations" who would display God's love and glory.

Sanders next suggests this misunderstanding of Jewish law arose from a deeply ingrained anti-Semitism. Luther (and countless Christians afterward) had drawn a gross (and uninformed) caricature of Jews and Jewish law. This reading both influenced readings of Paul's letters and was "reinforced" by these misreadings. The critical mistake, Sanders notes (apart from interpretive bias and ignorance of Judaism), was "mirror reading" the letters of Paul. True, in many of Paul's writings, Paul is arguing that Jesus, even as the Jewish messiah, provided, via his death on the cross, salvation to all nations. True, as well, many of Paul's letters argue forcefully against compelling non-Jewish believers in Jesus to keep Jewish law. Sanders observes, however, that this is quite different from a blanket condemnation of Judaism or an assessment of Judaism as fundamentally inadequate for understanding God. Further, we must always remember that Paul's letters were written in the context of an argument. Were that not enough, we only have Paul's side. Perhaps many of his statements about the law would have been generally conceded. Does Paul mean "Mosaic law" every time he uses the word "law"?

Four different versions of Paul. Four different views about what Paul's major concerns were. Four different notions about the "center" of Paul's values. Four different ways of describing Paul's mission. In many ways, these views could be harmonized. In many other ways, however, they are incompatible. The point could, should space and patience allow, be drawn in even sharper contrasts. Biographies and articles on Paul written in the last century have identified the apostle as a homophobe, a closeted gay man, a loyal Jew, a rabbi, a marginal Jew, a self-hating Jew, a cosmopolitan and urbane member of the Greco-Roman world, a radical dissenter opposed to the Roman empire with an unmatched vigor, a man motivated by religious impulses and ideas, or a man motivated by political agendas (which he, very literally, "baptizes"). These complicated pictures of Paul are not only present in biblical scholarship. Think for a moment about the very different "interpretations" of Paul that we find in the popular culture around us. Consider, for example, the common image of Paul (stout-bodied, bald-headed, bearded, intense eyes, fleshy face) found in stained-glass windows. Compare this to the wild-eyed, shabbily dressed, disheveled, unkempt presentation of Paul in popular films (such as Scorsese's *Last Temptation of Christ*).

How can we account for so much diversity? How is it that so many pictures of Paul can be drawn? Even more, how is it that so many pictures of Paul can be drawn *and defended*? These various images survive (and attract attention, if not devoted followers) precisely because they can be defended from our evidence. How can a single body of evidence produce so many different pictures? If we were to answer quickly, we might say that this occurs because the biographers lack sincerity or qualification. Certainly, personal bias (and professional qualification) will effect the outcome of such a project. But it's too simple to suggest these are the only (or even the main) reasons.

In some ways, the situation is similar to the problems surrounding a sturdy biography of Jesus of Nazareth. The gospels in the New Testament certainly depict much about the life of Jesus, but much more is left out. Jesus in the New Testament is depicted in gospels that are, themselves, the products of over three decades of oral transmission, collected together by devoted followers, theologically motivated to present a picture of Jesus as messiah. While such writers can certainly produce works that enrich communities of faith in thousands of immeasurable ways, they hardly reach the standard of a scientific, detached historical presentation of "the facts." Indeed, there may well have been multiple ways of seeing Jesus, of understanding his work, in the ancient world. What would the "Jesus of history" be like? What could historians or objective biographers know about Jesus?

The problem was best articulated by a very young German scholar, Albert Schweitzer. Schweitzer surveyed the number of attempts at biography and found that there were key, often irreconcilable, differences. Each scholar came forward and presented his own view of Jesus. Each view was defensible. Yet each was unique. Schweitzer surveyed the data and found a central problem. We have no direct evidence from Jesus himself. All our information about Jesus has been filtered, second-hand, through others (each, in the process, constructing his own view of Jesus). The very polemic nature of the data produced a polemic reconstruction. As Schweitzer argued, later historians constructing "the historical Jesus" were forced to make value judgments of their own about what, among the data, "mattered," and how, within the process of history, the data "should" be evaluated. These decisions of the modern scholar were not value-neutral, nor were they conducted without personal bias. Indeed, Schweitzer found that most reconstructed "Jesuses" were very, very similar to the scholars who did the "reconstructing." Jesus was, again and again, addressing issues that were remarkably analogous (if not identical) to the issues surrounding the modern scholar. Jesus was, again and again, arguing in ways analogous to (if not identical with) the methods of the modern scholar. Jesus was, again and again, a re-creation of the modern scholar dressed up in historical garb. As Schweitzer famously observed, "we have looked down into the well of history, only to discover the face we glimpsed at the bottom was our own."

Some similar issues surround our data for Paul. One of the major concerns surrounding a "historical Jesus" is that our data all comes second-hand and from a much later period. Jesus himself never wrote a word. As with Jesus, we don't have much specific information regarding Paul's family (one source says he had a sister), about Paul's childhood, or even (unless we rely on much later Christian traditions) about his death. Still, one might hope for some more security with biographies of Paul. Unlike Jesus, we have much more immediate evidence for Paul. We have at least 13 extant letters that claim Paul as their author. Each of these letters claims to be directly from Paul's own hand.

So, we return to our initial question: why so *many* "historical Pauls"? The differences arise (in the largest part) for two reasons: (1) the nature of the evidence for Paul; (2) the various methodologies that govern how scholars view that evidence. Indeed, the problem isn't that we don't have information, it's that we have abundant, specific information, but the specifics are often in direct conflict. According to one New Testament book, for example, Paul makes multiple trips to Jerusalem after his conversion; Paul's own letter to the Galatians, however, says he did not go to Jerusalem until 10 years after his conversion. According to Galatians, Paul went to Arabia. Even a single document, the Acts of the Apostles, tells three different stories about Paul's conversion. A second problem is the nature of the data. Paul's letters are only one-way communications. What were the contexts of his writings? What insider information did he expect to share with his audience? What special controversies, arguments, ideas, inside jokes, cultural references, or personal history are in his letters? Finally, while we have several letters in the New Testament that claim Paul as their author, should we automatically assume that a letter claiming Pauline authorship was, in fact, written by Paul? Should we automatically assume that, if the letter is in the New Testament, it is authentic? The question becomes more interesting when we recall that there most certainly were ancient letters that claimed to be by Paul but that the church has rejected as forgeries.

In other words, the problem is what I have elsewhere called the "specific ambiguity" of our evidence for Paul. We do, in fact, have some wonderfully specific elements of biography (Paul's birth-place, the political context of his education, his "profession," the state of his health). But none of these elements is without some complication or puzzle; none of these elements can stand alone as decisive. Data that is specifically ambiguous is specific data that cannot be verified, or that lacks clear context.

Much like Jesus, the historical Paul that emerges is plastic. Scholars have to make choices about what evidence is authentic and what is not. Scholars fill in gaps in the evidence. Scholars make choices about conflicting points of evidence. Scholars reconstruct the historical, communal, political, and confessional context of the evidence (and, so, determine what the evidence "means"). In short, much like questors for the "historical Jesus," biographers of Paul, as modern scholars, must also "enter in" to the process in very unique (and intrusive) ways. I would also argue that the variety of "historical Paul(s)" that are constructed are, in part, also reflections of the scholars' own needs, agendas, and contexts. In many ways, a full, final picture of the "historical Paul" is impossible to retrieve.

Why, then, write yet another biography? And why title it "A Brief *History*" of Paul? One might expect "A Brief Biography." More than just a nod to uniformity within the series, the title for this book reflects a great deal about its content as well as about Pauline studies in general. This book will not survey the "life of Paul" per se, but the history of how Paul and his writings have been approached within Western Christianity. Paul's writings are intensely biographical. He draws his theology and ideology from his own experience and views his own life, his successes as well as his struggles, as both source and fullest explication of his theological ideas. Accordingly, subsequent scholarship has rooted any systematic approach to Pauline thought in Pauline biography. Each major move in the interpretation of Paul's writings has been attended by (either precipitating or based upon) a shift in Pauline biography.

In some ways, Paul has been more important for being the "principled" objector/reformer than for the specific content of his theology. Paul's letters represent him as a lonely but committed (and ultimately justified) resister of popular theological misconception within the community and of broad hostility from the world outside the community. Because of this, Paul has often been a role model for iconoclasts, and Pauline writings have served as the ideological "high ground" in battles over Christian identity and stable theological development.

Pope Benedict XVI declared the Christian year 2008–9 to be "the year of Paul." According to Catholic Christian tradition, this celebration marked 2,000 years since the birth of the apostle Paul, an early advocate of Jesus of Nazareth as messiah. Paul is identified as author of 13 of the 27 books found in the New Testament, and these writings form the basis for several key Christian doctrines. For nearly 2,000 years, scholars, theologians, pastors, and lay persons have pored over Paul's letters, trying to tease out his larger meaning and gain an impression of Paul the man.

Paul: A Brief History is a survey of scholarship on the apostle Paul from ancient Christianity to the modern day. The book is written for beginning students to provide a synopsis of major interpreters of Paul and Paul's influence on Western Christianity. In many ways, how readers interpret Paul's letters arises from how they understand the life and career of Paul himself. We will see scholars' reconstructions of Paul's biography – biographies of Paul vary widely. The array of views about "the historical Paul" reflect the location and needs of later scholars. Since this book is written for non-specialists (and is, as the title suggests, striving to be "brief"), I will not be able to survey every interesting or important person in Pauline scholarship. At times, I have reduced Pauline scholarship of an era to one particular theme, or perhaps two contrasting themes. Finally, I have made an effort to aggressively (but, I hope, accurately) simplify complicated debates, terms, and arguments. Individual scholars have been selected for closer attention because they exemplify a particular point being made. This book is intended as a "guidebook" or map. It is designed to awaken questions and discussion as much as to offer summaries written in a scholarly "end-of-the-matter" voice.

The first chapter offers a survey of the Pauline writings themselves and the problems scholars face in interpreting them. It opens with a quick sketch of "Paul" to orient ourselves. Next, it reviews several scholarly assumptions and methodologies that are needed to construct that view. Finally, it turns to the actual data. It organizes Paul's letters into their various chronological orders, provides a brief sketch of the churches and individuals who served as their audience, and outlines briefly the major contents and themes of each letter. There will be an additional survey of what the book of Acts presents about Paul and of the noncanonical sources for Pauline biography.

Chapter 2 deals with Paul's reception in the early church. Beginning with the controversy surrounding Paul in the first century, the chapter will also include the appropriation/interpretation of Paul by controversial figures in the second century (particularly Marcion) and the development of the Pauline school of interpreters (largely responsible for both manuscript preservation and the composition of the pastoral letters). It addresses how some early Christian scholars (such as Tertullian) almost gave up on Pauline thought completely, given its usefulness to "heretical" theologies, and how other early Christians wrote additional stories and romances about Paul in order to harmonize his thinking and "tame" the unruly apostle. The chapter then turns to how other early Christian writers, exemplified by Ireneaus of Lyons and Origen of Alexandria, sought to mainstream Paul's writings via standardized techniques of scholarly interpretation.

Chapter 3 reviews Paul in late antiquity. It surveys how early writers and theologians developed their doctrines of anthropology, soteriology, and ecclesiology from the Pauline writings. It also observes how Pauline literature (in collaboration with Johannine themes) became key for notions of a universal "church triumphant." Paul's language became the basis for the exclusion of Judaism and the development of Christian theologies of ethnicity, and two contrasting images of Paul – Paul the intellectual and Paul the mystic – began to develop in Christian literature. The chapter concentrates on how two key figures, Augustine and Pseudo-Dionysius, interpreted Paul and exemplify a dual development of Pauline biography.

Chapter 4 explores Paul in the medieval period. Paul's language in 1 Corinthians was pivotal for the development of doctrines such as transubstantiation. Paul became, to many medieval writers, a role model for monastic intellectualism, asceticism, and for medieval views of the spiritual reality of the everyday world. The chapter explores the role of Pauline theology and mysticism that led toward later themes and concerns found in the Reformation, particularly in central Europe.

Chapter 5 focuses on the role of Paul in the literature of the Protestant Reformation, with heavy attention on the figure of Martin Luther, one of the most important interpreters of Paul in Western Christian thought. This chapter looks at how Paul was used by Luther, noting how Luther positions himself (the man of reformation and "faith") against the church structure of his day, which he described metaphorically as the "legalistic" Jew. The chapter notes the heightened context of developing anti-Judaism that emerged at this time, as well as the economic notions of soteriology that developed (recalling, as well, the cultural climate of a financially expansive Europe).

Chapter 6 explores Paul in the context of the eighteenth- and nineteenth-century development of "higher criticism." Pauline authorship and the integrity of the Pauline writings were critical questions forming an early locus of concentration in higher critical study in Germany. Much of this pitted a liberal, progressive academy (a community, in many ways, directly descended from Luther's own models of private, individual inquiry) against a popular church community. With advances in "science" steering both biblical inquiry and general cultural shift (particularly with tensions between science and religion sparked by Darwin), Paul's radical self-positioning was, ironically, also taken up in a variety of liberal academic contexts, and even in the nationalistic politics of central Europe. Yet Paul was also a vital figure for a growing interest in Christian missionary movements, and advocates of these movements also argued for a historical reading of Paul. Contrary to the academics, they insisted on a historically reliable New Testament and an image of Paul the missionary that authenticated their own desires for colonial evangelism. The chapter concludes its review of Paul's influence on the era of colonialism with an exploration of how various readings of his letter to Philemon affected debates about the morality of slavery.

Chapter 7 explores Paul in the twentieth century, noting in particular how scholarship first questions the location of anti-Semitism in Paul as well as how prior scholarship has tended to isolate him from his own cultural and political world. The chapter explores the development of Pauline studies post-Krister Stendahl to include the much-discussed "New Perspective" on Paul.

The book concludes with an overview chapter that explores some summary themes from the prior survey. The "historical Paul" has shifted according to the cultural and ideological location and needs of the scholar. A brief survey of the variety of "historical Pauls" present in modern scholarship (not to mention those available from historical survey) will demonstrate the lack of coherence among scholars as to who "Paul" might have been. Casting real doubts on whether a genuine Paul can be located, the conclusion highlights, instead, the ways in which he has contributed to the development of theology in the West, both positive and negative. It stresses as well the importance of ethics in Pauline historiography; since we cannot locate with final certainty an objectively constructed "historical Paul," the ethical implications of our own scholarly quests become paramount.

Chapter 1

What Do We Know About "Paul," and How Do We Know It?

In some ways, we know a great deal about Paul, particularly given what history often records about most individuals. Most of the ordinary people of any era vanish without any trace. For example, we know little more than the names of the majority of the 12 men who the New Testament gospels say were chosen as apostles by Jesus. Yet, despite what seems, at times, like an embarrassment of biographical riches, telling the story of the "real Paul" of history can be surprisingly difficult. This chapter will be an overview of what data we have about Paul and some of the issues that arise when scholars try to tease a biography of him from that data. I will open with a brief sketch of my own of his career, noting how the New Testament picture of Paul differs somewhat from popular memory of him enshrined in stained glass and vivid icons. Next, we will turn to the problems inherent in our data and five major assumptions that affect how scholars review that data. We will next examine some questions that surround the authority of our data, and end with a survey of the canonical letters. By the end, I hope it will be clear that biographies of Paul must resolve very complicated questions that arise from the nature of the data and the history of its preservation. Were this not enough, personal assumptions and biases will, inevitably, color how we make sense out of what evidence we have. The major cause of scholarly disagreement over Pauline biography is the nature of the evidence and the process of historical inquiry itself.

Who Is "Paul"?

Paul, also known as Saul, was a Jewish man who lived in the first century of the Roman empire. He was born in Tarsus, located on the southern coast of modern Turkey. Paul believed that Jesus of Nazareth was the Jewish messiah ("anointed one") foretold in the Jewish scriptures. He traveled to several cities of the Roman world declaring this message, teaching, and writing. He refers to himself as an "apostle" of Jesus. The Greek word *apostolos* means a person sent under a commission as a herald or ambassador. Paul wrote several letters in a dialect of Greek called Koine, which was commonly used in the eastern Roman territories. Many of these letters are preserved in the New Testament. These collected letters are often referred to as the Pauline *corpus* (Latin for "body"; here: "body of work"). Later Christians awarded Paul the status of saint for his role in the growth of ancient Christianity.

Tradition and confession remember Paul as a vigorous mind and body, intrepidly traveling the world with the message that Jesus was the messiah. Paul is remembered as a powerful preacher, a bastion of rational thought, an expert biblical interpreter, and a tireless worker. He is remembered as a founder of churches and a wise and caring pastoral voice who nurtured the care and growth of these bodies. He is remembered as a prolific author.

Virtually all of these assumptions do not hold up to close reading of Paul's letters. Within his letters, Paul often remarks about his own fragile state of health. His illnesses were often observed by others, and he seems genuinely moved when the horrors of his physical condition do not evoke contempt. Indeed, he frequently seems to be physically ill. Scholars have suggested a variety of ailments – malaria, vision problems, tumors, even epilepsy. Paul's illnesses may have often hampered his travel plans (and his needs for convalescence may have caused the sense of isolation and separation that is expressed in many of his letters). Paul often writes of his toils and labors, and the fatigue in his words is palpable. We can be very sure: he was very often tired and taxed to the very limits of his own body.

As a world traveler, Paul didn't really get very far afield. Even allowing a certain provincialism that would understand the

Roman empire as constituting "the whole world," there is little evidence that he saw much of that empire by modern standards. The overwhelming majority of his career seems to have been spent in the large cities on the coast of the Aegean Sea. Records indicate that he made one trip to Rome and planned a trip to Spain, yet he most likely only arrived in Rome at the end of his life and never made it to Spain at all. While it is true that travel in Paul's day (particularly travel largely by foot) was more time-consuming and difficult than travel in our modern world, and, indeed, Paul did certainly cover a great deal of territory, we should very much scale back our historical memories; most of Paul's travel was limited to a range of about 600 miles. Paul's legendary literary prowess also turns out to be mostly legendary. We currently have only 13 letters that have serious claims as authentically Pauline. We have indications that there were perhaps two others. Again, in some comparative terms (the number of letters extant from the general citizen of the Roman world), Paul is well documented. Yet Paul's career may well have lasted for three decades. That would equate to about 500 words every other year. In comparison to other collected letters from antiquity (such as those of Seneca or Cicero), Paul wasn't much of a correspondent.

Reading his letters is perhaps another jolt. Paul actually cites and interacts with biblical text (the Jewish Bible) comparatively seldom. And when he does, in more than a few places his treatment of biblical text, though creative and innovative, would often fail modern standards for "reading in context." In terms of rhetoric and logic, Paul himself notes how often he was criticized for being plain of speech and simple in style (1 Cor. 2:1–5; 2 Cor. 10:1). While downplaying one's rhetorical skill is, itself, a rhetorical move, Paul's prose in his letters often bears sad testimony to how true this self-deprecation might be. Paul's grammar and style, when compared to those of other writers from antiquity, are crude and without embellishment. His logic is, more than once, a bit strained. Indeed, in his writings logic is, more than once, completely abandoned. Paul is not exclusively rational and logical. He has frequent outbursts of anger and emotion. He has a sharp tongue and is not above profanity; he considers his past achievements to be worth "crap" when compared to his present mission (Phil. 3:7–8). He relates his own personal acquaintance with mystic visions, charismatic celebration, and prophecy.

Perhaps most shocking is what his letters reveal about his churches.

To begin, our notion of "church" needs serious modification. Paul always refers to his communities as "the saints," or "the elect," or the "called out" (*ecclesia* in Greek, a word meaning a body summoned together for a purpose). The terms "Christian" and "church" were not yet standardized. "Christian," when first used, was used by outsiders to refer to the early movement; it was probably intended to be an insult (Acts 11:26, 26:28). These communities were not large, by any definition. They were mostly small collections, perhaps of a half-dozen family groups (or fewer) that met, scattered in individual homes. There were no central buildings where members from across the city regularly met. There were no formal and standard hymnbooks. There was no New Testament. Many assemblies might not have had access to copies of the entire Hebrew scriptures in Greek translation. While there was doubtless some affiliation between groups, there is also strong evidence of inter-group rivalry and hostility.

One particularly acute issue that plagued the early community was how non-Jews (called "the nations" or "gentiles") were to respond to Jesus as the *Jewish* messiah. The earliest followers of "Rabbi Jesus" disagreed over precisely how (or even if) Jesus was the promised "messiah," a figure come to redeem Israel and restore her fortunes before God. Among many disputed ideas (that the messiah would be a physical king, a military leader, a reforming priest), one central question involved the relationship of gentile and Jew post-messiah. Numerous passages from the Hebrew Bible were read as predicting that the arrival of the messiah would initiate a "new age," a golden age of divine rule and the re-establishment of the Jewish people. A central aspect of this new age was a rush of gentiles to God's authority. Zechariah movingly wrote of a new age when gentiles would "tug at the sleeve" of Jews going to Jerusalem for worship, begging to be allowed to come along (Zech. 8:23). Isaiah asserted that "the Nations" would pour into Jerusalem to worship God at the Temple (Isa. 2:2, 56:6–8, 66:18). The "wealth of the nations [gentiles]" would pour into the Temple stores as votive offerings from around the world, given in stunned devotion to the messiah, who had arrived (Isa. 60:4–7, 61:6, 66:12–14; Hag. 2:6–9). The glory of God, displayed by God's use of the messiah to restore God's chosen people, the Jews, would be so demonstrably present in the world that the gentiles would cast aside their "idols" in contempt and madly rush toward Jehovah in devotional frenzy.

Paul certainly seemed to share these hopes, as did a host of other early figures who traveled the world teaching about Jesus in synagogues around the empire. Yet Paul's thought also seems to have contained a key difference from these teachers. For Paul, the decision to follow Jesus was open to gentiles as gentiles, without any need for conversion to Judaism or any adoption of Jewish ritual, kosher regulations, or initiation (particularly circumcision). Others, however, seem to have agreed that the gentiles would flock to Jehovah, in awe of the messiah, but that they would do so by *themselves becoming Jews* and following all the customs and rituals of Judaism. The difference could not be more dramatic. In essence, Paul is saying that the inclusive embrace of the messiah was meaningless if it could not embrace gentiles as gentiles. For his opponents, the very notion of messiah (the anointed by God according to *covenantal promises* made by God to the Jews) was meaningless if it erased Judaism in practice and form. These latter missionaries, to make the matter more acute, seem to have come from Jerusalem and enjoyed the imprimatur of some of the earliest followers of Jesus himself (Peter and James).

Paul refers to the other missionaries as "Judaizers" who operate with the endorsement of "super apostles" (Gal. 2:4, 14; 2 Cor. 11:5, 12:11). He defends, often, his own status (one that seems, indeed, to be self-appointed: the result of a private vision of the resurrected Jesus) as an authentic "apostle" himself (2 Cor. 11:16–29; Gal. 1:11–24; Phil. 3:2–11). He also answers direct challenges to his Jewish credentials. More acute, however, he becomes bitterly angry at the thought that these other teachers come behind him to "his" churches (in his absence) and teach new ways of understanding the messiah (Gal. 2:4, 5:10–12 – note the extreme anger of verse 12). Even more alarming, they seem to have presented a compelling case; many of Paul's writings are to churches that are wavering on the fence of abandoning him (if not already more than a foot or two to the other side: Gal. 1:6–10). Were this not enough, Paul's authority was often challenged for completely different reasons. Within the first century, some in Paul's early communities seem to have had little hesitation in simply disagreeing with his views of ethics or of the meaning of the messiah, or the need to be involved in many of Paul's various programs.

One project in particular was clearly more important to Paul than to some of his churches. Paul seems to have come up with a program to ameliorate relations between his congregations and Jerusalem. He wanted to gather a collection of monies from various non-Palestinian communities as a contribution to the Jerusalem church (other Christian documents indicate that Jerusalem was in the midst of a famine). His motives were complex. In one way, he may well have been hoping to fulfill expectations that the "wealth of the nations" would flood into Jerusalem in the messianic age. In another, he may also have been attempting to achieve both harmony and personal credibility with the leaders of the Jerusalem church.

In Paul's letters we can trace the development of this program. He collects monies from some churches (Philippi). Some churches (Thessalonica) want to contribute, but are themselves in financial duress. The church at Galatia (site of his sharpest debates with the "Judaizers") seems to be absent from the program altogether (perhaps having abandoned Paul and taken on the teaching of his "opponents"?). His "wealthiest" church, Corinth, is remarkably hesitant. Indeed, it may have even made suggestions that Paul was intending to use the money for other purposes (2 Cor. 12:14–13:4).

And so we see the Paul that emerges from his letters. In his own day he was not the final voice of authority to the early community. Many other voices actively disputed with him. These alternate voices may have been much more persuasive. They may well have possessed all that Paul lacked: a formal, documented relationship with Jerusalem and the earliest followers of Jesus; a reasoned and persuasive use of Hebrew scriptures; polished skills in speaking and writing; an effective and widespread mission program and campaign strategy; good health. Perhaps the most jolting alteration to the image of Paul preserved by piety is that his letters did not carry a QED quality of final argument. In fact, more than a few times, Paul may well have "lost" the immediate debate.

To make matters even more tense, Paul's early history certainly factored into his relationships among early believers. He describes himself as a Pharisee (Phil. 3:5). According to one ancient source, he was trained by one of the most famous rabbis of his day, Gamaliel (Acts 22:3). When the early Jesus movement began in Jerusalem, Paul was an opponent. He describes himself as a persecutor of early believers (Gal. 1:13). One can scarcely imagine an individual willing to resort to physical intimidation of others as an individual who would not also be aggressive in argument against the same. Following his vision experience (again according to Acts [9:1–19], an event on the Damascus road) of the risen Jesus, Paul radically realigns to support the new movement (though as a self-appointed, iconoclastic devotee). In other words, he was viewed with anger and suspicion by both communities. To one group, he was a deserter. To the other, he was a famous persecutor. Surely, some in both camps doubted that Paul's "conversion" was genuine.

So, turning our eyes away from the beautiful images of Paul found stained-glass windows, and toward the black and white of the New Testament text, we see Paul in the ancient world in much more "human" illumination. For many, Paul is a larger-than-life hero. It can be hard to remember he was human, too. He faced a series of very real frustrations, disappointments, and discouragements in his lifetime. Like any person, he had his foibles and failings. Often ill, often broke, often criticized as an outlier, often seen as a traitor, often irrational, often freewheeling in his use of the Bible, often acerbic, often alone, often feeling abandoned, Paul staggered around the Aegean, intent on a mission. His first churches, like Thessalonica, were struggling. His most "established" churches, like Galatia, abandoned him for other teachers. His most cosmopolitan churches, like Corinth, argued with him and may well have split. His program for reunification (a financial outpouring from gentile to Jew) turned out to be something far, far less than his grand plan. Bloodied but unbowed, Paul determined to make a new start. He wrote to Rome, introducing himself and implicitly requesting financial and personal support for a planned trip to Spain (Rom. 15:23–4). To his Cilician, Greek-speaking, Roman–Jewish mind, Spain was the limit of his imaginable world. Paul wanted to make this move because he felt that "there is no more room to work" on his side of the Aegean (Rom. 16:24).

Sifting the Data: Five Starting Assumptions

As I wrote in the Introduction, Pauline biography is notoriously varied. I've suggested that scholars tend to craft an image of Paul that reflects modern concerns more than ancient realities. Can we now, so easily, create a "new biography" of Paul, one that is fully resonant with the outline I have just traced? Probably not. While it is clear (and nearly unanimous) that popular memory of Paul needs modification, the biography I have just traced, sketchy as it may be, is still, in virtually every aggregate element, under dispute among Pauline scholars. The differences of opinion arise from different views of both our extant data and the best methods for interpreting and evaluating that data.

For example, I am assuming certain reconstructed contexts of the Pauline letters. I am assuming that some elements they describe are historically accurate. Also, I am reading these sources in a particular, assumed, sequence and pattern. I am assuming that modern, popular elements of biography need to be read (or, even, for the moment, that they *can* be read) against an ancient context; I am assuming certain ways of critically reading biographies and biographical claims. Finally, notice the sources I use (and, more particularly, those I don't). I am reading with a basic assumption that modern, theologically driven impressions carry a burden of proof (and are not, prima facie, beyond challenge). Each of these assumptions merits closer consideration.

Assumption 1: The Nature of Paul's Letters

One of the first and most fundamental points to consider when reading the writings of Paul is that these are all letters. Scholars illustrate how Paul used standard forms from antiquity. Modern letters open with a salutation ("Dear Jennifer"), then present the body of the letter or the letter's main point ("I'll be home by 6 for dinner. Don't start without me!"), and ends with a closing signature ("Love, Rob"). Ancient letters have these elements (among others) but in different locations. Perfectly following convention, Paul (and, most often, his "co-authors") identifies himself as author at the letter's inception (often in the very first word as in Rom. 1:1; 1 Cor. 1:1; 2 Cor. 1:1; Gal. 1:1; 1 Thess. 1:1; Phil. 1:1, etc.). He then moves on to a greeting identifying his audience and often setting the themes for the letter that is to follow. He concludes with a series of greetings and personal notes (and sometimes another signature). Ancient rules of rhetoric and "literature" often added (or recommended) other forms or set structures, and Paul uses these from time to time as well. But his basic skeleton is the conventional ancient letter.

Paul's letters, however, are long when compared to most of our surviving examples of ancient correspondence. In many ways, his writings are more belles-lettres – collections of "letters" which are really personal essays, intended for a public audience and for close, philosophical reading and reflection – than ordinary notes. Paul's letters are more similar to collections of letters by Seneca or Cicero than to brief exchanges of news or pleasantries. That point granted, however, the letters of Paul are still very much one side of a situational moment of dialog and correspondence. While Paul's letters are often written for public consumption, they still reflect a whole host of "insider" moments and information. We have to realize that each and every letter arrived in a congregation filled with personalities we have never met, possessing a unique history we no longer remember, struggling with problems and issues we no longer care about, torn by painful struggles we could never imagine, and surrounded by a pop culture (the Greco-Roman world) we can only barely retrace. How many inside jokes are lost on us? What veiled references to a common past are we missing? When is Paul teasing? When is Paul being insulting? When is he addressing real questions? When is he addressing hypothetical cases? What conditions or rituals does he assume (or describe)? When is he making references to popular sayings, culture, art, etc.? Isn't it possible (better: likely) that we will misread something that is written, fail to notice something that wasn't (but was clearly implied), or misconstrue an entire subtext?

In other words, we must always remember that we are only "dropping in" on one half of a complex conversation. We're overhearing a theological, personal, political, and pastoral conversation being conducted over a mobile phone by a guy in the next row whom we've never really met, who's from a place we've never been, talking about issues we've never faced, and, for the record, using a language we didn't grow up speaking. We're missing more than we're getting. Were all this not enough, there is evidence that Paul was responding to letters sent to him (which we no longer have), wrote other letters (which we no longer have), and may have co-authored many of the letters we do.

Scholars must make assumptions about the context of each and every sentence of each and every letter of Paul. Though guided by data (and, hopefully reasonable), no reconstructed context is ever, demonstrably, final.

Assumption 2: The Sequence of the Letters and the Development of Pauline Thought

Paul's letters have a number of very specific elements. Oddly, none of them makes reference to a single date or precisely datable event. In a few cases, Paul makes reference to people we might (I underscore *might*) know about outside the New Testament. In Romans 16:23, he mentions an associate named Erastus who was a city treasurer. In the late 1920s, archaeologists found an inscription from first-century Corinth that mentions a man named Erastus who was an elected official of the city. Generally, however, Paul's letters float freely in time and space.

A seemingly benign point, this element of his work makes any reconstruction of Pauline chronology in any but the most generic terms extraordinarily difficult and perpetually tenuous. Paul often gives glimpses or guesses as to his whereabouts, but rarely anything specific. For example, he is clearly in prison when composing Philippians (Phil. 1:12–14). But where, when, and for what offense? He refers to the "Praetorian Guard" (the elite, personal army of the emperor); does this mean he's in Rome? If so, is this his final imprisonment? Is he literally in shackles, or is the phrase "in chains" a metaphorical way of describing guarded custody (as we see at the end of Acts)?

The effect of the timeless nature of Paul's letters is to make them seem "of a moment" and static. Many readers of Paul find this outside-time quality to be an invitation for an immediate, almost mystical connection. In the New Testament canon, Paul's letters are ordered in two sections: public letters to general audiences ordered from longest to shortest (Romans to 2 Thessalonians); private letters to individuals, again ordered from longest to shortest (1 Timothy to Philemon). The effect is that Paul's latest, longest, most developed and sophisticated letter, his letter to the Romans, is the first in our series, appearing hot on the heels of the Acts of the Apostles, which presents Paul as a rational, reasoned, and passionate missionary to the gentiles. Paul's truly strange letters, 2 Corinthians and Galatians, do not appear until later. His most pessimistic letter, Philippians, does not bring up the end of the series. Indeed, the "final word," his letter to Philemon, is optimistic and leaves Paul patiently awaiting resolution to his legal troubles.

The canonical order of Paul's letters conceals any development of his ideas and arguments. Did Paul's thinking about Jesus or the role of gentiles in the messianic age modify or develop over time, possibly as a result of conflict with his churches or opponents? For example, 1 Thessalonians is considered by nearly all scholars to be Paul's first letter, in fact, the first ever written document by a follower of Jesus. In this letter, he addresses a church that is clearly suffering and under pressure to abandon its faith. The Thessalonians have accepted Paul's message that Jesus was the messiah and that a new age has arrived, but their problems have not ended. Their troubles haven't ceased; they've increased. The Thessalonians seem to feel betrayed by the absence of a "cure all" and the delayed return of Jesus. Is this a result, in part, of Paul's early missionary teaching? Did a young, exuberant Paul oversell points – perhaps that the world would end soon and that Jesus would return at any moment? Did he learn from this and nuance his language in his later preaching? Reading the letters chronologically, the problem of too much excitement over the world's end doesn't seem to be addressed again in them. Paul's views about a number of issues (the consumption of meat, the value of circumcision, the role of government, even the role of the messiah) seem, from letter to letter, to change. Did they develop? Were his teachings nuanced by experience?

Many scholars have attempted to construct a chronological sequence to Paul's letters. We look for increasing sophistication of argument, correspondence to other data about Paul's missions (corresponding with the chronology of Acts for example), and a few specific points, such as the ongoing saga of Paul's collection program for the Jerusalem saints. Plans for a trip to Jerusalem run through Paul's late career. This planned trip is repeatedly mentioned in Acts 19:21, 20:16, and 21:7–14. When these are all matched with Romans 15:22–33 and most likely Galatians 2:10, we have the full picture. Paul wanted to collect money from his gentile churches to take back as an offering to Jerusalem. Curiously, Acts omits explicit mention of the collection of funds. This collection was among Paul's final acts as a free man. He rounded up funds on a final preaching tour around the Aegean, then arrived at Jerusalem. According to Acts 21, however, Paul was arrested within weeks of his arrival and delivery of the monies. After a series of trials (and changes of venue), he made an "appeal to Rome" (Acts 25:1–12; Roman citizens had the right to have any criminal charges adjudicated in the city of Rome itself). Scholars often "follow the money" to establish some sequence to Paul's letters. Finally, informed guesses or "gut instincts" almost inevitably play a role in fixing a sequence.

There are multiple reconstructions, but one of the more common series is 1 Thessalonians, Galatians, 1 and 2 Corinthians, Romans, Philemon, Philippians. Thessalonians seems very "raw" and mentions Silas, who, again according to Acts, was one of Paul's early co-workers. Galatia, as well, seems to reflect an early stage of the conflicts over circumcision and seems to allude to the collection, but lacks a real plan of action. 1 and 2 Corinthians mention Paul's collection for Jerusalem and Paul asks the Corinthians to participate (1 Cor. 16:1–4; 2 Cor. 9:1–5). In Romans, as we've seen, Paul refers to his planned delivery of the monies to Jerusalem. In Philippians, he refers to the collection as a past event (4:14–20). Philippians also refers, as we have seen, to Paul's incarceration and in it he seems, overall, in a retrospective mood pending a coming trial. Philemon seems to be of a piece with Philippians. If this reconstruction is accurate, the bulk of Paul's letters were written in the last two years of his 20-year career.

To summarize: scholars must assume whether or how Paul's thought developed over time. At minimum, did he develop the way he articulated his ideas? If so, scholars need to reconstruct the sequence of his letters. One common sequence is the one mentioned above: 1 Thessalonians, Galatians, 1, 2 Corinthians, Romans, Philemon and Philippians.

Assumption 3: Reading for History and Context

Our primary interest has been to construct a sense of "what happened" or a biography of Paul. Therefore, we've been reading with attention to the "historical sense" and data that arise from the letters. Implicit in our work has been the question "What really happened?" To begin, we should note that there is no formal requirement to read the Bible (or any other book) with such questions in mind. Modern readers are perfectly free to read in any way they wish, with any agendas or biases or interests. There are no "reading police" who will arrest the non-historical reader. A reading that has no interest at all in being historical is in no way less "valid" than a reading which is historical. For most of history, the Bible was not read within a set of historical or grammatical contexts. The New Testament often quotes passages from the Hebrew scriptures in ways that modern readers would assert are "out of context." The Bible doesn't even read *itself* according to the rules of modern historical interpretation. The overwhelming majority of Christians come to faith without even the slightest hint of historical sensitivity to the author's original meaning. Most Christians live out their entire lives without ever studying even an introductory book on the history of the Roman world. I doubt one in one thousand contemporary Christians can read ancient Greek well (if at all). Many today might argue that the

Bible can only "mean" what the original author intended. This is a chimera. The Bible can mean whatever anyone wants it to mean, and such ways of creating meaning are always what the Bible "means." Reading for the historical context of Paul's letters, making intelligent guesses at Paul's most likely intention, is certainly a possible approach to interpretation and one that many others will find convincing and useful, but it is equally certainly not the *only* way to read the Bible.

Should we decide to read historically (and there are good reasons to do so), we still have multiple problems to address. Some modern scholars argue that, given the language and cultural differences between our own day and Paul's, we cannot accurately interpret his meaning without understanding his culture. These scholars immediately turn to reading ancient texts contemporary with Paul in an effort to learn more about his context. While this is certainly a reasonable way to start, if we can't understand Paul because of his distance from us in culture and context, how can we understand those contemporary with Paul who are equally distant? Historical inquiry is not free from scholarly bias or interest. Scholars are not disinterested bystanders in these types of decisions. They play an active role in the construction of historical "meaning." They must. Indeed, the very choice to approach the subject "historically" is already a value-laden approach.

A second concern is that ancient texts may not reflect a broad range of popular feeling in the ancient world. Reading and writing were aristocratic activities. Only the wealthy had time, leisure, and sufficient education to enjoy the literary life. Do the ideas and values they represent reflect the ideas and values of the majority of people of their day? How many Harvard professors reflect the values of the average NASCAR fan? How universal were the views and ideas of ancient authors? Since theirs are the only texts that have been preserved, how could one even know how representative they might be? How does one compare and contrast? Again, the individual scholar and his or her decisions on what is and is not "relevant" play a critical role.

Chronology and geography are also issues. One example where this question is particularly thorny is the debate about the "role of women" in ancient society. What texts or evidence do we use to describe this status, and how representative is the evidence for women's experience? Women's access to social, economic, and political opportunities varied greatly over time and by region. Economic and social status were also important factors. Imagine asking "What is the role of women in the US?" Should we begin by using essays describing women's activities in the eighteenth century? Prior to 1970? In the north or in the south? Urban or rural? Wealthy or poor? The number of variations would soon surpass the number of any common themes.

When looking for cultural parallels to construct Paul's context, most careful scholars try to choose those that are most chronologically, geographically, and culturally contemporary to Paul. Ironically, we might get far more information about the social world of Paul from archaeology conducted in cities that we have no record that Paul personally visited, but that are located in the same region and time-frame as Paul's known activity. Further, simply visiting sites and gazing at ruins tells us nothing of real value about what the cultural context of *Paul* might have been. We must also admit the limits of both our reconstruction and our data. We possess less than one-quarter of all the literature we know once existed in antiquity. How much is lost even from memory? Archaeology is vital as a source, but, in some ways, it is even more limited; we only know about what we've found and often have to guess at its significance. We must admit the episodic nature of our data. We simply don't have records of everything we would want or even need to know. Indeed, some of what we would most like to know – the everyday items, popular culture, the jokes of the common people, the most popular plays and poems, everyday food items, everyday household items, what common people thought about government or religion – are exactly the sorts of things with the least evidence. Literature preserves the interests and values of the elite. Archaeological finds are still largely happenstance. The ordinary, the small, the common – the things that make up the vast majority of popular culture – are exactly what is deemed least important and, so, is least often preserved.

Were the simple vagaries of historical preservation not enough, Paul's contemporary world exists in fragments which survived by accident or which were preserved by someone later. In the latter case, for Europe, many of the preservers were later Byzantine and medieval Christians. They didn't think much of "pagan" culture, literature, and religion, so they saved little. Our modern reconstructions are always comparisons to what previous generations thought were most analogous to Paul and other early Christians. In other words, our modern evidence exists largely because previous (Christian) scholarship perpetuated it, and these scholars only protected it because they thought it illuminated Paul. Little wonder he fits so nicely into such a world.

No historical reconstruction is without bias or limitation. At minimum, scholars must determine what elements are relevant and which are not. This determination is done from a distance of over 1,900 years and based on partial data. Further, it is driven, more often than not, by theological interests. Finally, as we've seen, Paul's letters are notoriously difficult to date and are all situational communications. What elements of antiquity actually matter?

Scholars reading for "history" must admit that neither they nor anyone else is a disinterested, unbiased observer of free-floating historical "facts." Such scholarship must admit that any reconstruction is, at best, provisional and occasional; the village idiot of Corinth heard more of the cultural context of Paul's letters than the most erudite modern scholar could hope to discern.

Assumption 4: The Value of our Sources

As I have been saying, on first survey, we would seem to have an abundance of material on the apostle Paul, particularly given his relatively ordinary status in the first century. As I've mentioned, we have 13 letters with serious claims to be written by Paul. Paul is also the central figure in the second half of the New Testament's Acts of the Apostles, and figures prominently in several second- and third-century Christian writings. Scholars have to decide how, or whether, to read narratives about Paul alongside letters written by him. There is, of course, potential that information found from one source would corroborate information found in another. At times, this happens. There is also, however, potential for discrepancy. At times, this happens too.

According to Acts, Paul, whom we first meet under his Hebrew name of Saul, was initially an up-and-coming Pharisaic rabbi in Jerusalem and a zealous opponent of the followers of Jesus. He participated in the execution of Stephen (7:54–8:1). Not content merely to oppose the movement in Jerusalem, he solicited and received letters of introduction from the high priest in Jerusalem, authorizing him to arrest and try early followers of Jesus in the city of Damascus as Jewish heretics (9:1–2). On the road to Damascus, he has a vision of the risen Jesus; the vision shatters his sense of mission and self and leaves him physically blinded, as well. He retreats to the city of Damascus, where he is first healed, then baptized into the Jesus movement by Ananias, a local believer (9:3–19).

If, as many historians surmise, Jesus was crucified sometime in the early to mid 30s CE, Paul's conversion seems to have been sometime in the mid to late 30s. He then spends a bit of time as a student in Damascus, where he learns much (9:20–3) before being forced to flee as his life is threatened by his former associates (9:23–4). Paul returns to Jerusalem, this time as a believer, but is naturally met with suspicion until he is taken under the wing of a venerated member of the community, Barnabas, and introduced privately to the apostles (9:26–30). Paul attempts an early career as a teacher in Jerusalem, but controversy still surrounds him, and he is once again forced to flee for his life, this time back home to Tarsus (9:28–30). He then briefly drops out of the narrative of Acts.

After some undisclosed period of time, Barnabas, who had learned of a thriving young interracial (Jew and gentile) community in Antioch, travels to Tarsus, hunts out Paul, and brings him back to Antioch to work with that church (11:19–26). Paul spends a year working with the Antioch community of believers. According to Acts, a prophet named Agabus arrives at Antioch predicting an impending famine (11:27–30). Acts clearly says this was during the reign of the emperor Claudius (41–54 CE). This is one of the few potentially datable moments in Paul's career. There does seem to be evidence of a famine in Judea sometime around 45 to 48 CE. The church at Antioch (possibly, though Acts is ambiguous here) decides to send funds to Jerusalem and Judea for famine relief. Notably, in Acts, Paul does not collect or deliver the funds. His trip to Jerusalem for this episode is neither his first nor his final visit. He has also, according to Acts, not yet begun planting churches at all, but is part of the Antioch community, and Acts is not clear that the contribution is a collection of monies from anywhere other than Antioch. Paul begins his "first missionary journey" in Acts 13. As a protégé of Barnabas, he is commissioned by the Antioch church to take the message of Jesus to the world. The pair visit major cities along the western coast of the Roman province of Asia Minor, what is now the southern and western coast of Turkey. They return to Antioch jubilant (14:24–8).

Sometime in the late 40s CE, a major division arose among early followers of Jesus regarding the role and status of gentile believers. A major council was held in the city of Jerusalem (presided over by James) to settle the matter, and a position paper was drafted (Acts 15:1–21). Paul, Barnabas and other members from Antioch were present. Antioch was a very cosmopolitan city, located on a major roadway between the areas of Judea/Galilee (the area many today call the Holy Land) and Asia Minor. Without doubt, the community of believers in Antioch contained a mix of both Jewish and gentile followers. Paul and Barnabas were nominated by the council to circulate a letter reporting on their findings (15:22–9). Acts reports that others were commissioned, as well, but does not name them. Presumably, representatives from particular "regions" carried the letter back to their home provinces. The council decided, according to Acts, that gentiles could become members of the community without converting, first, to Judaism. Gentile believers were only required to avoid idolatry, abstain from sexual immorality, and avoid meat containing blood or from animals that had been strangled (most likely aspects of ritual sacrifice). Paul and Barnabas pass through Antioch again, then revisit the churches they first established along the eastern Aegean coast. Once again, they return to Antioch (15:30–5).

"After some days" (Acts 15:36), Paul and Barnabas begin making plans for yet another visit to these churches. Barnabas agrees, but wants to bring along another young protégé named John Mark.

Paul mistrusts Mark, since on an earlier trip Mark abandoned them and returned home. The two senior missionaries quarrel, and decide to make separate trips. Barnabas leaves with Mark (and vanishes from Acts). Paul takes along his own young students, Timothy and Silas. On this trip, Paul has a dream where a "Macedonian man" calls for him to come over and evangelize (16:6–10). Macedonia was a province on the northern peninsula of Greece, the southern boundary of Europe. According to Acts 16:11–18:17, Paul obediently presses into Greece, starting churches in Macedonia and pressing down through Philippi (also in Macedonia) then into Borea and the regions of Achaea and as far south as Athens (where he has very limited, but some, success), then on to Corinth (where he has more luck). Along the way, Paul encounters various problems with local leaders and with Jewish communities. Acts reports that the former are worried that Paul's message is a threat to the vitality of their own religious communities. The latter are simply jealous of Paul's successes. One Greco-Roman leader is mentioned by name. In Acts 18:12, Paul is examined by Gallio, the proconsul (managing governor) of the region of Achaia. Gallio governed from roughly 51 to 53 CE. Paul resides in Corinth for about 18 months. Concluding this journey, Paul returns, once more, to Antioch (18:18–21). While there, Paul meets another missionary pair, Aquilla and his wife Priscilla. Oddly, Acts also reports that he cuts off his hair as part of a vow. Most likely this is not a Nazarite vow since Paul does not dedicate the cut hair in the Temple (as described in Numbers 6:18). He seems to be fulfilling some Jewish practice that would involve abstention from cutting his hair, but exactly what the ritual might have been remains a mystery.

Paul, having fulfilled his mysterious vow, leaves for Ephesus, the capital city of the province of Asia Minor (18:19–19:41). Ominously, he is uncertain, on his departure from Antioch, if he will ever return again. He establishes a school in Ephesus and resides in that city for two years, teaching publicly in the Hall of Tyrannus (19:9). He also makes occasional trips to churches in Macedonia. Acts describes several adventures of Paul on this particular trip, noting that he is opposed, once again, by threatened worshipers of pagan deities and jealous Jews. Paul decides to make another trip to Jerusalem (Acts 20:17). Acts does not disclose any motive. He begins this journey, visiting congregations along the way. At several points, there are ominous signs and portents that his trip will not end well.

In Acts 21:17, Paul arrives in Jerusalem and has another visit with James. James suggests Paul sponsor some local believers who are undertaking a Jewish vow. James suggests the idea in order to quiet tensions between Paul and the Jewish believers in Jerusalem (21:18–26). Paul agrees to not only pay the relevant expenses, but to take on the vow himself. Things go awry, however. Paul is accused of bringing a non-Jew, a companion named Trophimus, into the Jewish-only courts of the Temple, a defiling act. A riot ensues, and Roman soldiers (the "police" of Jerusalem) intervene. Paul makes a public speech to explain himself, but the crowds become even more angry, so he is taken into protective custody by the Romans (21:27–22:29). After some time in the protective custody of provincial authorities, Paul invokes his status as Roman citizen to have the venue of his hearing (presumably, on the charge of being a participant in disturbing the public order) changed to Rome (25:10). Several of the officials who hear Paul's case are known outside the biblical text; the particular group mentioned ruled in Judea during the late 50s CE. The balance of Acts narrates Paul's harrowing trip to Rome in Roman custody, and Acts ends with Paul in a rented apartment in Rome under house arrest, awaiting his trial (28:11–31).

As a missionary, Paul is presented in Acts as often opposed, at times by Greco-Roman, pagan locals, more often by "jealous" Jews who disagree with his teaching. His Jewish opposition are not "Judaizers" (who would argue that one must convert to Judaism to truly follow the messiah) but Jews who resist even the idea of Jesus as messiah. Paul is a miracle-worker of no little ability (19:11–12). He casts out demons (16:16–18), has dreams from God (16:6–10), heals the infirm (14:8–10), survives a poisonous snake bite (28:1–6), and once even raises the dead (20:7–12). He is arrested (for civil disturbance – always unfairly, however) more than once, beaten (often "off the radar" by local thugs or magistrates who try to run off this missionary vagabond), and faces horrible hardships from travel. He remains confident and poised throughout.

If we compare the picture of Paul found in Acts to the content of his letters, there is a great deal of corroboration. In both traditions, as we've seen, Paul is born a citizen of Tarsus; in both he is trained as a Pharisee. Paul describes his early career in essentially the same terms as we find in Acts; the basic skeletal narrative of persecutor–vision–conversion–missionary is intact. Also, Paul refers to the many hardships of his travels and alludes to resistance met from both Jewish and gentile communities. He writes to cities generally noted in Acts as "his" churches. Paul, as we have discussed, is concerned with taking and distributing a collection of money for the Jerusalem church. He also focuses his ministry on issues surrounding the inclusion of the gentiles. He writes from Roman custody (imprisonment). A rough (very rough) chronology of his travels is generically compatible with his letters. Most of the key associates of Paul in Acts are also mentioned in his letters.

There are, though, some discrepancies between the two pictures. In Acts, Paul is never shown as a letter-writer. In his letters, Paul never refers to himself as a miracle-worker or exorcist. In Acts, Paul's teachings build around the promise of the messiah found in the book of Isaiah. In his letters, he deals much more with Genesis and the figure of Abraham. Many of the cities Paul visits in Acts are not referred to by him in his letters; many of his associates mentioned in his letters do not appear in Acts at all. Paul doesn't write about his long stay in Ephesus, nor his extensive work with the church in Antioch. He never gives the same detail surrounding his own conversion story that we have recorded in Acts. Acts omits any discussion of Paul in heated (and repeated) conflict with other Christian teachers over issues of doctrine. In Galatians 2, Paul describes an open conflict with Peter/Cephas and suggests conflicts with James. Acts never mentions these. Acts omits any sense at all that Paul was accused by other Christian teachers of being unqualified to teach. Paul never discusses his own baptism or his own healing in his letters. These letters frequently discuss his health problems, but Acts never shows him ill or infirm beyond his initial temporary blindness, and never to the extent that he cannot travel. Indeed, in Acts, not even stoning or a venomous snake bite slow Paul down. Paul describes an early trip to Arabia (Gal. 1:17); this trip is never mentioned in Acts. In Acts, he is depicted as a Roman citizen (from birth – a key plot point) and a student of the immanent teacher Gamaliel. In his letters, Paul mentions neither point, despite the fact that he often defends his "Jewish credentials" and his previous social status. In 1 Corinthians 15, Paul refers to engaging in ritual practices (baptism for the dead, for example) that are otherwise unknown in Acts. His collection "for the saints of Jerusalem" is located, in Acts, prior to the Jerusalem council or any of Paul's missionary journeys. In Acts, Paul's final trip to Jerusalem is never explicitly associated with the collection and delivery of monies, though, somehow, Paul has enough money on hand to fund multiple Nazarite vows at the Temple.

What should we make of this? Before deciding, we should notice that there are a few out-and-out, irreconcilable conflicts. In Acts, Paul is a powerful (and polished) orator; in his letters, as we have seen, he denies having such an ability. Some of his moments of incarceration seem to be out of sequence (or not mentioned at all by him). Paul, in Acts, positions himself as a "suffering servant" in the vein of Isaiah. In his letters, he more often casts himself as Jeremiah. In Galatians 1, he insists (very emphatically) that he was not taught his "gospel" message, but Acts shows him often in instruction, first by Ananias, then by Barnabas. Also in Galatians 1, Paul insists that, after his conversion, he never met the "super apostles," nor did he visit Jerusalem until 10 years after his conversion. In Acts, Jerusalem is one of Paul's first stops following his conversion and he is promptly run out of town. In Paul's letters, his main opposition arises from within the Jesus movement itself – other, more persuasive, teachers, rival missionaries, "Judaizers." In Acts, opposition to Paul always comes from outside his communities. Again, according to Galatians 2:1, Titus seems to have taken the role of Timothy in Paul's appearance at the Jerusalem conference in Acts 15, and, despite Paul's remarks in Galatians 2:3–4 regarding Titus, Paul himself circumcises Timothy to prevent conflicts with other Jews (Acts 16:3). Also, in Acts 15, Peter is the principal speaker on behalf of gentiles at the Jerusalem conference. In Galatians, Paul puts himself in that role, and even describes a public shouting argument with Peter over the issue in Antioch.

It will be helpful here to provide a brief summary of our argument. The New Testament preserves information about Paul in the Acts of the Apostles and in several of Paul's own letters. Without Acts, Paul's letters are without any real context. Comparison between Acts and Paul's letters shows some agreement, but also reveals disparity and outright factual conflict. Some scholars and believers assume Acts is a reliable account of the life of Paul. This may well not be the case; there are enough conflicts and disparities to awaken suspicions. Even if Acts is a generally reliable history, the differences and disparities suggest we must be cautious in how Acts and the Pauline letters are used together. In other words, the confidence that the New Testament documents are all historically accurate and can corroborate one another is merely an assumption.

The problem is greater than simply coordinating Acts and the letters. Reading through just Paul's letters, we also see some internal disparity. In 1 Thessalonians, Paul insists that there will be no signs preceding Jesus' return. Jesus will arrive like "a thief in the night" (5:1–11). In 2 Thessalonians, he gives an outline of the events which will harbinger Jesus' return (2 Thess. 2). A substantial portion of Paul's letter to the Colossians is repeated verbatim (preserving even the word order of the Greek) in his letter to the Ephesians. The letters 1 and 2 Timothy and Titus (often called the "pastorals" since they are presented as personal letters to two of Paul's protégés, young pastors in training, about issues of congregational life and management) have a common style and vocabulary. That style and vocabulary, however, are markedly different from those of Paul's other letters. The pastorals mention individuals and travel itineraries that simply cannot be reconciled with the balance of Paul's letters (or even with Acts itself). On the surface, the pastorals seem the most intimate of the writings attributed to Paul. 1 and 2 Timothy are addressed, "to my loyal child in the faith," "to my beloved child"; Titus is penned to "my loyal child." Paul explains his immediate plans (1 Tim. 3:14), requests his books and papers, and inquires about a forgotten cloak (2 Tim. 4:13). Timothy is given personal encouragement (1 Tim. 4:12) and advice about his character, public presentation (1 Tim. 6:11–19), and physical health (1 Tim. 5:23: "Take a little wine for your stomach"). Titus is invited, with the tone of one pained by separation, to "do your best to come to me" (Titus 3:12). We might hope to develop from these letters a side of Paul saved for his closest colleagues.

At the same time, however, they are *too* intimate in places, referring to events and people we know nothing about. (1 Timothy 1:18 refers to a time of "prophecy" regarding Timothy, predicting his future work, which is without other record.) They refer to conflicts among early Christian leaders of whom we are otherwise ignorant (2 Tim. 1:15, 2:17). They refer to Paul's travel to places that we have no other record of his visiting, and these journeys are nearly impossible to coordinate with accepted Pauline chronology. Paul places himself in Nicopolis in Titus 3:12, but we are told nothing about his ever having traveled there, and he mentions a trip to Crete in Titus 1:5 which is equally mysterious. The conclusion to 2 Timothy is replete with unexpected and unidentifiable referents. At times 2 Thessalonians, Colossians, and Ephesians seem so different from 1 Thessalonians, Galatians, 1 and 2 Corinthians, Romans, Philippians, and Philemon that some scholars suspect that they were not actually written by Paul at all. For example, the pastorals instruct Timothy to silence opposing voices of all women (1 Tim. 2:11–12). Indeed, women are not even to ask questions in public, and Paul indicates this is his normal modus operandi, despite the fact that, in his first letter to the Corinthians, Paul allows women to pray and prophesy in public (1 Cor. 11:2–16), though with their heads covered. Paul frequently mentions, and praises, female missionaries as "fellow workers" (more than nine are mentioned in Romans 16 alone). He emphatically writes that gender (and ethnicity) are no longer binding in the new messianic age (Gal. 3:28).

We have evidence in Paul's letters for omissions, alterations, and worries about forgery. He worries about whether the Galatians would receive a teaching concerning Jesus "from himself" that differed from his initial teaching (Gal. 1:8–9). He notes a few times that he has signed his letters "by his own hand" (Gal. 6:11;

Philem. 1:19). 2 Thessalonians refers to letters circulating as "Paul's," but which are fraudulent (2 Thess. 2:2–3). In Colossians, Paul refers to a letter he wrote to the church at Laodicea (Col. 4:15–16). We have and ancient letter claiming to be from Paul "To the Laodiceans"; it is not in the canonical New Testament, and scholars regularly date it to the second century, at the earliest. In 2 Corinthians, Paul refers to an "angry letter" he wrote the community (2 Cor. 2:3–4). 1 Corinthians, though firm at times, does not seem to be that letter. Once again, however, we have a non-canonical "to the Corinthians" purporting to be from Paul; once again, scholars unanimously believe the document to be later.

These vagaries, omissions, discrepancies, and conflicts must be, somehow, reconciled or addressed for any biography to exist. The conflicts in fact between Paul's letters and Acts, as well as the complex relationship of the letters to other letters, are simply present. To articulate as much is not a matter of skepticism or of faith; it is simply to articulate what is, in this case, in "black and white." Scholars must choose how to reconcile these conflicts (even if that choice is to attempt to deny the conflict is present). How one chooses to reconcile these problems – indeed, even if one recognizes any problems exist at all – reflects one's assumptions.

Assumption 5: The Burden and Nature of Historical "Proof"

As we have seen, the letters of Paul, themselves, reveal worries about the potential for falsely attributed letters. Also, we do not have all the letters we suspect Paul wrote. At a later point in Christian history, letters and stories were written to "fill in the holes" of Acts and the Pauline correspondence. Could this have happened in the earliest centuries? Could some letters written in Paul's name – perhaps written by a pious student of Paul who intended to craft a literary production that would suggest how Paul would speak to a later church circumstance – have inadvertently been identified as "authentic" and accepted into the Christian canon as Pauline? Finally, what about the picture of Paul in Acts? Acts was written, most scholars agree, decades after his death and has a clear, thoroughgoing thesis: Christianity is a reasonable view, continuous with Judaism, and not a threat to Roman civil order. Might the picture of Paul in Acts also have been selectively presented to make him appear more "mainstream" and accepted than he was in the early decades of Christianity? Is it possible that the author of Acts might not even have known all, or perhaps any, of Paul's letters? I remind the reader, the New Testament – and, for that matter, printed publications of any sort – did not exist in the first century. The early writings were hand-made copies of copies that circulated very slowly. Might a desire to rehabilitate Paul's reputation have even been an impetus for some revision of his writings or even for the composition of some new writings?

Clearly, the answer to all the above questions must be, at least at the hypothetical level, "Yes." Historians know that written records are always subject to problems. They may have been altered. They may be polemical and biased. They may be missing key portions. They may preserve only part of a larger story. They may erroneously report factual data, or even their own origins. Could this have happened for New Testament documents? Again, hypothetically, the answer is a simple "Of course it could have." Many will have theological reasons, however, to insist that it did not. Many, indeed most, Christian interpreters throughout history would suggest that God through the Holy Spirit oversaw the process of New Testament collection and preservation. After all, the pious faith of generations of manuscript copyists, scribes, scholars, and so on has been to endeavor, as much as possible, to preserve the record, as completely and as accurately as possible. Their faith led them to extreme care concerning the documents they viewed as theirs in trust from God.

But there are two sides to piety. Surely it is also possible that faith prevents some people from asking tough questions regarding the historical reliability of the New Testament. Even if determined to remain balanced in their assessments, being human, they also simply could have erred. Were this any book but one currently regarded as "holy" and "inspired," there would be no arguments about these possibilities; the easy rationality of these sorts of historical questions would be accepted as the norm. Such questions, of course, would also wildly complicate a reconstruction of Paul's biography. Taken to extremes, they might even undermine confidence that Paul ever actually existed. Yet the historically skeptical could be, in their turn, answered that history is not normally written about mundane events and figures. Who preserves the story of a relaxing morning off work, followed by a nice brunch, a few hours of idle reading, some shopping, a pleasant walk in the woods, a delightful dinner, a good book, and an early bedtime? History is always written about the improbable and unusual. Historical figures are often historical precisely because some aspect of their nature and career is "larger than life," and such stories are necessarily complicated. Many scholars would continue the counter-argument by observing that the New Testament is no less reliable as a historical source than any other ancient text. Few people write bestselling books about the "historical Socrates." Many of the apparent discrepancies could also be the product of our own limited data; they only seem to be problems because we don't know how they properly "fit." Finally, should we expect total agreement between a biography and the biographee? Wouldn't too much agreement, in fact, be a strong indication that the biography was less than objective? As we have said, we know a great deal more about Paul than we know about many ancient figures. Should we, then, be any less confident about a "reconstructed Paul" than about modern biographies of any figure, chosen at random, from the ancient world?

Perhaps two brief "parables" of my own will best illustrate the scholarly debate and discussion. Assume you have found a series of letters which identify me as their author. In some cases, they present startling and amazing facts about my life and my ideas. How would you determine if I were indeed the author? Assume, as well, you found a brief biography of me, and assume, further, that there are some differences between this and the letters. Which is "accurate," the letters or the biography?

Your first move would be to see if there is any claim, within the letters themselves, that I wrote them. Indeed, you find just that in my signature line. Of course, since the letters are typed, you cannot compare handwriting, but the letters claim to be my own. But couldn't this claim be fraudulent? Finally, let's assume you have copies of other letters that claim to be by me but which are clearly not and, for that matter, the content of my own letters suggests I am worried that such copies could or do circulate. Some form of additional verification will be required.

To advance any further you would need to read the letters closely. Do they use language consistently? Are there expressions or manners of speech or idioms or grammatical oddities that are consistent throughout? Do I talk about issues in similar ways? Do the letters show some consistent range of literacy? Do I use the same words intending the same general sense? What if I suddenly veered off into radically divergent ideas, say suddenly alternating between Democratic and Republican politics? Do I refer to people and places I could actually have met or visited? Do I greet people I could, conceivably, have met and known? Are there factual errors? What if the biography is incorrect but my own letters are accurate? What if, because I'm angry or embarrassed, I leave something out of my letters? What if I write differently when writing to a close friend than when I am addressing a public audience? What if my style or ideas develop and change across my public career or in response to changing issues in the world? Did I use a secretary for my writing? Are there any other scholars, authorities, or experts who know me who quote from my work or write about me?

What you would have to collect would be: (1) textual concerns (Are the letters consistent in copy? Do they appear to be edited or modified?); (2) stylistic consistency (Do I use a consistent vocabulary and grammar throughout?); (3) thematic or ideological consistency (Do I use the same general range of ideas?); (4) internal coherence (Do the letters present ideas or factual data that are divergent?); (5) external coherence (How do the letters correspond to any other data from a third party?); and (6) verification (What do other contemporaries with unique information about the subject suggest?).

In biblical studies, these are the central questions for Pauline authorship and biography as well. A careful reader will note (perhaps with frustration) how none of these questions can be answered beyond debate. I vary my writing style all the time, and to make an assessment of my prose would require a substantial body of literature for comparison. I vary my themes and ideas all the time in my writing; I may even, in time, come to modify or even disavow something I wrote earlier. Biographies are often wrong. Further, there are an infinite number of reasons why I and a third party could disagree over how to interpret or understand events of my own life. Errors in one or two facts do not invalidate the historical merits of a given source in respect to other areas; wrong once does not mean always wrong. Finally, which "experts" should be trusted? Can't they make errors (pro or con) as well?

It is important to admit that no single element, alone, can produce certainty; any question, challenge, or critique can be answered. Further, even if viewed collectively, the list above cannot produce absolute certainty. The best we can hope for is a reasonable argument of what *probably* is the case, and that argument will always be provisional, pending the discovery of new data.

To illustrate this point further, I offer my second parable. Behold, I tell you a mystery – a murder mystery, in fact. One morning, my long-time best friend is found murdered in my living room; a bloody knife (the murder weapon, on investigation) is found next to the body. Am I guilty? Certainly, the police will want to talk slowly and seriously with me. It is, after all, my knife and my friend and my living room, but I'm in no danger of handcuffs yet. On investigation, I have no certain alibi for the time of the murder. On a spur-of-the-moment idea, I decided to take my dog and go camping that evening, alone, as we often do. No one I know saw me. Am I guilty? Not yet, but it looks grim. As the investigation widens, the police learn that I had publicly and angrily quarreled with my friend the day before the murder over a financial deal that had gone badly. I punched him in the nose, and he bled. I stormed off and went camping that very night to clear my head after the fight. Since he was my long-time friend, he has left me a large amount of money in his will. Can my guilt be proven yet? No, but there is motive now, and my lack of an alibi is becoming more of a problem.

Let's make the situation even more sketchy. Forensics verifies that the living room was the site of the murder; there is a broken window latch in the kitchen, but otherwise, there are no signs of forced entry. My friend had a key to the house, and I assert I know nothing about the window. Is my guilt certain? Again, no. Windows do break, and my friend had a key. Perhaps, while I was away, my friend came to my home (to apologize?) and surprised a burglar who, after killing my friend, escaped as he had entered through the window. Finally, examination reveals my fingerprints on the knife and traces of his blood on my clothing. That means I must be guilty, right? I still have an answer: my attorney points out that we should expect both. It was my knife (I don't dispute this) and the blood came from our earlier fistfight.

Given the above, can we say for certain that I am guilty? Perhaps not. But I absolutely must expect to be charged and most likely arraigned. No one item is, by itself, convicting. Each one can be readily explained in a way that defends my innocence. Yet the whole weight of them all combined doesn't look good for me. I should be finding a very good lawyer and getting prepared for a dramatic day in court. While each element can be explained, in the end, my friend is found murdered with my knife in my house after our quarrel. I can't offer an alibi, I have motive, my fingerprints are on the murder weapon, and I've got my friend's blood on my clothing.

What would happen in a trial? Well, much would depend on the way the evidence is presented and on the standard and burden of proof. In the US, the burden of proof is on the state and not on me. If it were otherwise, in the case I just describe, I would be unable to prove my innocence short of finding the actual murderer. Also, for a capital charge, the case against me must be such that, by unanimous vote of the jury, there can be no reasonable doubt as to my guilt. In the above, we might agree that I could establish this doubt (though the wrong set of lawyers with the wrong jury could prove disastrous for me). I might be in more trouble, however, if a civil suit is filed. In that case, the standard for proof is not "beyond reasonable doubt," but "preponderance of the evidence." In other words, the accusers must make the case that it is more reasonable (even if only just a bit more) to assume that I committed the crime than that I did not. Finally, they need only convince a simple majority of the jurors, not all.

In the above scenario, the standards and burden of proof are established by prior law. But what if they were not? They aren't a priori established in cases of historical and literary study. Much like the murder mystery above, as we have seen, there is a legitimate and defensible reason to "arraign" Pauline authorship of some letters and the credibility of Acts. Given the concerns Paul expressed, the differences between Acts and the Pauline corpus, and the actual possession of fraudulent letters, we have a case we must investigate. Not to do so would be intellectual irresponsibility. Also, much like the above case, as we apply the "standards of evidence" (consistency, style, witness, etc.), we find some problems, but no single, final, complete "proof." Taken individually, each charge can be answered, but what about their cumulative weight?

As historians, we must also decide who bears the burden of proof. Is it the scholar who is refuting more than 1,900 years of church tradition? Surely, the ancient Christians who canonized these works were much closer to the events in terms of both culture and chronology. But, again, they were also heavily biased toward faith, and the claims they make about Paul are, to say the least, bold. A fairly standard convention in philosophical argument is that the person who is advancing the more improbable claim carries the obligation of proof. Extreme assertions require extreme evidence. Must the dissenter prove that 1,900 years of history are wrong, or is the biblical Paul *too much* larger than life? Which is the more extreme assertion?

Finally, what is the standard of proof? Must we reach a position where no other reasonable argument is valid? If so, historians, on the whole, are in a very bad spot. Given the circumstantial and spotty nature of our data, absolute certainty for either side is impossible to argue in strictly historical and literary terms. Is it merely "preponderance of the evidence"? If this is the case, what makes evidence "preponderant"? According to the assessment of whom? And according to how many? Is something "true" simply because most people say it is?

Biblical scholars disagree over whether critics or defenders of tradition carry the obligation of argument. This disagreement is, doubtless, affected by faith concerns of all sorts. In addition to sorting through all the data to determine if and where a decisive "problem" occurs, scholars have to make further choices about how to contextualize and interpret the data. Who carries the burden of proof? What is the standard of proof? The various permutations of possible answers to these two questions are legion. That variety is also exactly why scholars, by necessity, bring their own biases into the process of reconstructing a historical Paul. There is no vantage point for a value-free, perfectly "objective," scientific, and absolute assessment of Pauline biography. It is unavoidable that a scholar's own needs, concerns, questions, agendas, biases, hopes, fears, assumptions, ideas, beliefs, background, worries, limitations, and expectations will influence and shape how they evaluate our evidence and how they read Paul.

Scholars simply have to decide whether or not to give the Bible (and church doctrine) the benefit of the doubt from the start, or if the Bible must prove and defend its claims. This assumption, which is unavoidable, will fundamentally affect how one reads Paul. No one is "forced" to make a conclusion because of value-neutral historical "facts." The very way "facts" are identified, collected, and analyzed is a subjective process that reflects assumptions about the burden and nature of "proof" itself. The rest of this book will examine how scholars have reconstructed Paul, often oblivious of their own intrusions.

More Problems: The Question of Canon

The very first "biographies" of Paul are lost to history because they were most likely never written down at all. Paul's letters were written to churches. Delivered by associates, the letters were read aloud to the entire house church. As we've seen, these letters were also most often written to communities in conflict, often conflict over Paul's message and even over Paul himself. Our modern imagination of these readings has likely been shaped by more than 1,900 years of hearing Paul's voice as the voice of authority. The majority of Christian believers today would recognize Paul's word as the end of the matter.

Such would hardly have been the case in the first century. Much of the conflict that Paul addresses had arisen precisely because some other teachers or voices from within the community were saying different things than Paul, perhaps even questioning his authority or good sense. These voices did not passively shrug at a "word from Paul" and concede. To the contrary, they very likely began spirited rebuttals to his letters as soon as the reading ended, if not interrupting its progress. No doubt, there were also supporters of Paul and his ideas. We must remember that the movement behind Jesus of Nazareth as messiah was still very much in its infancy. Very, very few formal doctrines had been articulated or even thought through. Most of the narrative of Jesus' life and teachings was still oral story. No single community would have been privy to all the teachings we find in our modern New Testaments. Every community would have been subject to a host of cultural and ideological pressures and experiences we can only now partially imagine. The debate was a lively and active one.

The very first Pauline biographies and theologies began in this crucible. One side would argue that Paul's ideas were incorrect, that he was unqualified to teach, that he was an outlier (if not, more fully, a false teacher). Others would certainly have argued the opposite. They would have insisted that Paul's life and words bore the stamp of God's spirit. They would have asserted that he declared his gospel was given to him directly from God and the resurrected Jesus. Debate over the meaning, authority, and role of Paul's letters began almost as soon as they were made public. Debate over Paul's letters began, almost immediately, to inspire debate about Paul's biography.

I remind us of this tension not merely to make a trivial point, necessary for some academic's exhaustive (and often exhausting) scruple. I do so because these early believers who were engaged in active, contemporary debate over Paul's life and thought are the *very same* people who preserved and first circulated Paul's letters. The *content* of these letters leaves no room for doubt that Paul was opposed, often bitterly, within his lifetime. Indeed, he was openly scorned, disputed, and rejected by many. Yet the *reality* of Paul's letters – the fact that they even exist today at all – is testimony to another view of Paul within the early church: he was clearly respected, revered, and heeded by someone. We can't say which side had the more adherents in the first century. We can, however, assert that *someone* felt Paul's ideas were important enough to preserve his letters. And someone felt it important to collect some of the letters together. Perhaps this was one of Paul's associates or co-authors. Perhaps it was a collective, grassroots movement of several small cell-groups who collected and preserved a letter, shared this letter with others, and collected letters in turn. In time, a small corpus emerged.

What we preserve or archive from a person's life is a form of interpretation of that life, a form of biography. What do we leave out, and why do we leave it out? Preservation is also a form of interpretation. Much the way a familiar picture is "changed" by rematting and reframing, the way in which material is collected, edited, and ordered highlights some elements and downplays others. This process, innocent and unavoidable though it may be, is a form of interpretation and "biography"-making. Of course, the ascription of "canon" status to Paul's letters is also a form of interpretation – it implies a value ascription and a perspective on the work as a whole.

Many disliked Paul during his lifetime. After his death, his chief supporter was a man later orthodox Christianity remembers as an arch-heretic. What followed was a long intramural debate among Christians. Were the "heretics" reading Paul correctly? If so, he was best disregarded. Were they misreading him? If so, clear boundaries needed to be established for "proper" interpretation of his letters. These boundaries could be achieved by judicious editing of his works, careful collection of "appropriate" Pauline letters, biographical details that provide a skeletal frame for the correspondence and theological systems that interpret and control the rich potential meanings in them. Much of this "Pauline reclamation" occurs in traditions and texts that originate during the second century. Some comes from theological and polemical documents. Some, though, comes from the selection, preservation, and preparation (perhaps even composition) of the primary texts themselves.

Sorting through the Data: The Range of Scholarly Views

For many contemporary scholars, Paul's 13 letters can be divided into two groups: the "standard" or "authentic" seven (1 Thessalonians, Galatians, 1, 2 Corinthians, Romans, Philippians, and Philemon) and the "disputed epistles" (2 Thessalonians, Colossians, Ephesians, 1 and 2 Timothy, and Titus). Colossians and Ephesians are often called the "Prison Epistles," since, in each Paul seems to be writing while himself a prisoner in chains (Eph. 3:1, 6:20; Col. 4:10–11). As we have seen, 1 and 2 Timothy and Titus are called the pastorals since, in each, Paul is writing to one of his protégés, offering advice for pastoral ministry and the administration of local congregations.

While there is nothing at all like unanimity among scholars on the question of Pauline authorship of the disputed epistles, there are general trends. Scholars with a strong bias toward a historically rooted faith (in other words, those who are active members of most Evangelical and some Roman Catholic communities) tend heavily toward arguments for Pauline integrity. In general, they point out that no one complaint against Pauline authorship is, in the end, convincing. Further, they tend to argue from a perspective that challenges to Pauline authorship bear the burden of proof. For these scholars, to alter received Christian consensus, particularly regarding the authorship and, by implication, the authority of the Bible is so grave an act that the evidence must be simply overwhelming.

Pauline scholars who do not have a strong bias toward a faith that can be rooted in historical actuality are, in turn, much more likely to find the cumulative weight of the inconsistencies, curiosities, and complications most convincing. These scholars do not tend to respect Christian tradition simply because it is Christian tradition, though many often *do* take long-standing confessions and assertions into consideration. These may well be the beginning point for their inquiry, and they will concede them until there is reason to suspect them. But these traditions do not carry final authority; they are not, in other words, sacrosanct and beyond need of defense. Such scholarship finds the bold claims of

Christian tradition as the "more difficult assertions" that require the burden of proof. Tradition must defend its assertions of Pauline authorship.

The differences between these groups cannot be boiled down to some rudely simplistic formula such as "liberal scholars hate submission and faith and are trying to destroy the authority of the Bible and God" or "conservative scholars are insincere about facts, ignorant, and blinded by faith." It is true, however, that confessional and other worldview issues shape the discussion. Scholars disagree largely because of their fundamental disagreements over data and its assessment, but this disagreement, is, of course, related to their other ideas, views, and values. It is too simple to reduce the disagreement to just doctrinal (dis)loyalty. Liberal religious views, for example, are not necessarily responsible for creating or shaping liberal scholarly views on the question of Pauline authorship. Both views could be dependent on a larger, more fundamental idea: authority systems – even long-standing, deeply religious ones – are not above challenge. Certainly, "liberal scholars" did not create the discrepancies that can be found in the text, even if they do find them more problematic than "conservative" scholars might.

Another point that merits consideration is the occasional challenge that critical scholarship on Pauline authorship is somehow a "new" concern (or, when seen as an "old" one, a reiteration of some previously settled question now brought back up by "troublemakers" or people just looking for a fight). This is no more true than the assertion that those who defend Pauline integrity are illiterate or gullible. As we will see, Pauline authorship and authority have been disputed questions *from the very first century.* There has really *never* been a time in Christian history when these questions were not discussed. It is true that there have been times and places in history when Christian critical scholarship was formally (or implicitly) constrained; many scholars may not have been allowed to make public arguments about some of these issues. Since the Renaissance, scholarship in all fields – including biblical studies – has been moving toward values of unfettered intellectual freedom. As a result, more and more essays critical of any received idea, even a religious one, have been written and published and seriously discussed. Critical essays on Pauline authorship have increased with each century as well. They blossomed, in particular, when certain religious and doctrinal constructs were shaken by the scientific explosions of the eighteenth and nineteenth centuries. It is not true, however, to say that these arguments are new, nor that they're the products of nineteenth-century hyper-critical scholarship. Critical scholars are, on the whole, not "out to get" anyone or anything. They are also not going to quietly overlook historical questions or concerns that are intellectually reasonable.

The major seven letters listed above are considered "authentic" by nearly all scholars. While these letters do display some occasional complexities, they also present a relatively consistent grammar, style, theme, ideology, and structure. They tend, as well, toward a generally high level of chronological coherence and have a very good "reputation" among ancient scholars and critics. While they may occasionally trigger one of our "authenticity warning lights," they do not awaken dramatic or frequent concern.

Opinions over the authorship of Colossians, Ephesians, and 2 Thessalonians are more divided. These letters light up more than one "inauthentic" indicator light (and/or strike one of these lights rather forcefully). Some scholars consider all three to be later compositions, written in Paul's name. Other scholars consider all three to be precisely what they claim – straight from the pen of Paul. Many, many scholars have something of a "compromise" view: that Paul may be the author of much of the text, but that major portions of the letters have been altered or edited by later hands. There is no strong consensus. The pastorals sharply divide Pauline scholars. By far, these are the most frequent of Paul's letters to be seen as inauthentic. They exhibit the most inconsistencies and variations. These letters light up nearly every problem light, and strike multiple lights very forcefully. Scholars who defend their authenticity, however, do so vigorously and aggressively. These letters, indeed, have proven critical for much Protestant theology and liturgical practice. Scholars who dispute them, likewise, argue as if their concerns are obvious. Arguments about the authenticity of the pastorals are also complicated because the strongest claim the Bible makes for its own authority is found in 2 Timothy 3:16–17. If this claim for biblical inspiration occurs in a letter that is, itself, not authentically Pauline, many feel that the consequences to biblical authority are dramatic and dire.

The question of Pauline authorship is often linked to the "authority" of the writings. This linkage is particularly true for Christian theologies that depend on the "Bible alone" as the source for Christian authority. For such groups, the Bible is the only authority for the believer because it is seen as the word of God delivered through selected, inspired men. Communities that locate "authority" in group consensus, however, are often far more open to arguments against Pauline authorship. Christian communities, they would argue, have selected these texts regardless of the actual author. Therefore, these texts have authority. In other words, biblical authority is not solely based upon the direct inspiration of a particular person; the *text* is recognized as authoritative. This claim, they counter-argue, is what is strictly promised in 2 Timothy 3. The letters could easily be considered inauthentic in terms of authorship, but still be regarded as authoritative because of canon. To put it bluntly, these letters are authoritative because the church *says* they are authoritative. Actual authorship is a secondary question.

Other readers feel that if the letters claim Pauline authorship but are not, in fact, written by Paul, then they are deceptive and fraudulent. If inauthentic, they are lies and ethically unfit to be guides for anyone's faith. If inauthentic, we must concede, they would not meet modern standards for "truth." Yet this need not mean they are unfit ethical guides in every case, nor even that they are "lies." No modern Christian community would argue that any human apart from Jesus of Nazareth has lived an ethically unimpeachable life. Flawed humans meet with flawed humans to embrace, together, a redeeming God. Why would flawed texts be, prima facie, unfit?

The letters might also have been written by someone else in Paul's voice but with no intention to deceive anyone. Recently, I heard a radio interview with Thomas Jefferson, third president of the United States. Mr. Jefferson was talking about his favorite books. The interviewer always referred to him as "Mr. President." Was this interview a falsehood? Strictly speaking, yes it was. It was clearly a Jefferson impersonator. Jefferson is long dead and died well before recording technology was invented. Was the interview a "deception" or a "lie?" Of course not. It was a theatrical and instructional production. Someone, an expert in Jeffersonian thought, was presenting Jefferson's ideas in a creative and entertaining way. It wasn't a lie because there was no real intention to deceive. Any person educated enough to follow the conversation should be very aware that Jefferson is long dead and that this must be an actor.

It is very true that the pastorals could have been written by a later person fraudulently attaching Paul's name to his own document to achieve more authority. It is very true that the pastorals could have been written to rehabilitate and "mainstream" a radical Paul. It is also very true, however, that the disputed Paulines could have been written or edited by later followers of Paul who were trying to reinterpret him for a new context (to say "Paul would have said …") or to develop what was generally understood to be Paul's practice but not written elsewhere, or to articulate what were known to be his oral teachings, or to reinterpret him as a standard figure of the community's theology. Such would not, prima facie, be an attempt to deceive. The author, a literate student of Paul or a member of a "Pauline school," might well have expected his potential audience to know very well, that Paul was long dead. Once the "letters" began to circulate more broadly, they were adopted and read by people not "in on" the literary device.

The potential for such a "Pauline school" and later Pauline traditions is exactly why this whole debate is relevant to the question of Pauline biography in the early church. First, such a community would be an ideal candidate for role of collector and editor of the Pauline corpus. Second, this community would be particularly interested, as well, in crafting a sense of Pauline identity. Third, this community (or individual), if responsible for the redaction or composition of the disputed epistles, is directly constructing a biography of Paul at the same time.

As a final note, many scholars suggest that there is also the possibility that any of the Pauline letters (disputed or otherwise) might have been altered in the process of collection and preservation. Words, sentences, or even paragraphs may have been moved, omitted, or added to the preserved copy by a later editor or redactor. Such changes, though seemingly small, can have a dramatic effect on the final image of Paul that emerges. A key example of this can be seen in 1 Corinthians.

In 1 Corinthians 14, Paul is addressing the question of spiritual gifts, particularly speaking in tongues. Apparently, the ancient church had some aspect of its worship or community meetings where the presence and power of the Holy Spirit were miraculously displayed by believers speaking (ecstatically?) in a strange language (perhaps the famous "tongues of ... angels" discussed in 1 Corinthians 13). Paul is concerned that some of the believers, seeking to show off their spiritual power, are chattering in these tongues during key parts of the service or while someone else is speaking. He worries: the group will not be edified by the message but confused; the display of "greater spiritual power" is unseemly and antithetical to Christian ideals of humility; outsiders who stumble upon the group at worship and, hearing such a cacophony, will come away not only without any real information about the group but also thinking that everyone present is mad. Paul concedes that speaking in tongues is valuable. He moderates this, however, by indicating that services should be "decent and in order;" no more than two or three individuals should speak in tongues at any given meeting, and "interpreters" (those with the gift of making sense out of this ecstatic speech) should always be present (and allowed to do their work).

At the apex of Paul's argument, he interrupts himself in verses 34 and 35 to talk about women. He suddenly asserts that all women should be silent in the assembly. They are not even to ask a question; they must wait until the service is ended and they are back at home. The sense is one of stunning suppression, and it comes as quite an unexpected surprise. In Galatians (3:28) Paul had earlier written that there were no distinctions in status between men and women "in Christ Jesus." True, this is not necessarily a conflict (Paul may be saying there is no distinction *in essence*, not necessarily in role and activity). But it does suggest a more egalitarian Paul than we see in 1 Corinthians 14. More surprising, though, is that, earlier in 1 Corinthians itself, Paul addresses the problem of how men and women should dress while leading worship. He is particularly concerned with women praying and speaking prophecy in mixed assemblies without having their heads covered. He insists that women, in public, must cover their heads when praying and prophesying. One can't help but wonder, however, that, if 1 Corinthians 14:34–5 means what it clearly says, if it is as universal and as matter-of-fact as it claims to be, *and* if it was written by Paul, something seems to be lost in context. Why would Paul go to such effort to tell women *how* to speak in public (with covered head) when he opposed them speaking *at all* in public? Why wouldn't he just tell them to sit down and hush?

Verses 34–5 are surprisingly abrupt in the flow of 1 Corinthians 14 as a whole. One can easily see my point here by reading through and skipping from verse 33 to verse 36. Not only is there no perceptible gap in argument, it works better for the omission. On small research, we can quickly discover additional complexity in the ancient manuscripts. Some manuscripts do not have verses 34–5 at all. Others have this sentence in different locations in chapter 14. All of this may very well suggest that these two short verses were never part of the original, but were added by the later editor or redactor. The sentiment of 1 Corinthians 14:34–5 is certainly consistent with prohibitions on women's speech and ministry found in 1 Timothy 1. Indeed, 1 Corinthians 14:34–5 may well have been composed and inserted into 1 Corinthians *precisely* in an effort to make Paul appear more consistent across his letters. Once again, how one collects, frames, and edits a work certainly shapes the final image and biography of the author.

(Finally) A Brief Tour of Paul's Letters

For the collection, as it stands, we both know a great deal and lack a great deal of data. Paul's letters are both compellingly evocative and annoyingly vague. To sense the image of the Pauline figure the New Testament describes, a brief survey of the surviving letters may help.

1 Thessalonians

1 Thessalonians is a short letter written to the church at Thessalonica, a city on the southeastern border of Macedonia. Paul's missions to Macedonia seem to have been his most successful in terms of reception and long-term viability. Conversely, from his letters, the community there seems to be among the poorest and most pressured. 1 Thessalonians is almost universally considered to be Paul's first letter. If so, it is the oldest surviving document written by a believer in Jesus. It was likely composed in the early to mid 40s CE. Paul does not discuss his plans for a contribution for Jerusalem. He also addresses problems that have arisen over Thessalonican worries about the imminent return of Jesus. Some have died, and the survivors are concerned that the dead will miss Jesus' return. This view reflects what scholars call a belief in the "imminent parousia" (or any-minute-now return) of Jesus. The earliest followers of Jesus (Paul included) seem to have expected Jesus would return within a few weeks or months, certainly within their lifetimes. The longer the delay, the more pressure it placed on the early community. Paul is writing, in part, to quiet these worries. He is also addressing a community that, overall, feels oppressed. It is suffering personal and economic hardships. Some of these may be a direct result of the choice to follow Jesus. 1 Thessalonians, Paul's earliest letter, is written to a fledgling community struggling to maintain cohesion and faith in the face of suffering and pressures (internal and external) and discouraged by the delay in Jesus' return. Paul writes to encourage its members to maintain faith. From 1 Thessalonians, one might reasonably guess that Paul's earliest message was a radical call to believe in Jesus since the new messianic age had clearly begun.

Galatians

The exact audience of Galatians is uncertain. Paul may be writing to churches in either the highlands of central Turkey or on the southwestern coast of Turkey. Both regions were called "Galatia." He is certainly writing in answer to an immediate crisis. The letter may date from the early to mid 50s CE. Paul had established his congregations, then moved on to work elsewhere. In his absence, some other teachers from Jerusalem (perhaps affiliated with Peter and James), whom Paul calls "Judaizers," have come along behind Paul and, in their view, corrected his teaching to the Galatians. These new teachers have argued that gentiles who wish to follow Jesus must first convert to Judaism and then observe Jewish law. Many of the Galatians are agreeing with the new teachers. Word of this has gotten back to Paul. Furious, he writes the letter to dissuade the Galatians from their course of action, defend his own credibility as a teacher, and counterstrike with angry outbursts against his opponents and fearsome threats and insults toward his congregants.

The letter is hard to read in many ways. Paul's voice vacillates from anger to pleading. He relates in cooing terms the "honeymoon" days of his work in Galatia. He was ill when he arrived, but the Galatians still embraced him. Their mutual love was warm and affectionate. Now, they have cooled to him. Paul declares his wish that advocates of circumcision would err with the knife and castrate themselves. He shouts at the "stupid Galatians" who must, clearly, have been "bewitched" to have rejected the logic of his first teachings to them. Anyone who teaches differently than Paul should be "accursed," literally "cast aside" by the divine; periphrastically, "Goddamn them." Paul may be conceding a charge against him: that he does not have "Jerusalem connections" to teach and that his gospel is unique, different from the one taught by others. He sarcastically and bitterly reiterates the history of his conversion, conceding that he has no Jerusalem connection – his commission comes directly from Jesus. His gospel is unique; it comes, again, directly from Jesus. And Paul is confident enough in his positions to publicly shout down Peter, or anyone else, who opposes him.

Once again, the letter does not discuss a collection in process for Jerusalem; Paul briefly (and obliquely) mentions that he has agreed to take up some sort of similar project (and, that though the idea was suggested by Jerusalem leaders, he had planned to do it anyway). Galatians clearly reflects a sharp division between Paul and some other teachers regarding Jesus and the relationship of gentiles to the new covenant, a tension that may have lain at the source of his contribution plans. He is also clearly pulling out all rhetorical stops to try to dissuade the Galatians. Notably, after this letter, Paul does not again refer to Galatian churches as supporters of his work. Very possibly, he lost this argument and his churches in Galatia adopted new practices.

1 and 2 Corinthians

1 and 2 Corinthians make up our most extensive remaining correspondence by Paul. Our extant texts, however, are only a portion of the whole. Scholars believe the letters were written within the same year, perhaps in the early to mid 50s CE. The congregations of Corinth seem to have been overwhelmingly gentile; Paul makes few references to the Hebrew Bible but often appeals to "logic." This might be because he can't assume his audience is familiar with the Jewish scriptures. The issues of 1 Corinthians are mostly issues central to a pagan convert who would not, at first, know the rules and expectations of Judeo-Christian ethics and who would still need to navigate the social world of paganism. In Corinthians, Paul rarely speaks of Jewish or conversion issues. Guesses (and we have little more than that) are that 1 and 2 Corinthians were written while Paul was in Ephesus.

As 1 Corinthians 1:7 indicates, the Corinthians have written a letter with questions for Paul. Some reports, and probably even the letter itself, arrived via "Chloe's people," most likely mutual friends, believers who met at her house, or some of her slaves. The questions concern "spirits" (most likely beliefs in pagan gods), spiritual gifts, how to conduct family and business relationships post-conversion, social and political ideas, living among pagans, and other matters. For example: could one attend a banquet or symposium being held in a pagan temple? In addition to these issues, Paul has also heard of some practices which he wants to correct. The Corinthian congregations have divided into factions for some reason. According to Paul, the Corinthian believers are corrupting Christian liturgy and worship. They use spiritual gifts on display to establish a spiritual hierarchy. Believers have sued other church members in court. Their worship is tainted by appeals to status. In the ancient church, the "Lord's Supper" was very likely observed in the context of a large, possibly pot-luck-style communal dinner. At Corinth, people are refusing to share food and drink. Wealthy believers are going away drunk and full while the poor go away hungry. Paul sees disunity, selfishness, and division as the root of all these problems; he encourages greater unity and love, most famously in chapter 13. There are some (slight) indications that Paul is less credible to some at Corinth, and they seem to think he is less formally trained, less "rhetorical" or "philosophical" in his presentations, less "documented" in his missionary message than other Christian missionaries or teachers at Corinth.

Paul's greatest ire, however, is reserved for examples of what he regards as sexual immorality still present at Corinth; as a Jew, he very likely equated "idolatry" with sexual and social excess. He is also acutely concerned that the Corinthians present a "distinct" community to outsiders. He is, therefore, horrified at the "sexual immorality" found in Corinth. First, the Corinthian men are still visiting prostitutes. They would argue, very likely, that this was quite proper; they had paid the agreed-upon sum after all. Paul, to put it mildly, disagrees. An even greater worry to Paul, though, surrounds a man who is in an apparently monogamous sexual relationship with a woman who was (formerly?) his stepmother. The Corinthians are not only tolerant; they are proud of their inclusivity. Paul is aghast. Indeed, this issue seems to exemplify many conflicts between him and the Corinthians. He was, some felt, less "urbane" and cosmopolitan than many believers. He may well have also had much less formal education, have been less wealthy, less elite, and was thus to many less than credible. He orders the member be formally (and publicly) rebuked; if he does not immediately comply, he is to be expelled from the group. This is Paul's most heavy-handed command to the Corinthians.

It didn't go over well. 2 Corinthians opens as a letter of conciliation. Paul has apparently made a trip to Corinth and had a very vivid, painful, and confrontational exchange with some members. It may have been regarding the "immoral brother." It may have surrounded Paul's credentials and qualifications for ministry. It may have involved his spirituality, his theology, or even his status as apostle and voice of authority for the Corinthian community at large. It most likely involved aspects of all of these. Whatever the exact conflict, it was bitter. Paul and others said harsh and painful things to one another's face. 2 Corinthians is written after cooler heads have had a chance to prevail. Perhaps some of Paul's supporters at Corinth have sent a first, conciliatory letter of their own. Paul is hardly apologetic (unless, that is, "I'm sorry you made me do that; please don't make me have to come back there and rebuke you a second time" strikes one as a meritorious apology), but he does seem interested in peace, regretting not only his earlier "painful visit" but also a previous "painful letter."

2 Corinthians makes an abrupt shift in chapter 10. The last four chapters are bitter, angry, and acerbic. Scholars have long pondered this sudden shift in tone. Some have suggested that Paul paused in the midst of writing a polite letter of reunification (perhaps for sleep or a meal), learned of more trouble in Corinth (a sudden visitor with news) and, enraged, began to scribble out a new, harsh ending. Such a view is ludicrous. It assumes, if nothing else, that the letters of Paul are all first, single drafts without any thought or revision; ancient epistles are not email. A second hypothesis is that two letters of Paul have been edited together into a single document with the concluding greetings of one and the opening greeting of another elided during the editorial process. Perhaps, then, 2 Corinthians 10–14 is the "angry letter" Paul earlier composed and seems to regret sending.

At any rate, it seems clear that a good number of the Corinthian believers did not accept Paul's authority, and his relationship with the Corinthian church, as a whole, was tenuous. Clement of Rome, an ancient Christian writer active more than 50 years after Paul's death, wrote a letter to the church at Corinth raising some of the very same issues. Paul does seem to have retained a few loyal followers. Someone, after all, kept the letters. Yet he also seems to be generally ignored by others and openly confronted by some. A particular concern surrounds the contribution for

Jerusalem. The Corinthians, whose congregations may well have had some quite wealthy members, are hesitant to contribute. Paul has to "remind" them frequently. He cites the example of his churches in Philippi and Thessalonica, though he concedes, implicitly, that these churches are less wealthy, to "spur them to jealousy." The reader can decide if this bit of applied child psychology would have been effective. In 2 Corinthians 12:14–13:12 Paul has to reassert that the money is not for his own use, though he bitterly remarks that he is entitled to such support. As we have seen, he has to clarify that the money is traveling to Jerusalem by means of a third party (Titus). He also asserts – in the very same context – that uncorroborated accusations should not be considered. The indication is that some of the Corinthians have accused Paul of being a huckster scheming for money.

Romans

Romans is the last letter of Paul to mention the contribution. Paul is planning to take the money he has raised to Jerusalem and then strike out anew on his work. His hope, he writes to the Romans, is to go to Spain. Paul is writing to the Romans, at least in part, to acquaint them with his teachings (his Christology and his understanding of the role of gentile believers), and to "inform them of his plans." This latter point is a very unusual move. Paul did not found any communities in Rome. Indeed, there is no clear evidence that he had ever been to the city before. Why would they have cared about what his plans might include? Along the way, he more than once makes a subtle appeal for support, asking explicitly for prayer and moral support, implicitly for financial support. He may also be looking for any "political grease" the Romans could apply to help his planned travels. He wants to move further west since "there is no longer any place for me to work here."

That last statement is curious. Paul has clearly indicated in other writings that he prefers (and sees his gifts as surrounding) the role of congregation starter; others teach and expand (1 Cor. 3:6). Staying put for a decade or two at one church is not in his vocabulary. Even granting that, is he suggesting there is not a single city or location around the Aegean where the message has not gone? This could hardly be the case. Perhaps, though, there is no longer any place for *Paul* to work effectively. Indeed, from a survey of his letters, we see clear indications that, after 20 years of work, Paul's churches are small and he has generated more than a few enemies. He wants to start over. If Acts reports the history accurately, Paul will never make his planned trip to Spain. As he returns to Jerusalem with the offering, he is arrested and, eventually, transported to Rome for trial. We will examine the evidence more closely in our next chapter, but every indication from antiquity is that Paul is executed in Rome in the early 60s CE during the reign of the emperor Nero.

Paul may also be writing to the Romans to address a particular problem in those churches about which he feels uniquely qualified to speak. In 49 CE, the Roman emperor Claudius had expelled Jews from the city of Rome because of disputes surrounding a person later historians name Chrestus. Our primary source for this is a Latin-speaking historian from the early second century named Suetonius. The expulsion is mentioned, but without explanation, in Acts 18:2. *Christos* is a Greek word, understood by Greek-speaking Jews to mean "anointed (by God)." Chrestus is a common Latin name. The mistake could be easily made by an ancient Roman historian. Some modern scholars have argued very persuasively that it was. These disputes, they argue, were among Jews disagreeing about the messianic status of Jesus. If so, then early Jewish followers of Jesus and all the other Jews had been thrown out of the city in 49 CE. At Claudius' death, these Jewish believers returned to find the communities filled with gentile believers. The result was a community divided along ethnic lines. Paul speaks to this division as he articulates a theology relating Jew to gentile (particularly in chapters 9–11). Of course, this motive for writing need not be distinct from the earlier "letter of introduction and support request" model.

Romans is Paul's longest, best argued, most complete, and most clear presentation of his teaching (what he calls his Gospel). His use of biblical text in Romans is the most careful, precise, and integrated into his argument. His thoughts reflect maturity and practice in articulation. In many ways, Romans is Paul's masterpiece. He argues that Jesus as messiah was a revelation of God's glory and grace to the whole world. God has fulfilled God's promise to the Jews despite the apparent faithlessness of some, proving God's consistency and fidelity; God has included the gentiles, despite their earlier practices of sexual immorality and idolatry, proving God's patience and mercy. Jesus was messiah, a reality proven by his resurrection from the dead. As messiah, Jesus was the central sacrifice and vicariously able to redeem others by/through/from the observance of law. Baptism offers the believer a chance to vicariously participate (mystically) in both Jesus' faithful act of submission (his death) and God's greatest commendation of Jesus (the resurrection from the dead). As a result, we live ethically in a new world as new creations.

Philippians and Philemon

Paul never got the chance to spread this gospel to Spain. In Philippians, one of his last letters, he is in prison (as he writes, "in chains"), or at least protective custody. He is beset by rival teachers and abandoned by his former associates. He seems tired. He speculates on his coming trial and indicates it could go either way: he could be freed or he could be executed. Though he comes down on the side of exoneration, he may well be talking himself up; he hardly seems unshakably confident. The Philippians have sent him a financial gift to cover his expenses while in custody. A mutual friend who was visiting Paul had been taken ill, but is now recovered. Paul is writing to the Philippians to thank them for the gift, commend their common friend, and offer some news of his current situation. Though the present gift seems to be for Paul's personal use, he mentions his gratitude for the support of the Philippians in the past, particularly for his effort to collect funds for Jerusalem.

Philemon is a very brief letter written while Paul is also in prison. The context, setting, and circumstance are generic and briefly stated. The letter is almost impossible to date or definitively set in context. According to traditional interpretations, Paul has met a slave named Onesimus (Greek for "useful") while in prison. Onesimus belongs to a gentleman named Philemon. Paul has converted Onesimus to Jesus and is sending him back to Philemon. The letter accompanies Onesimus and uses heavily manipulative rhetoric on his behalf, encouraging Philemon not to discipline the returned slave but to embrace him as a fellow believer.

An overview

From the "accepted seven" letters, we see a picture of Paul as a man driven by obsession. He is concerned, above all, with spreading the message that Jesus of Nazareth was/is the promised and prophesied messiah, and he is certain of his calling, despite many hardships and bitter debates. Paul is more oblique than direct about what, theologically, "anointing" might mean. He says very little of what Jesus taught and less about what Jesus did; his focus on Jesus includes: assertions of Jesus as the fulfillment of prophecy, celebration of Jesus' perfect obedience, declaration of Jesus' messianic status which was confirmed by his resurrection, and appeals to the vicarious effects of all these. Taken as a whole, these confessions, Paul asserts, result in the sanctification – the "being made holy"– of a believer who "unites" with Jesus. This promise is open to gentiles, as gentiles, in fulfillment of the promise to Abraham in Genesis. Abraham is also key to the modern messianic age: the inclusion of the "whole world" in the people of the Covenant is, for Paul, the ultimate fulfillment of God's promise to Abraham that he will have countless descendants.

Paul faced many physical setbacks. At times he was physically ill. By his own admission, he was not sophisticated in his display of formal logic and rhetoric. By his own description, his mission was iconoclastic. He viewed himself as directly and personally called by God; no doubt, outsiders accused him of self-appointment. His career was often embroiled in controversy. He clearly had a temper. As for his churches: his "successful" congregations were small, struggling, and impoverished; he very likely lost his congregations (or at least a major percentage of their members) in Galatia; he struggled through a painful "church split" in Corinth and failed to get those communities completely on board with his agenda. Perhaps discouraged, perhaps worn out, or perhaps simply realistic in assessment, he decided that he had no more room to work in the Aegean areas, so he planned to strike out to the "other side of the world" and appealed to the Romans for support. He very likely never made it to Spain. From the letters, his career seems to have been beset by controversy and challenge, small, iconoclastic to the point of being isolated, and marginally successful.

But the "disputed letters" complicate the picture of Paul that emerges from the other seven. Paul would likely concede much of the picture I describe above, but he would also likely challenge the words "marginally successful." Even within the undisputed letters, we find him granting that his work seems small by "human" estimation; yet one added believer, for Paul, is a stirring success. If nothing else, he has the critical characteristic necessary for a missionary: a very thick skin for feelings of ineffectiveness and "defeat." A missionary must endure scores of outright rejections before finding one person even interested in conversation. This characteristic is even more notable in the disputed letters. In addition, they often bring Pauline theology away from iconoclasm and more toward the center of what emerges as a "received" Christian theology (in other words, more consistently in resonance with other New Testament documents). At minimum, each letter contributes to (at least minor) inconsistencies and complexities in Pauline thought. Some scholars have suggested that these letters were written (or compiled/redacted) to interpret Paul for new problems and changes in the fledgling church. Perhaps they offer overviews of Pauline thought. Some scholars, more cynically, have suggested that these letters (particularly the pastorals) were written specifically to reframe and reconstruct Pauline identity.

2 Thessalonians

2 Thessalonians is a prime example of this process. In his earlier letter, Paul addresses numerous issues surrounding Thessalonican discouragement. He writes to spur them on and to awaken resolve to fidelity. Along the way, he addresses one (among many) of their discouragements: fears about potentially missing the reward

of Christ's return (after such determined allegiance). He openly notes that there are no indicators of the coming end of history; it will be sudden and unpredictable in its arrival. This "radical" expectation of the immediate coming of Jesus seems, many scholars suggest, to have been the norm in the earliest communities. The first believers, by every indication, believed that the end of the world as it currently existed was very, very much at hand.

Yet, as we now can easily see, the end of the world didn't occur. History has marched on, frustrating believers with what Tina Pippin has called a "refusal of the world to end according to schedule." Not only this, but the world that has stubbornly continued to exist has not gotten notably "better." The inequities, injustices, and moral standard of the world, as a whole, have remained unchanged. If anything, the struggle has gotten worse in the minds of many.

By the end of the first century, believers in Jesus had developed (or, at minimum, begun to more fully articulate) substantially more elaborate and sophisticated notions of time and the end of history. In essence, borrowing in part from ideas common in Greek philosophical literature, the world was segregated into realms of the physical and the "spiritual," mirroring Platonic divisions between the "real" and the "ideal." Our perceived world might indicate one reality, but the "spiritual truth" of the world was often quite different. While Christians seemed small and ineffective by "physical" or "human" standards, they were actually powerful and victorious in "spiritual" measures. A major example of this bifurcation is the Apocalypse of John. Rome appears, from a human standard, to be powerful, glorious, and overwhelmingly oppressive to dissident ideologies. Yet from a divine eye of revelation Rome was, quite literally, bestial and crude and awaiting the actualization of God's already made but not yet enacted judgment of wrath. The "signs" of that judgment were within the world already, to the discerning eye. These signs are not harbingers because God is tipping God's hand; instead, they are the indications, to the spiritually discerning, of the real spiritual state of the world.

2 Thessalonians represents this ideology. In exact contrast to his earlier remarks about the unpredictability of the end of history,

Paul lays out the signs of what is to come in a pattern very similar to the one found in the Apocalypse and other writings associated with John. He predicts a coming "Man of Lawlessness" and other signs of spiritual disorder which will occur as signs of the end. In other words, to elaborate and clarify his earlier remarks that there would be no signs of the end of the age, Paul lists the signs of the end of the age. More than a few readers and scholars have found this, to say the least, confusing.

Many scholars feel that this elaboration reflects later eschatologies because it is itself a later writing, perhaps inserted into 2 Thessalonians, or perhaps because 2 Thessalonians was written precisely as a "delivery vehicle" for the idea. This, matched with alterations in typical Pauline vocabulary, style, and structure, have led some to question 2 Thessalonians' authorship. While, again, we can not say conclusively, there is a real logic and coherence to the argument. It may well be one example of how some Pauline traditions were manipulated to construct a more uniform Christian theology. Simultaneously, the (re)construction brings Paul more into the mainstream of what the New Testament represents as a consistent worldview and theology.

Ephesians and Colossians

One of the first and most curious elements of Ephesians and Colossians is their remarkable verbal affinities. A major portion of Colossians is repeated, verbatim, in Ephesians. Greek (like Spanish or French) is an inflected language. The respective parts of speech in a sentence are not communicated by rigid rules about word order for syntax. Instead, a root stem of the word is modified to indicate its function in a sentence. As a result, authors in Koine Greek used word order to indicate emphasis or nuance. Word order, in many cases, was as variable as word selection. The repeated sections between Colossians and Ephesians preserve *both* vocabulary *and* word order. The best explanation for this is some sort of literary interdependence. Ephesians is the longer of the two. Scholars have long puzzled over whether Ephesians is intended as an expansion and elaboration of Colossians, Colossians is a summary of Ephesians, or both depend upon a (now lost) third document. Why would Colossians omit some of the key elements of Ephesians' ethics and practical theology? Why would Ephesians, so expansive about the glory of God and the supreme role of Jesus, omit Colossians' strong suggestions that the "Christ identity" of Jesus was a part of God from creation and pre-exists the physical incarnation?

That latter point, again, was a key assertion in Christian writings of the late first and early second centuries. It was particularly integral (indeed, crucial) to emerging Christian orthodox teaching about Jesus. It is also absent from the undisputed letters of Paul. The closest one can find is Philippians 2, where Jesus did not consider "equality with God" something to be "maintained" or "seized." The underlying Greek of this expression ("seized" or "grasped") is ambivalent. Further, Paul may be indicating (in sympathy with his idea in Romans) that Jesus was the perfect human. Unlike Adam, who Genesis says consumed the forbidden fruit to be equal with God in knowledge of good and evil, Jesus resisted this temptation. While many scholars would feel a more natural reading would stress the harmony between Philippians and Colossians, once again, we must consider at least the possibility that the Christology of Colossians has been composed and elaborated within a Pauline frame (or edited in a manner that reframes it and makes it central) by later hands to foster a notion of theological harmony. If so, it also recasts Paul himself as less iconoclastic and more mainstream.

Finally, many key ideas and themes in Colossians and Ephesians are unique in Pauline thought and many other ideas are used in variant ways. The vocabulary and style are, once again, distinct. Scholars debate whether there might be a central Pauline core which has been altered with theological and Christological expansions or edited/redacted into a new letter form and associated with Paul.

The Pastorals

The pastoral letters, 1 and 2 Timothy and Titus, are radically different from other Pauline writings. As we saw earlier, they also are homogenous among themselves in terms of style, vocabulary, and argument. They are often regarded as a distinct group within the Pauline corpus. Their vocabulary, style, syntax, and literary structure are remarkably different from those of the other Pauline letters. The variation is so pronounced that the effect is even visible in translations.

The pastorals refer to people and places that are otherwise unknown in Paul's life. They offer a timeline that is almost completely irreconcilable with a chronology that has Paul arrested, tried, and executed all in a single phase. To read them in any way compliant with any possible reconstruction of Pauline chronology and career, we would need to assume that Paul was initially tried, exonerated, and released, and that he traveled on to Spain. He was subsequently rearrested, and this time he was executed. Many early Church Fathers argued exactly this. They based their argument, in part, on Paul's "expectation" in Philippians and Philemon of his impending exoneration (Phil. 1:19–26; Philem. 1:22). They were also more than a bit candid about the fact that such a hypothesis was the only real way to make sense of the facts mentioned in the pastorals.

The pastorals are the most "homogenizing" of the Pauline letters. Paul is brought into a consistent community with his teachings on women (that they have no voice in the leadership or teaching of the early church). He comments on second-century structures of church office (elders, deacons, and "widows") and touches on issues that were sharp points of controversy in the second century. Were this not enough grounds for indictment, the pastorals are not cited by early "heretical" writers who valued Paul in the early second century *nor* are they cited by the opponents of those "heretics," even though these opponents are arguing about some of the *exact* issues the pastorals address. In fact, no one seems to quote or even know about the pastorals until the latter decades of the second century. Why would someone pass on an opportunity to quote from a "favorite" author of an opponent when that favored writer is writing explicitly and exactly in contradistinction to the very point the opponent is himself advancing?

Some radical scholars of the nineteenth century argued that the pastorals were composed deliberately as forgeries by early church leaders to refute opponents who prized Paul. The pastorals bear a strong literary affinity to the writings associated with an early bishop, Polycarp, and some suggested that he was the author. Less cynical scholars have suggested that they were written by a pious student of Paul who wanted to interpret or frame contemporary debates as, he or she felt, Paul most certainly would have, had he lived long enough. Others suggest that the student of Paul was collecting ideas and instructions Paul actually gave, but never wrote down; the student used the letter form as an organizational device. In either event, once again, the pastorals certainly reframe Paul. By this point, he is no longer a voice from the margins of the mainstream thought of the first century. Quite the contrary, he is the prescient voice of orthodoxy. If he had been marginalized during his career, it was only because his centrally orthodox greatness had been rejected by "hard-hearted" believers. Given that Paul also was framed to have argued against "Judaizers," this movement of Pauline literature toward what was constructed as an "authentic center" of Christian thought also sowed seeds of anti-Semitism deep within the soil of the earliest movement. Those openly unreceptive opponents of Paul were hard, calloused, jealous, and blind Jews.

The Acts of the Apostles

Sometime in the late first century or early second century, an author whom history remembers as Luke, the companion of Paul described in the pastorals and in the latter parts of Acts, investigated the "history" of the earliest movement and set about composing what he called an "orderly account of the things which have happened among us" (Luke 1:1–5) What emerged was a two-volume work: the Gospel of Luke and the Acts of the Apostles. The gospel deals with the career and teachings of Jesus. Acts deals with the spread of Christianity "beginning in Jerusalem, then to Judea and Samaria and unto the ends of the earth" (Acts 1:8) The two-volume work opens with a scene of a priest quietly going about his duty in the temple of Jerusalem, and ends with Paul the apostle in the bustling city of Rome proclaiming the arrival of the messiah. How did this message go from the quiet, inner conclave of Jewish religiosity to the bustling center of the empire? Luke/Acts narrates the tale.

We have already summarized the bulk of Acts' narratives about Paul. Acts relates his conversion on the road to Damascus and his adventurous career as a missionary, ending with him under (liberal) house arrest and awaiting trial in Rome. Beginning in chapter 16, the narrative of Paul's travels begins to shift in and out of the third person ("he went in," "they arrived at") and into the first person ("we set out from," "we arrived at"). Scholars have puzzled over the change. Traditionally, this is where the ascription to Luke of the authorship of both volumes arises. From analysis of the narrative, Luke emerges as the most likely candidate who would be qualified to articulate "we." Many modern scholars have posited that, among many sources for the two-volume work (the Gospel of Mark, Q, L), "Luke" had access to a travel narrative by Paul or one of his associates.

The narrative of Paul reads with the excitement of a novel. These stories are not simply a historical record of the early expansion of the movement (though they are our only glimpse into it). They are written to both entertain and to edify. They are also written to advance an argument via narrative. It's primary agenda – to articulate how a promised *Jewish* messiah would come to be a hero to a largely *gentile* empire means that it must deal, centrally, with the translation of Jesus from redeemer of Israel and fulfiller of the promise to Abraham to savior of the world and redeemer of all humanity. Paul's career as an early missionary with a message of gentile inclusion in the people of the Covenant of God during the messianic age was integral to that narrative. Also, Paul's "blended" status as both Jew and Greco-Roman citizen made him uniquely qualified for this role. Finally, Christianity faced a real challenge in its appeal for popular acceptance. The movement venerated the teachings of a man executed by the state for sedition and treason. Many Jews did not acknowledge Jesus as messiah. Finally, there were often controversies surrounding this outspoken and idiosyncratic group advocating what, to a Roman eye, must have seemed like a "newfangled cult." Acts is taking great pains to present a narrative that implicitly argues Christianity is peaceful, harmless to civil order, and "reasonable." The author of Acts is trying to tell "our side of the story."

In order to accomplish this, Paul must also appear peaceful, harmless to civil order, and reasonable. Any suggestion of challenges to his credentials or status from within the movement itself need to be quieted or explained. He must be both charismatic and spiritually powerful. Acts produces such a figure through the device of very careful storytelling. It stresses those elements which support this image and downplays others which might conflict with it. As we've already seen, this produces a certain discontinuity with much of Paul's own writings. His acerbic temper is downplayed. Dissent in his churches is ignored or blamed on someone else. He is shown in complete harmony with the Jerusalem leaders Peter and James. When trouble arises, it is always due to circumstances beyond Paul's control, or because of jealous enemies.

Some scholars, to be sure, argue that Acts, while clearly following an agenda of getting its side of the story into the record, is still highly reliable as a historical document. Any disagreements, omissions, or variations from what we find in Paul's letters are minor and represent, at most, the difference in perspective of the storyteller or writer. To say that there are variations does not, of necessity, mean that one or the other is "wrong."

Very true.

Yet it also indicates that neither complies with a simplistic idea of "historical fact." It would mean that "facts" of history are not neutral things, free-floating in the universe and stable to the degree that any and all informed and sincere collectors of such facts (historians, say) would present the same picture. Acts is telling a particular story that needs a particular perspective of Paul. Finally, many historians, particularly those who do not have a confessional or theological allegiance to Christianity as "truth," wonder about how Acts' improbable stories of miraculous visions, healings, resurrections, and exorcisms could ever be real or true.

Yet there are additional factors to consider when reading Acts as a "history." Even within itself, Acts does not always present a consistent picture of events. Acts first narrates Paul's Damascus road vision, and then twice later has him repeat the story. To begin with, repeating a story *three times* in the same work is a strong indicator of how key that story is for the author. In Acts, this story is the fundamental basis for Paul's authority to teach and evangelize. Yet, reading Acts closely, we notice that the stories vary in fact *even within Acts*. At first, in the story told by the narrator of Acts (9:1–19), Paul and those with him hear God's voice, though only Paul sees anything (9:7). Later, when Paul retells his own story, his companions see the vision, but do not hear the voice (22:9). Still later, when Paul again recalls his own story (26:12–23), there is no mention of his companions at all and the words of God are different. All three cannot possibly be "true" in a simple, literalistic way. Still closer reading reveals, however, that each of the three stories changes by context, and changes in a way that is exactly resonant with the immediate issue. Acts is not a narrative that conforms to modern, newspaper-like precision. When considered alongside the discrepancies we've already noted with the letters, reasonable historians could readily shift to emphasize the letters for Pauline biography. Certainly, many scholars have pondered these variations with an eye to seeing consistency in Acts, and they have come up with numerous suggestions, some plausible, some not. Yet the point remains: Acts is not treating its own "facts" the way some moderns might desire.

Acts may not conform to everyone's expectations regarding historical precision, but, to put it bluntly, if we did not have Acts to provide *some* skeletal framework for the life of Paul, the letters would be almost totally unintelligible. For example, notice how, above, I have depended on Acts' account of Paul's arrest in Jerusalem (on delivery of his collection) to construct sequence. Even more, we totally depend upon Acts to even begin to understand what the collection itself actually was. Acts is essential as a base, a foundation, for discovery of the "historical Paul," even if only to add structure to his letters. But, if Acts is, indeed, reframing Paul, then we, yet again, glimpse the problem of Pauline biography in any exact sense. The picture of Paul found in modern Christian memory is both constructed and reinforced, but the "historical Paul" is already obscured even by the very device, the New Testament canon, that preserves any memory of him at all.

Hebrews

Before leaving the subject of Pauline writings in the New Testament, I should also note a final letter, written generically "to the Hebrews." This letter is anonymous. It bears no real affinity to Pauline theology, omits key Pauline terms, concepts, and vocabulary, cites liturgical texts (and other Hebrew Bible materials) Paul never uses, and constructs a highly supersessionist view of Judaism against Paul's "dual covenant" model, where Judaism is expanded – not superseded – by gentiles. Hebrews doesn't even look like a letter; it reads much more like a baptismal sermon. It doesn't begin with any address or author identified. It does, however, conclude with a greeting which mentions "Timothy."

Hebrews had a difficult time making the Christian canon. Early Christians felt its theology was too extreme, radical, and idiosyncratic. Its authorship was unknown. Some of its citations of the Bible were clearly from memory, others were clearly tendentious. Because of a reputation that Paul was a radical voice supporting gentiles *to the opposition and exclusion* of Judaism, and because of the reference to "Timothy," many second- and third-century Christians argued that Paul was the author of the letter.

The argument was a hard sell. Even in the late third and early fourth centuries, many early Christian scholars didn't buy it. Origen, one of the most famous early Christian interpreters, studied the work very closely, noting all the problems with Pauline authorship. Still, he wanted very much to adopt the theology of Hebrews, and he was nothing if not a loyal churchman. After summarizing the debate, he famously concluded that "only God knew" the author of Hebrews, before almost audibly shrugging his shoulders and taking a dutiful turn toward arguments that Paul was its author. In essence, he seems to say, "It doesn't look like Paul, but that's what they tell me." Origen is hardly an enthusiastic supporter of Pauline authorship of Hebrews.

The ascription of Pauline authorship to Hebrews was very likely what secured the book for the New Testament canon. Placing arguments of Hebrews, particularly its strong anti-Semitism, as the product of a Pauline pen radically reframe how one reads Galatians and Romans 9–11. Modern scholars – even Evangelicals – are almost unanimous in denying Pauline authorship of Hebrews. The correction is a long time coming. To my mind, not only is Paul not the author of Hebrews, he would have disavowed much of the work. Yet Hebrews has still played a critical role for some in the history of Pauline biography.

Chapter 2

Paul in the Ante-Nicene Church

The sea called Euxine, or hospitable, is belied by its nature and put to ridicule by its name. Even its situation would prevent you from reckoning Pontus hospitable: as though ashamed of its own barbarism it has set itself at a distance from our more civilized waters. Strange tribes inhabit it – if indeed living in a wagon can be called inhabiting. These have no certain dwelling-place: their life is uncouth: their sexual activity is promiscuous, and for the most part unhidden even when they hide it: they advertise it by hanging a quiver on the yoke of the wagon, so that none may inadvertently break in. So little respect have they for their weapons of war. They carve up their fathers' corpses along with mutton, to gulp down at banquets. If any die in a condition not good for eating, their death is a disgrace. Women also have lost the gentleness, along with the modesty, of their sex. They display their breasts, they do their housework with battle-axes, they prefer fighting to matrimonial duty. There is sternness also in the climate – never broad daylight, the sun always niggardly, the only air they have is fog, the whole year is winter, every wind that blows is the north wind. Water becomes water only by heating: rivers are no rivers, only ice: mountains are piled high up with snow: all is torpid, everything stark. Savagery is there the only thing warm – such savagery as has provided the theatre with tales of Tauric sacrifices, Colchian love-affairs, and Caucasian crucifixions.

Even so, the most barbarous and melancholy thing about Pontus is that Marcion was born there.

(Tertullian, *Against Marcion*, 1.1)

What is "Ante-Nicene" Christianity?

Quintus Septimus Florens Tertullian was a prolific early Christian writer from northern Africa. He was born about 152 and died around the year 222. He was the son of a career military man, raised in a very pro-Roman household as a non-believer, and trained as a lawyer. He converted to Christianity in his early adulthood and subsequently devoted his life to teaching and writing about his new faith. He wrote *On The Trinity*, a work that explains the triune relationship of God the Father, Jesus, and the Holy Spirit as three persons in one substance. Tertullian was the first to coin the term "triune" for God. He also wrote the *Apology*, where he defends the rationality of the Christian faith and argues that any formal Christian persecution was irrational and violated the best Roman ideals.

Tertullian also wrote a five-volume work titled, accurately if unimaginatively, *Against Marcion*. Marcion (ca. 110–60) was born in Pontius on the Black Sea coast. He taught for a while in Rome and later returned to Pontius as a self-appointed bishop of his own church. Tertullian didn't like him. Many others didn't either. Marcion, apparently a very persuasive teacher and writer and a very, very independent thinker, had been expelled from the church in Rome because of his teachings, which were denounced as heretical. None of his own writings have survived intact; we only know of his teachings through the responses to him which often quote him. His major work, *Antitheses*, was rebutted by several writers.

In addition to Tertullian, he was also opposed in writings by Irenaeus and Hippolytus, two Greek-speaking, heresy-hunting advocates of Christian thought also from the second century. These writers argued that Marcion's ideas were "wrong" and deviated too much from the received faith, and many modern believers would agree. Most certainly, Marcion's ideas varied from what is now considered "orthodox" Christian theology. Many people in today's churches believe, as Vincent of Lérins once argued, that "orthodox" Christian thought is what has been believed by "all Christians at all times in all places." Modern scholars rightly question whether there was ever any belief that would meet that definition, and suspect that later believers have superimposed their "orthodox" ideas back onto some writers (say, for example, Paul) and eradicated the evidence of divergent views either by heresy trials and rules or by the destruction or non-preservation of alternate documents. At minimum, however, the evidence is clear that Christian beliefs and practices in the first two centuries CE varied widely, and that Christian doctrine – at minimum, the articulation of its ideas – evolved over time. For example, the central concept/term "Trinity" does not appear to pre-date the third century, and mostly evolved as a result of controversy and dispute. In other words, while Christians today talk about "orthodox" Christian theology, in the first centuries of the Common Era these views were not clearly articulated. Many scholars of ancient Christianity question whether they ever existed at all. The unarguable presence of sharp dispute suggests more than a little variation in belief, and the complexity of ancient Christian confession and practice is becoming more and more evident with each new element of data that comes to light. Diversity, far more than uniformity, was the rule of the day.

"Orthodox," as a term, describes a strategy of Christian authority more than it denotes a list of approved doctrines. The word "orthodox" is Greek for "straight" or "linear teaching." It is making an implicit assertion that the ideas go back in a straight line to Jesus and the first apostles. "Heresy" is from the Greek for "choice" or "alternative." It was used to describe ideas that someone felt were "progressive," or innovations in the previously accepted teachings of Jesus and the apostles. In the early fourth century a group of Christian bishops met at the city of Nicaea to sort through all the various claims regarding Jesus and determine which were orthodox – which went "authentically" back to the earliest apostles. The result of their work was the Nicene Creed. We have no record of their deliberations, only of their results. We have no way of evaluating their evidence for the line of continuity in their teaching, nor why they excluded some other alternative claims. Many modern believers are confident that the Nicene bishops were led by the Holy Spirit. Others, less confident of the Spirit's role, suggest that political and personal agendas entered the evaluation process. Our evidence suggests that the Nicene Creed is certainly continuous with written evidence of ancient Christians, but it also shows substantial development of its own. More and more, scholarship is seriously questioning Nicaea's claims for linear continuity. The period prior to Nicaea is called "Ante-Nicene" Christianity (*ante* is Latin for "before" or "prior to").

Some Ancient "Heretics": Marcion and the Gnostics

Some moderns may want to defend the freethinking of Ante-Nicene "heretics" and are suspicious of authority claims made by the orthodox. Yet even the most ardent supporter of free thought will blanch a bit at Marcion's teachings. Marcion is often called a Gnostic, but this isn't strictly accurate. Gnosticism, if it existed in the second century, is better used to describe another "arch-heretic" named Valentinus. At any rate, "gnostic," like "orthodox," doesn't so much denote a single set of ideas as a generic strategy for authority, vaguely analogous to the way we use a modern term like "evangelical" (though, most certainly, in terms of content it is quite dissimilar). Gnostics also had a variety of highly symbolic and speculative myths about creation and human origins. Many scholars argue that Gnostic mythology is too complex to have any real "core." If there is any "Gnostic pattern," the one proposed by Bentley Layton seems the most reasonable.

Bentley Layton has argued, for example in *The Gnostic Scriptures*, that Gnostic mythology had general "movements" or "acts"; some are similar to some of Marcion's ideas. The first describes a primal, pre-time origin of all deity, the "Monad." The Monad is a swirling source of divine energies and being. This Monad begins to emanate various divine beings. These beings are called the "Fullness" or the Pleroma (in Greek), which existed in a state of perfect harmony and balance. One of these divine beings, often named Sophia (Greek for "wisdom") took it upon herself to give birth to another being, often named Ialdabaoth. Ialdabaoth was very powerful, but also limited in his knowledge. He created the physical world and humans, and thought that he himself was the only god. He was a terrible, wrathful god; he is the God described in the Hebrew scriptures. Humans have two natures. Those descended from Adam's son Cain (who, in the biblical text, murders his brother Abel) are mired in physical reality and possess none of the divine spark of the Pleroma. Many Gnostics believed that those descended from Adam's son Seth are spiritual and possess the divine spark, though they are blinded by ignorance since they are trapped in physical reality. To correct this ignorance, the Pleroma revealed itself in human form via Jesus. Those who are descendants of Seth and possess the divine nature will recognize the Pleroma in Jesus ("Gnostic" is from the Greek for "knowledge," or "familiar recognition"). Some Gnostic myths suggest that Sophia partners Jesus (the Logos) in this saving role. This knowledge will save them. Aware of the true nature of the cosmos, they will, on death, transcend the physical world just as, in life, they transcended spiritual ignorance. They will return to the Pleroma. Humans who recognize Jesus do so because they are privy to secretly passed down, esoteric teachings from Jesus, not found in the majority of the writings. There are dozens (perhaps even hundreds) of variations as to the ethics (or their lack) that such gnosis requires, the names and natures of various deities, and the secret arcana that impart knowledge of the "real" universe.

In Colossians 1:15–20 we read that the "fullness [*pleroma*] of God" was revealed in Jesus who transcends "the powers." Paul asserts in Galatians that Jesus was "in" him (Gal. 2:20, 6:17). He writes that the Jews are "under a veil" of ignorance that is lifted by Jesus (2 Cor. 3). He says his accomplishments as a Jew are inferior to the "knowledge [*gnoseos*] of Christ" (Phil. 3:8). He writes about how Jesus undoes the limitations of Adam (Rom. 5). These and many other passages were likely seized on by Gnostics.

Marcion was an avid reader of Paul and seems to have been drawn to some of these same passages, but he was not fully a Gnostic. He does not seem to divide humans by their descent from Adam's two sons, does not discuss Pleroma, and does not speculate about a primordial mythology. That granted, his teachings do sound some similar chords to Gnosticism. Marcion asserted that the God found in the Old Testament – named Yahweh – was a deity of wrath and judgment. By nature, he was vengeful, jealous, and wrathful, and tyrannically imposed an irrational set of laws and rules on a specific people whom he then took pleasure in torturing. To counter him, the God of love and mercy – "the Father" – sent Jesus. Jesus' mission was to reveal the real loving, gracious, and ethical nature of the Father. He also ransomed humans by paying their debt to Yahweh through his own crucifixion. Believers who participated in Jesus' death were redeemed, literally bought back, from sin and death. For Marcion, Judaism was inherently flawed. There was some, limited good in some of the stories from the Hebrew traditions, but Jewish religiosity itself was bankrupt. Jews were to be pitied at best, and opposed in extremes. They were gullible and enslaved and unable, by being observant Jews, to really understand God, morality, or ethics. Christianity was vastly superior in ethics and morality. It was liberating, where law was destructive. It was hopeful, where Judaism was restrictive. It was from the real, true God of Love. Judaism was best eradicated; it offered nothing but division, wrath, and judgment. The anti-Judaism of Marcion can scarcely be oversold.

Marcion and the Gnostics are examples of two debates in Ante-Nicene Christianity. Many were asking which were the "correct" books to read. They wanted to know which books, from a surprisingly varied array of candidates, best represented the teachings (public or esoteric) of Jesus and his earliest followers. Once these books were identified, however, they still needed to be "correctly" interpreted. The balance of this chapter will be an exploration of how some Ante-Nicene Christians answered these two questions.

Marcion's Paul

Marcion was opposed to the "Jewishness" he found in many of the early traditions, stories, and writings by first-century believers in Jesus. He wanted to marginalize these texts and traditions. Accordingly, he compiled a list of what were "productive" writings for his followers to read. For this, he edited out his own gospel based on Luke/Acts. He edited away the parts that seemed "too Jewish" in Jesus' teaching. He focused on Jesus' birth, death, and resurrection. Marcion's Bible also included most of the letters assigned to Paul. He does not include the pastorals, and called Ephesians "Laodiceans." Apparently, he built a major portion of his doctrines of atonement, sanctification, and the relationship of Judaism to the worship of Jesus largely on the basis of Paul's writings. Marcion's ideas were extremely popular. His new churches exploded in membership, and he created his own hierarchy and official structure. His views remained, despite a vigorous counter-response from his opponents, persuasive for hundreds of years. Refutations of Marcion were written in Greek, Latin, and Coptic: the array of languages used by his opponents testifies to the spread of Marcion's ideas. Tertullian's angry and extensive rebuttal was composed nearly 50 years after Marcion's death, strong testimony to both his popularity and the depth of the nerve that Marcion had touched in many.

Marcion, while crafting a new theological understanding of Jesus and God, was also at work on crafting a biography of Paul. In it, he chose to construct a Paul who was in opposition not just to the circumcision of gentile believers in Jesus, but to Judaism as a whole. He also emphasized the "mystic" elements of Paul. Paul writes, for example, how Jesus appeared to him personally (Gal. 1:12–13; 1 Cor. 15:8). In Galatians, as we have seen, Paul asserts he can re-present the crucified Jesus in his own body. He fully believed that Jesus "lived in" him, "putting to death the old man." Paul sees this mystic union as so strong that he uses it as the basis, in 1 Corinthians, for forbidding visits to prostitutes: Christians are so united with Jesus that Jesus would be having sex with the prostitute too (1 Cor. 6:12–20). The Pauline literature and traditions were so central for the theology of Marcion (and the later Gnostics) that Tertullian, exasperated, referred to Paul as "the Apostle to the Heretics" (playing on the conventional "Apostle to the Gentiles").

Marcion's opponents were also crafting (counter-)images of Paul. Tertullian, stopping just short of advocating a wholesale rejection of Paul, went so far as to advocate that the reading of Paul should be limited because of the ease with which the Marcionites and Gnostics could construct their theologies from his letters. Other ancient writers went even further. One author wrote a letter as if from Peter to James that has Peter complaining about and denouncing Paul. "Problem passages" in Paul, the elements of arcana and mysticism, are often downplayed (or ignored) by modern theology, but they were hotly debated in the early church. One major reason for this debate was reaction to Marcion. The early Christian "heresy-hunters" Hippolytus and Irenaeus counter-read Pauline texts in their own heresy-denouncing tomes. Some scholars even suggest that the pastorals, with their emphasis on following the "real" bishops – and not self-appointed ones such as Marcion – may have been written (or may have gained wider credibility) as a result of these debates as well.

Marcion's Bible

Marcion is the first person we have on record to have compiled a Christian canon of authoritative writings. "Canon" is from the Greek for "measuring rod" or "rule." A canon of writings is a collection that establishes the "standard" or "common denominator" for doctrine. Ideas which do not arise from or conform to those in canonical writings are, by definition, regarded as false. Ironically, given Marcion's other views, the idea of a collection of documents recognized as original and according to the tradition of the elders was long established in Judaism. Evidence indicates that, by the Common Era, Jews had settled on the five books of Moses (the Torah), the writings by and about the prophets (the Nevi'im), and a fairly stable collection of other writings (the Ketuvim). The earliest followers of Jesus may have begun collecting various writings, using them as part of the Ketuvim or planning a nascent fourth part of the Bible which would deal with the messiah. Marcion, in effect, borrows the idea of a Christian canon from Judaism. Various collections of writings existed before Marcion's canon, but the idea of collecting a restricted canon of the letters of an apostle of Jesus but not restricting this collection to stories or sayings associated with Jesus seems to be his own innovation. It is, however, highly analogous to the organization of the Jewish canon. According to Tertullian, Marcion was the first person to gather the Christian writings into a distinct collection apart from the Hebrew Bible. Marcion also carefully ordered the Pauline letters, placing Galatians, Paul's most aggressive letter in terms of opposition to Jewish ritual, to the fore.

Some scholars, such as Edwin Blackman and Elaine Pagels, have argued that Marcion is the among the first followers of Jesus to even think of the idea of a Christian canon. Certainly, collections of documents had existed prior to Marcion. 2 Peter and 2 Thessalonians seem aware of a collection of Pauline writings. But Marcion places these on a restricted canon list, indicating that the books not only had authority, but that *no other books equaled* that authority. This seems to be an innovation on his part. In other words, Marcion is trying to define a single, authoritative teaching that excludes alternative views of Jesus. In another ironic move, the first person history records as a Christian arch-heretic was also among the first heresy hunters. Also, he was the impetus for both the articulation of "orthodox" theologies and the construction of counter-canons. The intertwining of heretical and orthodox is complicated indeed.

Marcion did not include the pastorals, which include repeated instructions about hierarchical authority in the emerging church, an authority Marcion was flaunting. The pastorals forbid debate and dispute; Marcion was frequently the center of both. The pastorals revere continuity; Marcion rejected conventional notions of the continuity of faith and authority. 2 Timothy 3 asserts that the Bible is "God-breathed" or "inspired." In context, 2 Timothy is referring to the Hebrew Bible, a text Marcion had rejected. We can readily guess what might have prompted Marcion to avoid these works. Yet, oddly, *none of Marcion's early opponents cites the pastorals either.* This dual silence has prompted many to suspect that the pastorals either did not exist or were not widely known in Marcion's day. Some scholars (most famously, the nineteenth-century critic Ferdinand Christian Bauer) suggested the pastorals were composed precisely to counter Marcion with the mouth of his own, favorite author. Few contemporary scholars would put the composition of the pastorals so late.

It is equally possible that Marcion knew them but deliberately rejected them. Marcion demonstrates, if nothing else, a readiness to disregard texts others considered sacred when they were not in keeping with his theological views. He was perfectly ready to throw away the entire Hebrew Bible, and he rewrote the gospels; we can scarcely place selectivity regarding Pauline letters beyond his reach. Some scholars suggest Marcion's opponents make allusions to (but don't directly quote from) the pastorals, and seem aware of their content and teachings. Marcion's opponents may be avoiding direct citation because the letters were not widely known. If so, we are left to wonder whether or not Marcion omitted letters of Paul which are now lost, or whether he altered any of the letters he retained.

Lessons from Marcion

Marcion's heavy-handed restriction of "authoritative" books is a healthy caution against thinking of heretics as freethinking liberals advocating a positive, open-minded, "live and let live" attitude toward theology. Marcion, at least, could be just as dogmatic and closed in his thinking as his detractors; we should not imagine him as one who prized wide-ranging thought for its own sake. Indeed, he seems equally concerned with establishing his ideas as "from the original source," rooted in arcane and esoteric teachings directly from Jesus. He asserted that his teachings were the obvious and normative way to read Paul and to understand Jesus. In many ways, he argued for a tradition more "apostolic" and closed than did many of his orthodox detractors. He also clearly valued some sense of apostolicity. Marcion conceded that Christian teaching needed to be rooted in a tradition that went back, as closely as possible, to Jesus. Though he saw different meanings in Jesus' words, he agreed that Jesus' original ideas trumped innovative revelation.

We also notice in Marcion a pattern that will become more than merely familiar in the study of Paul. To adapt Tertullian's adaptation of Galatians 2, Paul seems very often to be the "Apostle to the Ideological Outsider." Marcion's attraction to Paul may not have been merely doctrinal; he may well have seen himself cast in a similar role: an outsider maverick, rejected or criticized by the "authorities," challenged as unqualified, possessing a unique understanding of the role of Jesus, hemmed in on all sides and oppressed by others in the community but doing it all for God. Christian theology seems to provoke or inspire a sense of the hesitant but called prophetic voice for "truth" and right theology, of the iconoclastic but noble defender, the outsider arguing that he is, instead, the "real" center. Obliged by the ignorance and resistance of others, the iconoclast must speak the truth, even in the face of hostility and rejection (indeed, may well even provoke the hostility). Paul fits this model.

Marcion, despite all his challengers, is difficult to overrate in terms of his influence on the development of Christian thought and the Christian canon. He in many ways determines both the issues and the "rules of engagement" that will be followed for centuries to come. As we have seen, he is first on record to argue for a closed canon. Second, he argued that his ideas were based on readings from the text and arose from "natural" and obvious interpretation. He also argued that his ideas were not innovations but could be traced, through Paul, to Jesus. Finally, he foregrounded three major tensions in ancient Christianity. What is the relationship of Christianity to Judaism? Is the presentation of God found in the Bible consistent? What is the relationship of Jesus to God? Tertullian resolved the latter two in his trinitarian model. Later orthodoxy embraced this view. Orthodoxy also ended up embracing many of Marcion's supersessionist views of Judaism, establishing its own canon, and asserting that *its* views were those of Jesus' first followers. In other words, orthodoxy rejected most of the *content* of Marcion's teachings, but accepted most of his *methods and concerns*. In effect, Marcion won the debate but lost the argument.

Paul Outside the New Testament

The context of debates between the proto-orthodox, the Marcionites, the Gnostics, and others made the second and third centuries a fertile time for the composition of texts revealing the hidden lives and teachings of the apostles. Stories are written to address what biblical characters looked like, what happened to some "missing" characters such as Thomas, Mary Magdalene, Bartholomew, and others absent from the biblical Acts of the Apostles. The "missing years" of Jesus' youth? Again, stories were written. Several "Acts" of the first generation of believers were written, along with several collections of letters. Paul generated his share of extra-canonical writings. One ancient collection, for example, pretends to be a series of letters between Paul and the famous Roman philosopher Seneca. Generally, these writings fill "gaps" in the record. Paul mentions another letter to the Corinthians, so a 3 Corinthians was composed. Paul mentions a letter to the church at the city of Laodicea, so a "To the Laodiceans" was composed. The "missing years" of Paul's missionary career are recorded in elaborate narratives. Who were Paul's opponents? Stories about some of the more notorious ones were written. What about the apparent tensions between Paul and Jerusalem, between Paul and Peter and James? Were these ever reconciled (or reconcilable)? Stories were written depicting both alternatives.

There is no ancient record for the founding of the church in Rome. The city of Jerusalem was destroyed by the Romans in the year 70 CE, no doubt a disruption to the church in that city (and to its influence). The congregation in Rome, the capital of the empire, seemed a logical replacement to many. Paul is last seen (by Acts) in the city of Rome. The two New Testament letters assigned to Peter are also vaguely associated with Rome, and there were extra-biblical stories, such as the Acts of Peter, that asserted that Peter ended his life in Rome as well. Such an important congregation needed to have its history intact. Once again, stories and traditions were written. If, indeed, Marcion (or others) were constructing biographies of key figures and casting themselves in similar role and costume, clarity regarding these lacunae was even more critical. The first generation of believers was dead or dying. Very few who could even remember having seen a living apostle were still alive. Tradition was emerging as the new ideological battleground; tradition, therefore, always fragile, needed codification, collection, and inscription.

An example of this process was the Acts of Paul, composed, according to Tertullian, by a pious (but misguided) bishop, probably around the year 160. The Acts of Paul survives as a collection of texts. It tells stories that explain some cryptic references in

Paul's letters (such as 1 Cor. 15:32 or 2 Tim. 4:14). Paul's teachings on sexual expression and marriage are developed. Paul appears to have traveled beyond his first incarceration in Rome. We even have a physical description of him. According to the Acts of Paul, he was "a man little of stature, thin-haired upon the head, crooked in the legs, of good state of body, with eyebrows joining, and nose somewhat hooked, full of grace: for sometimes he appeared like a man, and sometimes he had the face of an angel" (AP II.3).

Other extra-biblical writings preserve stories of Paul's martyrdom by beheading outside the city of Rome off to the side of a road, the Ostian Way. According to most traditions, Paul was condemned to death by the Roman emperor Nero, which would date his execution to the early 60s. These stories reinforce (or assume) Acts' report that Paul was a Roman citizen. Roman citizens were entitled to trial before the emperor and to beheading if condemned to death. This may seem like small consolation until one remembers that many others who were condemned to death were thrown to beasts or tortured. The tradition that Paul was beheaded in Rome is late but tenacious. A fourth-century historian, Eusebius of Caesarea, was aware of a second-century authority (Caius) who asserted that the church knew and still venerated the tombs of Peter and Paul in Rome (*Church History*, 3.25). Peter was buried in the city near where he had been crucified at Nero's command; Paul was buried near a roadside outside the city, where he had been beheaded. Ancient Christians in the late second century (and later) built sites for worship at both locations. Eusebius' citation of Caius is hardly definitive. Eusebius was writing his history more than 150 years after Caius, who was himself writing 100 years after the death of Paul. Still, the tradition is affirmed by other scholars both before (Tertullian, *Against All Heresies*, 36) and after (in a catalog of scholarly notes on Paul by Jerome) Eusebius – and the report, itself, that Paul died in Rome is not so remarkable. An anonymous writer in the third century wrote a story of Peter and Acts in Rome that affirms the skeletal assertion regarding Paul's death. Scholars today speculate that Paul may have been killed in a general persecution against the Christians under Nero. While the ancient texts are uniform, there is, however, no non-Christian evidence or corroboration for these assertions.

Paul's opponents, the "Judaizers" of Galatians or the "super-apostles" of Corinthians, were not rival sects of Christian missionaries whose presence would give the lie to assertions of widespread, ancient uniformity and ancient veneration for Paul. In the extra-biblical literature, they are nearly always jealous Jews or Greco-Roman priests. In general, extra-biblical traditions also soften the conflicts between Peter and Paul. There are a few, notable, exceptions, but on the whole the acuity of the conflict is hidden beneath assertions of mutual respect. In some cases, there is also a clear point-counterpoint quality to Pauline doctrines embedded in the extra-biblical narratives. Paul is shown directly refuting teachings later associated with "heretics" such as Marcion. Scholar Elaine Pagels, in *The Gnostic Paul*, has pointed out that the Gnostics, as well, were writing texts that celebrated Paul's central role to their own theology. These texts offered Gnostic readings and interpretations of Pauline themes.

Paul is often quoted in doctrinal writings from the second and third centuries as well. Anti-Marcionite critics – Hippolytus, Irenaeus, Tertullian – struggled to root Paul (and Paul's biography) back in the pastoral letters and in Acts. They wrote about Paul's connections to Judaism and stressed his language about Christianity as a "natural" outgrowth of Judaism. They argued for "proper" ways of reading Paul. Irenaeus, in particular, struggled to claim the flag of Paul's support for broader theological themes reflected in other parts of the New Testament. For example, Irenaeus argued that any Gnostic readings of Colossians or Philippians were misreadings and distortions. Far from being "Gnostic," they were ignorant and incorrect distortions of Paul's points. Irenaeus felt himself to be in a battle for the Truth of the very movement around Jesus, and Gnosticism was insidious. He lamented that "Gnostic" Christians often sat beside "orthodox" Christians in churches. Some even made the same confessions, sang the same hymns, and read the same Bible. But, Irenaeus laments, "they *mean* something completely different." He accordingly sought to stabilize Pauline "meanings" and doctrines. In doing so, he also argued decisively that any Pauline biography that allowed a Gnostic Paul was the wrong one.

Pseudepigraphy: A Closer Look

As I have noted, the period from the second to the fourth centuries saw a fairly wide-ranging production of books written about New Testament characters in general, along with "new" writings by New Testament characters, many of which contain records of "secret" or esoteric teachings by these figures. New Testament scholars refer to these extra-biblical writings as "pseudepigraphy" (literally "falsely written") since these books often claim to have been written by notable figures while in actuality they were not. "Pseudepigraphic" is actually a more accurate term than "extra-biblical" or "extra-canonical." The final, formal "canon" of New Testament texts was still under debate in Ante-Nicene Christianity and, strictly, didn't really exist yet. Also, as we saw in Chapter 1, some books which, in time, were listed as "canonical" may have been, themselves, pseudepigraphic.

Certainly, some of the pseudepigrapha were produced as a cynical ploy – they were forgeries – designed to reinforce some individual's particular position. During the period we're discussing, separate churches or separate individuals held copies of some books. It is entirely plausible that some communities – many of whom might well have read and revered books that later were included in the New Testament – may not have even known that other "New Testament" books existed (or, indeed, may have rejected them as forgeries). Certainly, some communities read and revered books that the church would later reject as forgeries or false. In this context, it would be easy to produce a pseudepigraphic document in order to enforce one's point. Some may have even been written by pious individuals writing down what they were "sure" a biblical character "would" have said or written, or perhaps what the character, according to oral legends, was remembered to have taught or said. It is also easy to see how early believers would have found such a morass confusing and would have very much desired someone, somewhere, to sort it all out and decide what was "genuine." Three examples of Pauline pseudepigrapha are worth a closer look.

The first is a series of letters exchanged between Paul and the Roman Stoic philosopher and statesman, Seneca. Seneca was exiled to the island of Corsica in 41 CE by the Roman emperor Caligula. In addition to his larger philosophical works, Seneca engaged in an extensive correspondence with a number of other statesmen, philosophers, friends, and family members. His letters are not just "news of the moment." Seneca wrote long letters that discuss the nature of friendship, the essence of beauty, and his own views on morality and ethics. Paul, as well, wrote several long letters on similar themes.

Someone apparently thought that these two great figures and letter-writers from the first century should meet, so he or she wrote out a correspondence for them. Seneca begins the exchange, writing that he has heard of Paul and heard of Paul's great learning and philosophical skill. Seneca writes, curious to learn more if Paul is willing or has the opportunity to answer. What follows is a series of letters exchanging ideas. At one point, Seneca sends Paul a copy of his newly written book on rhetoric. Paul apparently also sent Seneca drafts of some of his own work.

Scholars are unanimous and confident that this exchange of letters is absolute fiction. Even many ancient Christians doubted the letters' veracity. Yet their very existence reveals something of how Paul was viewed by some in the ancient church. He is shown as an exemplar of rational thought. Though he is consistent in his views about Jesus, he is also able to discourse at the highest level with one of the most famous pagan intellectuals of his day.

A second, fascinating, work is the Apocalypse of Paul. In 2 Corinthians 12, Paul refers to a mystic vision where he was transported to heaven. What did he see there? The Apocalypse of Paul describes it. According to that fascinating text, Paul was given a tour of heaven and hell. His visions very much influenced later medieval writers, particularly Dante, and we will discuss this work more closely in a later chapter. I bring it here up to demonstrate something of the range of interest in Paul. He was remembered by some for his intellect and his letter-writing. In some ways, this view of him has survived with the most vigor in the West. Yet others, even among the proto-orthodox, celebrated his mysticism.

Each of these sources presents a slightly different Pauline biography. And each, by its biography, shapes and interprets Pauline thought. My final example is one of the best examples of this process of reinterpretation via the rewriting of biography: the Acts of Paul.

In 1 Corinthians 7, apparently responding to a question sent to him by the Corinthian believers, Paul dispenses some advice regarding marriage. He tells the Corinthians that if they are married or engaged to unbelievers not to divorce but to remain devout in their faith and perhaps, in time, to persuade their partners. He tells people who are single, however, to consider remaining single since a single person has the most flexibility in the service of God. He doesn't say it here, but if he truly believed the world was going to end at any moment, marriage and family would have been less important. Paul grants that this advice to remain single is basically enjoining celibacy. Some, he asserts, have a "gift" of being able to tolerate celibate living. For others, the rigors and temptations of celibacy would become, themselves, a distraction. He advises these individuals to go ahead, become engaged, and marry, but to be sure to marry another believer so that their values will be reinforced.

The basic story of the Acts of Paul revolves around Paul's teachings about sex and marriage. In that book, he is teaching in a town. His core message is about sexual abstinence, celibacy, and the rejection of marriage. He is overheard by a young woman named Theckla. Theckla is a major character in the work, in many ways more so than even Paul; it is often called "The Acts of Paul and Theckla." Theckla is persuaded by Paul's teaching and refuses to marry her betrothed (a fairly wealthy and well-placed young man). As the story unfolds, she is brought up on charges by the state for her refusal to marry and for her Christian leanings.

The Acts of Paul reinterprets the views expressed in 1 Corinthians. In the Acts of Paul, celibacy itself is a virtue and not the by-product of another choice (singleness) made as an expedient means to a larger end of service to God. This is remarkably different. According to Tertullian, the document was written by a bishop in Asia Minor. Many people were misled, however, into believing it was very old and authentic. The bishop in question was removed from office for his work, and he did offer an apology. His intention, he said, was to produce a delightful and pious document to illustrate his sermons and teachings. Pseudepigraphic works were not always well received by ancient Christians. Many considered the process to be forgery and manipulative. Still, it also illustrates how many people would compose such works with innocent intention *and* how many later readers could be – indeed were – deceived by these works into thinking they were "authentic."

Many books were written in Ante-Nicene Christianity that claimed to be authentic stories or lost writings associated with or written by biblical figures. Many of them are associated with Paul. These books preserve ancient ideas and traditions about Paul. They also often produce radically different pictures of him or new interpretations of his writings. Several groups began to compile lists of which books were "authentic." Marcion produced the first "canon" list. Others produced their own lists. Informal lists exist from the early fourth century that generally resemble the modern New Testament canon.

The Developing "Science" of Biblical Interpretation

The identification and preservation of "authentic" texts was a major concern of many Ante-Nicene Christians. There were limits to how many new stories and texts any given community would accept. But what was accepted still needed to be read. And what was read needed (proper) interpretation. Christianity, venerating apostolicity and the preservation of "authentic" texts, soon needed to develop a technique, a "science" for reading these texts. Two major systems or "schools" of biblical interpretation emerged, each identified with major cities. In both cases, the schools began as centers for the instruction of catechumens (provisional converts to Christianity). Each was also a center for the publication of Christian scholarship.

Antiochene Christian interpretation

One of these major schools was associated with the city of Antioch in Syria. As I noted in Chapter 1, Antioch was a very early and very cosmopolitan Christian community. Paul's early career was spent in this church, and Antioch sponsored Paul's first missionary trips. Syria in general, and Antioch in particular, had a long-standing tradition as an intellectual center. This "Antiochene" school of early Christian interpretation focused on the literal sense of the text. Scholars and theologians such as Diodore of Tarsus, John Chrysostom, and Ephraim are examples of Antiochene biblical interpreters. This school stressed reading texts in their historical context and strongly preferred to reconstruct an author's intended meaning. Its adherents did not, however, tend to emphasize studying the Jewish scriptures in Hebrew; instead, they tended to rely on the common Greek translation.

Antioch and the regions it served was something of a crucible for the training of bishops in the region of Syria and Asia Minor. It was also associated with some popular and persuasive preachers and prolific authors. Antioch was obviously proud of its history. Its bishops, writers, and teachers tended very much to support a "canon list" that foregrounded figures associated with Antioch and the southwestern coast of Asia Minor. One of the major figures in that literature and history was, of course, Paul. Christian scholars and bishops from Antioch more consistently supported a canon list similar to our modern New Testament. They also sent a very large number of bishops to the Council of Nicaea (and the later Council of Chalcedon). In the history of biblical interpretation, Antioch's major contribution is its insistence on literal reading and historical context. In terms of Pauline biography, Antioch tended to produce a more rational, intellectual, and pastoral Paul. The region is also very commonly associated by scholars with the pastorals. More important, perhaps, Antioch made popular a series of canon lists that focused on Paul.

Alexandrian Christian interpretation

The second major center for ancient Christian interpretation was the city of Alexandria in Egypt. Alexandria, like Antioch, was a very cosmopolitan city and, again like Antioch, had a long-standing reputation as a "university town." It had a prominent and very important Jewish community. We have very little information about how or when Christianity entered the region. Prior to Nicaea, Alexandria may have been slightly more prominent than Antioch. Alexandrian interpretation allowed methods of interpretation beyond literal reading and historical context. Two of its favorite approaches were allegorical reading and typology. One of the best ways to introduce Alexandrian biblical interpretation is via one of its most famous sons, Origen.

Origen was a teacher of young converts in Alexandria. We know of him in part through a biography of his life written by one of his devoted students, Eusebius of Caesarea. Eusebius also wrote one of the most ambitious and extensive histories of ancient Christianity to have survived into the modern world. Origen, according to Eusebius, was a highly contentious and pious young man. In one story, for example, a young Origen, living in a city where Christians were being rounded up for persecution, was bent on becoming a martyr. He was only stopped by his devoted mother, who hid all his clothing so that the young Origen would be too embarrassed to go outside. In another (often disputed) anecdote, the devout Origen castrated himself so as not to be sexually tempted or gossiped about as he interacted with young female students.

We know a great deal more about the mind of Origen, however, from his own hand. He was a copious writer and a meticulous scholar, relentless in his development of biblical commentary and interpretation. He wrote major commentaries and scores of other monographs on the Bible, and even today scholars review and use his work. Origen, a careful reader trained in biblical languages, seems to have found every critical textual problem, translation issue, or debatable point in the texts on which he wrote. Despite Alexandria's reputation for "free" interpretation, Origen, ironically, had more control of the historical context and grammatical complexities of the biblical text than virtually any other ancient Christian scholar.

Origen consistently conceded to the confession of the church (as he understood it) in resolving biblical problems. One famous example is his treatment of the (later canonized) epistle to the Hebrews. Some early scholars said – largely because of a reference to Timothy in chapter 16, that Hebrews had been written by Paul.

Yet the grammar, style, vocabulary, themes, and doctrines of Hebrews do not, in any way, seem similar to other Pauline writings. Origen pored over these discrepancies and noted every major one; he followed each with a careful analysis of his findings. In the end, he concluded that Paul could not have been the author. As to who was, he famously asserted, "God, only, knows." As we saw in Chapter 1, he then decided that since one couldn't say Paul *wasn't* the author (and since, to his mind, the doctrine of the book seemed to agree with Paul) *and* that many in the church insisted Paul *had been* the author, one should side with the church.

Origen found in Paul a model for a systematic way of reading the Bible. For Origen, reading the Bible needed controls. Yet these controls should not be too confining of God's revelation. His commentary on Paul's letter to the Romans is a substantial work of scholarship that offered a frame for later standard doctrines of the church regarding the role and work of Jesus in the salvation of the believer and reconciliation with God. He advocated several techniques of interpretation, each exemplified in Paul's letters as a technique of Paul's own biblical interpretation. First, he sought the literal or plain sense of the text. "Problem texts," those that are unclear or those that are clear but, if read literally, contradict other parts of the Bible, were to be read as allegories. All texts held a "spiritual" meaning that transcended the meaning of the literal words. Literal readings were a necessary step toward this enlightened meaning, but the literal sense could also be transcended by the spiritually mature. Origen found his model for allegory in Paul himself.

In Galatians 4 Paul quotes from Genesis 16–18 and argues – against the literal meaning of Genesis – that Jews, as descendants of Abraham's son Isaac, are sons of "slavery" because they are bound by circumcision and the law. From an Antiochene perspective, Paul does not seem to be at his exegetical strongest in this argument. His argument falls absolutely flat against a literal reading of Genesis, where Isaac is *clearly* the "son of the promise" to Abraham. Ishmael, Abraham's son through his wife's slave, is *clearly* the "son of slavery." Circumcision is not a sign of bondage, but a sign of covenant. And *both* sons – slave and free – are circumcised.

Paul's interpretation of the passage couldn't, in its literal sense, be more wrong. But Paul is searching for an allegorical reading, a spiritual truth. Isaac is associated with Judaism. Paul is arguing that Judaism, with its allegiance to Covenant law, is a form of bondage when compared to a "law of grace." I leave to the reader to determine if Paul is fully convincing in arguing that Judaism is "bondage." My point, at present, is simply to point out how allegorical arguments "work." Antiochene scholars (and more than a few modern ones) would argue that allegorical readings could be dangerously circular. Paul might get away with it, since he was an apostle, but we should not try. Origen, however, taking Paul as his model, defended the practice. For Origen, if it's in the Bible, it's authorized. When a text's literal sense affirms doctrine, then that text should be read literally. Origen believed that texts also had spiritual meanings alongside (or hidden within) their literal meanings. Using methods of allegory and typography, he sought to ferret out these deeper meanings.

What, de facto, results from such an approach is that divergent texts are harmonized, and potentially "heretical" interpretations – even those that follow a literal reading of the text – can be brought back into line. In one sense, any poppies that might have grown too tall would be "mown down" by the rule of the "orthodox" teachings of the church. Paul played a critical role in this in two ways. First, a major edifice for the standard rule and doctrine of the church regarding confessions about Jesus was derived from readings of Romans. Second, any pesky "Gnostic-amenable" readings of Paul were controlled. Paul was suddenly harmonized into the "consensus" of the early confessions about Jesus while at the same time being presented as the intellectual star of the movement.

Origen's biographer, Eusebius, offers us insights into the source for the final need for a consistent, uniform Christianity. First, texts were required. Second, a canon (which serves as both inclusive and exclusive rule) needed to be established. Finally, a standard system of reading (a system which constrains as much as, if not more than, it permits or enables) needed articulation.

Eusebius' *Church History* records much of the process I have been describing. Eusebius was writing under the authority of the (Christian sympathetic) emperor Constantine I. Eusebius recorded not only the history of the Christian movement, but many of the debates which surrounded that history. He devotes no small amount of space and time to exploring issues of the developing canon. He indicates that a list of books (noting all 27 of the current canon) emerged which contained the texts universally accepted as apostolic. By this point, however, "apostolic" was understood as, in part, antique (i.e. going back to the original apostles of Jesus), but also in accordance with "true" or "orthodox" doctrine.

What "orthodox" meant is a fair question. Strictly, the word (used by Irenaeus) is Greek for "straight teaching." It was "straight" because, it was argued, it was a consistent and unbroken line of transmission all the way back to Jesus. While everyone was aware that some key Christian terms (such as Tertullian's "sacrament" or "Trinity") were not present in the biblical text, the argument was that these concepts were very much in keeping with the earliest communities of believers. Paul, in other words, would have agreed with a trinitarian notion of God the Father, Jesus the Son, and the Holy Spirit (where all three are of the same substance, co-eternal). Perhaps one can argue that the rudiments of the concept are present in Paul. Still, one must *argue* as much since Paul never uses those words or terms. Such is, yet again, a construction of a Pauline biography where "Paul" is seen as an early believer who would affirm "orthodoxy." The essence of "orthodoxy" is articulated at the famous council in 325 in the city of Nicaea.

Certainly, prior to Nicaea, Christians didn't agree about the nature of Jesus. If they had, there never would have been a council. To settle disputes among Christians regarding Jesus' identity (particularly in terms of the Trinity), Constantine called leading bishops from each major church to come together and establish one basic confession of faith. The disputes prior to Nicaea had been so severe – some sparking riots in the streets – that the business and progress of the empire (not to mention those of the churches) were being hindered. Nicaea established an "orthodox" theology. Interpretations of Paul's writings (and the central biography of Paul in the canonical Acts) were fixed to be in accordance with orthodox theology.

Under Constantine, the church flourished with wealth, schools, and political and social influence. With influence, came the ability to control. Orthodoxy was born.

The image of Paul which was currently in vogue (sympathetic to the Paul of Acts, associated with Peter and Rome, defender of chastity, opposed by Jews, and supersessionist toward Judaism) became, in many ways, "canonized" itself.

Chapter 3

Paul in Late Antiquity

Western and Eastern Christianity

Late antiquity is a critically important era for the history of the West. The term refers to the historical period of, roughly, 300 to 600 CE, though the exact boundaries are a bit nebulous. As a historical frame, the epoch was first used by German classical scholars and made popular to English readers by the work of Peter Brown. The hallmark of this era is synchronicity. A variety of ideas and religiosities merge together in an organic fusion of cultures. It is also a critically important era for the development of Christianity. Christians began to enjoy unprecedented levels of public support and funding, and Christian arts and letters flourished. Among other things, late antiquity saw the development and expansion of Christian monasticism, and major councils, such as Chalcedon, nailed down the language of Christian orthodoxy. The Bible was translated into Latin, the vernacular language of many Christians, and the canon of the New Testament was fixed.

Economically, the period is marked by initial rapid financial growth but also by later economic over-extension. Roman emperors had pressed well into central Europe, North Africa, and Britain. This brought huge colonial revenues, but demanded increasing amounts of military support and control. Rome resorted to broadening definitions of "citizenship" and use of mercenary groups. In time, the military and political structure collapsed into itself. The western half of the empire was thrown into turmoil in August 410 when Rome fell to barbarian invaders led by King Alaric. The eastern empire and its capital, Constantinople, remained fairly strong and would remain independent until Islamic conquest in the seventh and eighth centuries. The western empire and North Africa remained, culturally, very "Roman." The eastern empire remained culturally and linguistically Greek.

These cultural and linguistic divisions parallel separations in religious thinking as well. Though united in many elements of doctrine, there were variations in practice, text, and focus. Eastern Christians were still neighbors with several Gnostic and Marcionite communities in eastern Europe, Egypt, and the Near East. Western churches were more homogenous. A rivalry between the cities of Rome and Constantinople began to develop. Rome argued, since it was the site of both Paul's and Peter's martyrdoms and had once been capital of the empire, that its bishop and its practice should set the normative standards. Constantinople did not concur. Eastern Christianity tended toward emphases on mysticism and growing to be like God in essence. Western Christianity tended (and I stress "tended") more toward doctrinal and ritual forms and growing to be more like God via stricter obedience and allegiance. In the West, where the dominant language was still Latin, many Christians could not read their Bibles nor understand the language of key rituals, all of which were originally in Greek. In the East, where many spoke Greek, there was a resistance to translation. In the West, there was a push, after the Council of Chalcedon in the fifth century, toward a standard canon of 27 books. Eastern Christians still read works such as "The Shepherd" (by Hermas) and an epistle attributed to Barnabas. In time, the Western church came to regard its practice as universal (or "catholic," to reflect the Nicene Creed). The East continued to stress its allegiance to "orthodox" belief. Paul's role would be pivotal in what emerged in both Catholic and Greek/Eastern Orthodox thought. The two communities would formally separate in the eleventh century, but the divisions between them had been brewing for centuries prior to that. Many of these differences would directly affect how Paul was understood in each community. In general, I would argue that two images of

Paul emerge from late antiquity, and these two images reflect the separating Christian communities. This chapter will explore these differences through the examination of two important Christian theologians from the period, Augustine of Hippo and Pseudo-Dionysius the Areopagite.

Canon Closure

One example of the separation of East and West is the "closure" of the canon. There has never been a single ecumenical council that permanently fixed the boundaries of the Christian canon. The Council of Trent did, emphatically, "close" the canon for the Western church; it was not, however, an ecumenical council. Early authorities tried, as we have seen, to articulate the texts they had before them and those that they felt were from the originals. By the fourth century (and even after Nicaea), the list was still under some debate and dispute. Eusebius records some of the earlier debates, but manuscript collections found by archaeologists and scholars testify that the debate continued until well into the fifth century. Later councils (Chalcedon, for example) also continued to discuss the issue, but more than a century later there were still manuscript variations. Two of our most important copies of the complete New Testament, both of which date to the sixth century, have the "standard" 27 books, but also contain additional titles. The famous Codex Vaticanus does not have 1 and 2 Timothy, Titus, Philemon, or Revelation. This may be because the pages are missing. Notably, though, these are also books whose authorship was under debate. Codex Sinaiticus has the standard 27-book canon, but also adds the epistle of Barnabas and "The Shepherd" of Hermas.

Athanasius, a prominent Western bishop, argued that the canon needed closure and, particularly, argued for the current 27 books (and no others). Despite pronouncements of Athanasius and their partial ratification at councils like Chalcedon, the closure of the Western canon was largely accomplished by the translation of the entire Bible into the vernacular language of the masses. As we have seen, closing the canon and, for example, excluding once and for all books like the Acts of Paul would have a radical impact on Pauline biography. Further, the endorsement of some letters such as the pastorals as authentically Pauline and others as not would undoubtedly affect how one understood Paul.

In the West and North Africa the main language had long been Latin. One scholar in particular, Jerome, felt strongly that a vernacular translation of the Bible needed to be undertaken. Unlike many others of his day, Jerome was well trained in both Greek and Hebrew. The majority of ancient Christians did not read the Old Testament in the original Hebrew; they read a Greek translation which had been produced in Alexandria Egypt in the second or third centuries BCE. Jerome agreed with Athenasius in many ways, particularly in his canon list, and these were the books he chose to translate. Further, his translations were heavily influenced by his theology. When faced with a problematic translation or an option, he consistently selected a translation sympathetic to Western theology. Few in the West, by Jerome's day, could read Greek. This was even true among major church leaders. Augustine wrote that his own Greek was sub-standard, though the "standard" to which he compared himself was high: even with his self-described "poor" Greek, Augustine probably knew more than the overwhelming majority of modern clergy. Books, even commentaries, were not widely available to Latin readers. Others, like the works of Origen, were only available in spotty, poor, and tendentious translations.

Jerome translated the standard 27 books of our modern New Testament. Other books, such as the Acts of Paul or the Apocalypse of Paul, were simply no longer available to Latin-speaking readers. Within a generation or two of not being read, many of the extra-biblical books which had been so popular in Ante-Nicene Christianity were forgotten by many. They became "strange" and suspect.

Jerome's translation fixed the listing of books about or by Paul. His translation choices ensured that some letters ascribed to Paul – 3 Corinthians and Laodiceans – were not read or remembered. Similarly, his translation vastly diminished awareness of the Acts of Paul (as opposed to the canonical Acts of the Apostles). It also concealed the remarkable differences in grammar and vocabulary found across the 13 letters and Hebrews. Jerome wrote introductory prefaces to each book. His remarks not only inclined readers toward noting specific themes (and these themes focused on Paul as an astute theologian) but made major assertions about Paul's views regarding Judaism and Jewish law. He argued heavily for Pauline authorship of Hebrews. This almost certainly altered how Paul was understood by Latin-speaking Christians. One gets a rather different picture of Paul's views on Judaism if one assumes Romans 9–11 is written by the same person who penned Hebrews 1–5.

Augustine of Hippo

Augustine (354–430), bishop of the North African coastal city Hippo, could arguably be called the central Christian theologian and interpreter of late antiquity and one of the most influential Christian writers of all time. Augustine's work was prolific, extensive, at times combative, and often effectively structured and elegantly written. Augustine left his fingerprints on the Pauline text. It would be fair to say that, in many, many ways, Augustine set the agenda for subsequent work in Paul. Indeed, at times, Augustine's Paul seems more often the subject of study than the New Testament texts of Paul himself. The philosopher Alfred Whitehead once wrote that Western philosophy was a "series of footnotes" on Plato. Adapting this assertion, the New Testament scholar Paula Friedrickson has remarked that Western Christian theology can be seen as a series of footnotes on Augustine.

Augustine was not a Christian from birth, though his mother, Monica, was a devout believer. Augustine spent his young adulthood as a lawyer and teacher of rhetoric. Very cosmopolitan, philosophical, and urbane, he was also very much an admirer of a community called the Manicheans, who sought a rational, philosophical basis for faith. The Manicheans blended Christianity with Neoplatonist philosophy, and denied the continuity between the Hebrew Bible and the New Testament. The former, they argued, was xenophobic, lacking in philosophical refinement, and presenting an image of God as an unruly, adolescent tyrant.

Augustine dabbled in this community until the death of his mother, a transformational moment in his life. He then began a slow journey toward orthodoxy. Baptized on Easter Day 387, he soon entered the clergy, then ascended through the ranks to become bishop at Hippo. Throughout, he remained a prolific writer and an active scholar entering into many of the interpretive and doctrinal debates of his day.

Augustine built much of his theology around Paul's writings. We could go further and argue that Romans was particularly key for him. Indeed, we could zoom in even more and note how pivotal ideas for Augustine are rooted in the soil of Romans 5–8 (particularly chapter 7). Augustine's arguments were driven by his biblical interpretation and articulated in vivid and engaging prose. He had, after all, spent a major portion of his life as a teacher of rhetoric and literary style. His views were the cornerstone for Christian thought in the Middle Ages.

Augustine shaped much of his argumentative and rhetorical style on Paul. He adopted Paul's technique (exemplified in Galatians and 2 Corinthians) of searching out the "spiritual" meaning behind the literal words of biblical narrative and text. Further, along with Paul, he affirmed that the whole of Hebrew scripture was a presentation – a typology – of the message and life of Jesus of Nazareth. Hidden teachings about Christ peeped from behind every word. Augustine also wrestled with Paul's remarks in Romans 1–3 about God's revelation. Jesus was the ultimate revelation of God, but not the sole revelation. Reason and nature were also vehicles of God's truth. Augustine read Paul as arguing that the natural world revealed God, even though willful humans turned away from that revelation and "worshiped the creation in place of the creator" (Rom. 1:24). Paul readily employed logic and reason to search out deeper truths about God. This, however, was not unfettered, critical "worldly" wisdom but was, as Paul terms it in 1 Corinthians 2, a spiritual wisdom. For Augustine, "spiritual wisdom" was the use of the faculties of reason from within the matrix of faith. Theology was, Augustine famously asserted, "Faith seeking understanding"; theology was reasoning out the nature of God from within an existing position of acquiescing faith.

Augustine also adopted Paul's use of personal reflection and experience. Paul's letters reveal several moments where, reflecting on his own life, he sought through that autobiography to explain or understand God's work in the world. Paul's letters express his own frustrations, disappointments, hopes, and temptations. He infuses these into his language about God. He reflects on his own shared history with his converts. For Paul, autobiography was a means of interconnection with the experience of the Gospel – so much so that he calls on the Corinthians to "imitate me as I imitate Christ" (1 Cor. 11:1). The most critical element of his theologized autobiography lies in his assertions about his own inner transformation. He writes in Galatians 1–2 how he made the transition from being a persecutor of the early followers of Jesus into a man who believed himself sent by God as an apostle of the very Jesus he once opposed. Paul seems to refer to this transformation multiple times, referring to his own past as one laced with sin, worth no more than rubbish, and himself as "one untimely born." In Pauline thought, this radical transformation serves as the basis for his zeal for Jesus, his confidence in God's election, and a demonstration of God's transforming power and constant love.

Augustine seizes on all these elements for his own rhetoric. What Paul began, Augustine develops almost to the point of exploitation. Augustine mimics Paul's use of didactic logic and analysis throughout his own writings. More than this, though, he took on Paul's autobiographical voice and filtered it through his own. In one of his most famous works, the *Confessions*, Augustine mimics both Paul's self-disclosure-as-theological-reflection *and* his turn to Jesus via a transformational encounter with God. Unlike Paul, Augustine was neither Jewish nor a former persecutor of Christians in any physical sense. His *Confessions*, however, is filled with his own guilt over having spurned Christianity as a less than philosophical and less logical way of living during his years as a Manichean. Augustine laments how he felt himself intellectually superior to the simple truth of the Gospel. It is not until he is transformed and humbled – he overhears a child outside singing "take up and read" and turns to the Bible in his study – that he sees the error of his own former arrogance, and sees this arrogance as the root of intellectual persecution of believers. This Spirit-led transformation, for Augustine, proved a critically powerful locus for his own reflection on God's grace and power, as well as a tangible proof of the same. In Augustine, autobiography becomes theology, and he develops this notion from a model he sees in Paul.

Cursory reading of Paul's letters reveals a context of doctrinal rivalry and contention surrounding his later career. 2 Corinthians and Galatians are written to combat what Paul saw as rampant immorality and a "false gospel" spread by rivals, respectively. 1 Corinthians, though occasioned by a letter of questions sent to Paul by the Corinthians, more than once veers aside to Paul's own agenda of correction of practices and actions that he deemed inappropriate. He presents himself as almost forced by the "truth of the gospel" to speak out via letters against practices and teachings he opposes. So does Augustine. A substantial amount of his writing arises from his own conscience-driven responses to other scholars, pastors, bishops, and theologians. Much as Paul did, Augustine also finds himself more than occasionally at the center of an argument. And, again much like Paul, Augustine works out many of his major doctrinal themes via the language of dispute.

Augustine used Paul to develop his techniques of autobiography and experience as means for theology. Yet the substance of Augustinian theology is also largely Pauline. A complete demonstration of Augustine's use and dependence upon Paul would require a separate monograph. For the present, I would like to trace out three major areas in summary. First, Augustine bases his views on Judaism directly from his own readings of Galatians and Romans. Second, Augustine's doctrine about the kingdom of God is rooted in his readings of Thessalonians and, once again, Romans. Finally, Augustine's doctrine of human nature is in constant orbit around his readings of Romans 5–8.

Augustine on Judaism

In Augustine's day, Jews were regarded by many with hostility and disdain. Blamed for the death of Jesus (largely because of texts like 1 Thessalonians 2:14–16), Jews were seen as stubborn and obstinate for rejecting Jesus as messiah. Many Christians argued that only Christians correctly read the Hebrew scriptures. The religion of Judaism was seen as a set of rules performed under compulsion and without any transformation or investment of one's inner self. These characterizations of Jews and Judaism were, of course, erroneous, but they were becoming commonplace in theological writings, popular sermons, and even in legal codes. A closer look at one charge in particular – legalism – demonstrates how Paul was used to support such characterizations. Legalism is the belief that an individual attains justification by God (salvation) by means of performing a set of predetermined actions. It many ways, it reduces salvation to an economic transfer. Jews, then as now, did not believe their salvation was effected by obedience to rules regarding special days or because they kept certain food rules (called *kashrut*) or even because of circumcision. Jews believed they had been chosen through the lineage of Abraham by God's free choice. "Salvation" depended on moral behavior and was open to all people, but election was demonstrated by keeping God's commands which were given to the Jews. In other words, Jewish actions and rituals are *markers* of God's election; they are done *because* one is among the chosen people of God, not to obtain God's favor. Furthermore, if followed, the laws of God mark a Jew off as distinct and different from other peoples and, so, proclaim and display the presence of God.

Paul actually seems to be arguing exactly this understanding in his own writings on the role of "works" and "election" (or "grace") in the life of the believer. He has made a critical switch, however: election is not based upon physical relationship to Abraham but, instead, on belief in Jesus as messiah. Works of law, Paul says (such as keeping kosher, or circumcision, or observance of the Sabbath), do not achieve salvation (a point many rabbis would concede). Paul concludes, then, that they are largely irrelevant and should never be enjoined on non-Jews (again, the latter is a point most rabbis would concede). For Paul, the central moment for salvation was faith in Jesus as messiah, the central fuel for sanctification (a life growing to be like God) was the presence of God's Spirit and the transformation of the self by the Spirit's power.

By Augustine's day, many Christian scholars and theologians had concluded that Paul was arguing that law was inferior, base, and useless. For example, Jerome argued that Jews had missed the point so badly that God would not – indeed could not – save them. They were utterly rejected by God because they had rejected Christ, and Jewish law had no purpose. The Jewish law, Jerome had argued, had been defective; it could not have any effect on the attainment of salvation, presently or even before Jesus. Jewish law could not effect a change in the heart of the believer, so it had been rejected and replaced by a "law of faith" found in belief in Jesus. Christian communities from Marcion to the Manicheans had gone so far as to completely reject the Hebrew scriptures, the Bible Jesus knew and revered.

Augustine disagreed. He came much closer to a balanced read-ing of Galatians than Jerome (and, indeed, upbraided Jerome for his misreading). He saw human experience with God as divided into four major eras: Before Law; Under Law; Under Grace; In Peace. Each era had its own, appropriate way to approach God. "Before Law" (in the age of the "Patriarchs" or "Fathers" of the faith – Noah, Abraham, Isaac, Jacob, and others), God dealt directly with specific humans, giving each a particular command. "Under Law" (and Augustine understood Jewish law as the mandates given through Moses in Exodus, Leviticus, and Deuteronomy), God engaged humanity via a chosen people, the Jews, through the means of a particular code of behaviors, rituals, holidays, and daily rules. This period, Augustine argued (reading Galatians) was a period for "training" an adolescent humanity in what God saw as ethical living. With the advent of Jesus (more specifically, at Jesus' resurrection), God began to interact with humans via "faith in Christ." This was the period "Under Grace." Those who believed, regardless of their nationality, were given the power of God's Spirit. Some (most) still struggled with sin. They would be ultimately perfected, however, in the age to come – following God's cessation of history. The faithful would live alongside the hosts of heaven, their natures so completely transformed by the direct presence of God that they could no longer sin. Humanity would finally live in total harmony with God's will; humanity would finally be living "In Peace."

In one sense, Augustine's views restored (some) inherent dignity and worth to Jews and to Jewish religion. The Hebrew Bible was understood to be a complete and stable revelation of God, without defect (though, to be sure, less than the revelation via Jesus). In its pages, a devout reader could find all that was needed to come to a saving faith (particularly since Augustine believed that a correct reading led one to recognize Jesus as the messiah). God moved through its words. The Hebrew scriptures were holy and were a revelation of God. As such, they held sacramental power. Augustine read the Hebrew Bible via a method called "typology." He believed that Jesus was not only predicted by the prophets, but prefigured in many characters, events, and settings. It was as if the whole of the gospels had been "encoded" in the Hebrew text, waiting for the discerning reader to discover the jewels held hidden inside. Granted, any such discovery was greatly enabled by a knowledge of Jesus; Jesus and the gospels were, in effect, God providing the "key" or the solution to the puzzle of the Old Testament. Our current "age" (the era of the church under grace) hinted at the glories to come in heaven. In a similar way, this current era of grace had been prefigured in the Old Testament. Jews, as well, behaved and believed and worshiped in a way commanded by God. Though, again, only figures of the glorious age to come contained the kernel (again, to the discerning) of Jesus and the church. As such, they were also a revelation of God and possessed sacramental power.

Consequently, Augustine argued that Jews should not be forced to convert to Christianity. Their texts were not invalid. Their faith was, at its core, neither irrelevant nor without power. They were a model of practice for Christians and, by their perpetuation, gave testimony to God's fidelity. Augustine was very much a supersessionist. Even though he restored some value to Judaism, he believed it was a second-hand value. Judaism was inferior to Christianity and Jews only had hope of God's favor because of the grace of God displayed in Jesus and mediated by the church. However, his readings of Paul did lead him toward a certain type of toleration of (and admiration for) Jews. He felt they were wrong; but they were reasonably wrong, and should be preserved as a witness to God. The church was the inheritor, ultimately, of

God's promises and God's fullest favor. Yet Israel "according to the flesh" (or "carnal Israel") still had a place. Augustine, it is true, argued for a value to Judaism. The value, however, lay largely in its service as a spiritual museum piece.

Augustine's readings were deeply rooted in his reconstruction of Pauline biography and Paul's world. He accepted the Acts of the Apostles and the pastorals. From these, he discovered a Paul who continued to value – and practice – his Jewish upbringing, its scriptures and ritual identity, even as he forbade the imposition of Jewish law on gentiles. In a more subtle move, Augustine saw Paul in Paul's own autobiographical moments reflecting on the process of transition from Jew to believer in Jesus; Paul, as well, was outspoken about his hopes for the next life and explicit in 1 and 2 Corinthians about how the next life is prefigured in this present life, even as Christ had been prefigured in the Old Law. The continuity of this one Pauline life became a model, to Augustine, for salvation history as a whole.

Augustine and salvation history

A second major theme in Augustinian theology arises from this reconstruction of salvation history. This theme was also, like Augustine's thoughts on Judaism, influenced by conflicts that surrounded him in his own day. Augustine lived in a changing political and economic world. Not least among these changes was the decline and destruction of the city of Rome. For many, Rome, as a Christian empire, was the actualization of the "Kingdom of God" spoken of by Jesus in the gospels. As the fortunes of Rome declined, many turned to a theological explanation. Surely, some argued, God was rejecting the faith of Rome, or perhaps, as others asserted, history was ending and Jesus was soon to return. The sacking of the city of Rome by the Goths threw fuel on already burning fires of religious speculation. Many were turning to obscure verses in the Bible to calculate the age of the earth and the specific time that remained. Others were abandoning the faith, finding current events (and, no doubt, the radical views of many apocalyptic believers) indicative of a rejection by God.

Augustine wrote his most extensive single volume, *City of God*, to explore these themes. Drawing very largely on the writings of Paul and on Genesis, Augustine argued that the decline of Rome neither demonstrated divine disfavor nor prefigured the end of human history. Rome had not been the Kingdom of God physically situated on earth. Indeed, no physical, literal Kingdom of God had ever existed or ever would. God's kingdom, God's city, was not a physical, earthly city. It would only be enacted in the age of peace in the actual city of God – the new, heavenly, spiritual Jerusalem.

Augustine's thinking was heavily influenced by his prior Neoplatonist ideas. Plato, a Greek philosopher from classical Athens, had divided existence into two general realms: the Real and the Ideal. The Ideal was just that, it was the perfect, conceptual – for Augustine, spiritual – realm. It was the location of the essence of things and of the realities of Good, Beauty, and Truth. The Real was the mundane, physical world in which we live, filled with material things. Matter was not bad, it was simply imperfect (particularly when compared to the Ideal). The concept or vision of an artist or a writer is always more rich, more nuanced, more complex, more perfect than the reality of what is produced. The idea of a chair always supersedes any real, material chair. Neoplatonism was a movement that revived these (and other) ideas of Plato. Augustine was greatly influenced by them and repeatedly turned to them in his readings of biblical texts.

Augustine turned to Paul's caution in 1 Thessalonians 5 against trying to calculate the hour of Christ's return or searching for signs of the coming end of an age. He rejected even the possibility of such calculation. Not only did such speculation fly in the face of biblical language (Mark 13:32–3), it was fundamentally wrongheaded. There would be no observable signs in the physical world because the Kingdom of God – being perfect – could not be in the physical world. At best, the realm of the Real can point, as a type, toward the Ideal. Rome was not God's kingdom. No human government or empire could be. Christ would not return to rule in this world. Christ's kingdom would be perfect, so it must be spiritual.

Certainly, reading Romans 13, Augustine conceded that human institutions and governments – the city of Rome, the church – could reveal something of the age to come and also had a purpose in this world. They provided mediating structure, stability, and tangible points for interaction with God. Governments controlled the unregenerate and the unbeliever by laws and armed troops. Governments effected peace, established order, and enabled trade, all of which allowed the work of God to flourish in the world. But governments should only have secondary allegiance from a believer (at best), and all governments would pass away in time. Government itself could enhance the work of God; governors, or any particular system of government, however, were human and therefore flawed and transient. The church alone received any sanction from God for constancy. The church was, of course, imperfect on its own and in its substance, much like the individual believers who constituted it. Humans, even saved humans, could sin. The essence of the church, however, was God-filled and Spirit-empowered. Human believers, though sinful, were still governed by God's Spirit (and evaluated by God's grace).

A central metaphor for this process, for Augustine, was found in Paul's treatment of the resurrection of Jesus in 1 Corinthians 15. Jesus, Paul asserted, had been raised from the dead, proving resurrection possible and serving as the "first fruits" of the resurrection. Paul here is referring to a Hebrew agrarian practice described in the Bible where a portion of the first harvest of the season was dedicated to God in an offering. This was, in part, a thanksgiving to God. It also served to symbolically prefigure the coming bounty of God and God's ongoing sustenance. A first fruits offering was a sort of "spiritual down payment" of the blessings of God. Paul argues that Christians enjoyed a "now but not yet" portion of God's regenerating grace. In Romans, Paul asserts that he has "died" to himself and that the "old man of sin" is dead and buried. The Paul which now lives is "alive in Christ." Clearly, this was not literally true. Paul did not believe that he had physically died and come back to life reanimated in body by Jesus' ghost. Augustine pointed out that this metaphorical (or spiritual) assertion was, however, still very much true. Paul writes that, in our present physical reality, believers carry the riches of God inside them as a "down payment" on the glories which they are to share in at the end of the current age (2 Cor. 1:22, 5:5; Eph. 1:13, 14, 4:30).

We carry these riches in our bodies as if they were rich treasures hidden away in clay jars (2 Cor. 4:7–12). Augustine saw Paul as arguing that we are, even though physical, already a type, a form of spiritual being. This full measure of salvation, however, is also "not yet." Believers still struggle, sin, feel loss, feel pain, doubt, feel distanced from God. In the age to come, however, Augustine argued that all these "not yets" would be accomplished.

Drawing on 1 Corinthians 15, Augustine argued that our physical, imperfect bodies (bodies that were subject to illness, hunger, sexual desire, defecation, and more) could not, themselves, inherit the glory of God's kingdom. As items in the realm of the Real (the physical), they could not share fully in the realm of the Ideal (the spiritual) without transformation. This transformation would be effected by God at the end of time. Humans in some sort of resurrected physical body (an odd and never fully explained alteration of Paul's specific point in Corinthians) would dwell in the divine, heavenly, New Jerusalem with God. *City of God* concludes with a re-reading of the first chapters of Genesis. In effect, Augustine is arguing that the world to come would restore humans to humanity's (Adam's) primal, first-created nature in the full image of God. Restored, humans would share in God's presence as God had initially intended (and as Genesis describes).

Augustine's readings of Paul, once again, reflect a particular Pauline biography. In one obvious sense, Augustine assumes that Paul's thinking, as represented by his letters (and Augustine considered all 13 letters of Paul to be authentic) is static. Augustine does not see a trajectory of development in Paul's thinking. Paul's views about the end of the age in 1 Thessalonians are as developed as his thinking is in 1 Corinthians, which is as developed as his thinking is in Romans 8. Augustine is implicitly assuming that Paul's message was essentially unchanged from the beginning to his final sermon. Further, Augustine is most certainly reading Paul through a Neoplatonic lens, which may not be entirely unfair or anachronistic; Paul himself may have been influenced by Platonic thought.

Finally, Augustine is not even considering what many modern scholars see as core to Paul's doctrines of the end of time (technically called "eschatology," from the Greek *eschatos* or "final"). Modern scholars argue that Paul, like many other early followers of Jesus, believed in an immediate and immanent end of history. Paul, modern scholars assert, very much believed himself to be living in the very last days of history. When he wrote 1 Corinthians 15, he asserted "we shall not all die," indicating his expectation that some of his first audience would be alive when history ended and God's kingdom would be very much, very literally, established. History didn't end; God's kingdom did not physically arrive. In fact as one scholar, Tina Pippin, has put it in *Apocalyptic Bodies*, the scope of ancient Christian theology was shaped by history's nagging refusal to end according to schedule. Augustine's reading, however, has Paul anticipate just such a delay. Augustine presents a Paul who really didn't expect an immediate end of history nor a physical arrival or locus for God's kingdom on earth (a reading many modern scholars also derive from Paul's later writings).

Augustine's view of "original sin"

One of Augustine's most notorious rivals was Pelagius. Pelagius, born in Britain but a leading theologian and teacher in Rome, has been denounced by later orthodox Christian thought as a heretic for his teachings on human nature, will, and the role of baptism. Yet during his lifetime Pelagius was apparently very popular and persuaded many people to accept his ideas. None of his works has survived to the present day; we know of Pelagius and Pelagianism largely from polemic opposing him written by Augustine. The ideas called Pelagianism – and their biblical and philosophical defenses – are very complex, and do not appear to have been original to Pelagius; many of the arguments can be traced to earlier writers such as Cyprian or to contemporaries of Pelagius such as Rufinus. They arose, in large part, from theological debates of a prior generation regarding baptism. By the late fourth century, baptism of infants (technically called "pedobaptism") was a common practice; it was most likely the routine form of Christian baptism. Biblical text is very explicit in linking baptism not only with inclusion into the community of faith and the moment of impartation of God's spirit, but also with forgiveness of sins.

Debates arose over what sin (if any) could be involved in the case of infants. Opinions ranged from arguments that infants did, in fact, sin (as they were capable, in their own way, of acting in defiance of God's will), or that the baptism was more preventive than regenerative in this case, to arguments that infants must inherit some form of sin. For many, suffering was caused by sin. Infants suffered. Therefore, infants must, somehow, be able to sin or have inherited a sinful nature.

Pelagius denied that infants were, of themselves, able to inherit sin. He rooted sin in human will and not in some inherited human nature. "Sin" occurred when a human acted in rebellion against God. For Pelagius, this was the end of the matter. There was no inherent corruption to being human, merely a stubbornness of will. For God to punish humans who were merely acting in accordance with some pre-inscribed will would lead to an ethical dilemma: God would be punishing people for something which they could not help doing. Pelagius argued that this would make God unfair and immoral, since punishment, if meted out morally, must be in response to some deliberate action. God would be commanding things that were impossible (piety and faithfulness), condemning things that were inevitable (human sin), and doing both to creatures (humans) that, in essence, lacked any free and independent will.

Augustine seems initially to have agreed. He was highly suspicious of arguments that humans, by their finitude, were somehow simply "evil." Recall that, as a Christian Neoplatonist, Augustine very much believed that the material world was inferior to the perfect spiritual realm. Inferior did not, however, equal "evil." Yet Augustine was also a devoted reader of Paul and found no other way to approach Romans 1–3 than to conclude with it that "all have sinned and fallen short of God's glory." Furthermore, scripture (particularly Romans) presents the sacrifice of Jesus for humanity's sin as inevitable and exclusive. In every sense, there was no other way for human salvation from sin apart from Jesus.

Augustine was struggling to articulate a theology of human nature that did not violate scripture's language (which he took as almost transparently clear on the matter), but that also did not create an acute ethical conundrum for God's judgment against sin and the central importance of Jesus' sacrifice. For Augustine, a key to the solution lay in the doctrines of election and Paul's treatment of human nature in Romans 5–7.

Scripture has several examples where God "elects" or chooses people for blessings. The most prominent example would be God's election of Abraham. According to Genesis, God simply "calls" Abraham to leave his home in the city of Ur and set out for a new land. God promises Abraham that God will give him numerous descendants and a land. As Genesis presents it, these descendants are the Jews and the land is Canaan. Scripture never really reveals why God selected Abraham. There is no record of Abraham's life prior to his call from God. Abraham seems to be a man with foibles and faults much like any other. He is faithfully obedient. He complies with God's commands – even irrational ones such as the command to sacrifice his son recorded in Genesis 22. Doing so, he demonstrates astonishing confidence in God. Augustine argued (initially) that God had selected Abraham because God had foreknown Abraham's faith. From this Augustine concluded that God's selection of individuals was based on God's foreknowledge. Other biblical passages (particularly in Paul) seem to suggest that God had also "elected" or "chosen" people to service to Christ. One of Paul's favorite words for Christian communities is "the elect." It would seem, then, that God had foreknown who would and would not be faithful. God had, in effect, predestined some to belief. By implication, some had been predestined, also, to damnation. But Augustine argued that this was not an ethical breach by God; God had not created people for the sole purpose of destroying them. God had elected those whom God predestined precisely because those were the people who would be most faithful. Human will, then, was the critical factor. God chose those individuals who would best use their free will to serve God. God preordained, but humans still had will.

Augustine then defined sin as the improper use of human will (using Romans 1–3). Humans used their will to do things against the will of God. When not in agreement, humans were in sin. A consequence or effect of sin was the perversion or corruption of human will. The effect was cumulative; multiple sins compounded the degradation of the will. This corruption could only be repaired by God's Spirit, who could only be attained by belief in Christ (and baptism). Christ's death both provided access to forgiveness of past sins (through Christ's atoning sacrifice) and means to the Spirit who regenerates human will and prevents future sin.

Pelagius disagreed. He agreed with Augustine (and both writers would continue to concede) that sin was rooted in human will. Even more, this disobedience arose from a fundamental desire in humans to replace God. Both Augustine and Pelagius understood, for example, that the primal sin of Adam and Eve was not purely the consumption of forbidden fruit, but the "desire to be like God." The forbidden fruit of Genesis 3 was a food that would somehow provide humans with a knowledge of Good and Evil. The rebellion, then, was the desire of humanity to know what God knows, to, in effect, replace God. Both Augustine and Pelagius also agreed that human nature, in itself, was not inherently corrupt. God had decreed, after the creation of Adam, that all of creation was "very good." A perfect God would, of logical necessity, create a perfect creation. Humans, furthermore, had been created "in the image of God." God was perfect; humans could not, by nature of creation, be corrupt. Pelagius wrote his own commentary on Romans, arguing such points. Humans chose to sin. Therefore, sacrifice was needed to atone for these sins. Further, for the whole equation to work, humans needed radically free will. Any other condition would place severe limits on God's ethics. Whatever "election" meant, whatever its basis, it could not mean divine predestination. Another implication was that Adam's sin did not and could not taint his descendants. Humans, even after the Fall, were still active free agents and there was no necessary corruption of the will (for Pelagius, this would be no different from arguments that humans were, from creation, incapable of obedience to God). Adam had set a bad example. Jesus, by contrast, had set the perfect example. Sin was a debt incurred through making bad choices. Humans were criminals facing punishment for these sins. Jesus took on the sentence of humanity, removing the guilt. Restoration to God was achieved via continued obedience to God's will and rooted in human effort and works.

Augustine countered, however, that Pelagius' views meant that humans could, conceivably, live without sin. Apart from being a flat contradiction (Augustine argued) of Romans 3:23, Pelagius' views meant that, conceivably, a human other than Jesus could live a faultless, sinless life and not need Jesus' atonement (a flat contradiction of Romans 3:23 and Ephesians 2:8–10). For Augustine, Pelagius could also not adequately interpret Paul's assertions that death had entered the world and all humanity through Adam's sin (Rom. 5:12), nor how faith in Christ could regenerate believers. Were that not enough, Augustine asserted that Pelagius viewed salvation as a reward for human faithfulness. This based salvation on works, not grace (against Rom. 4:4). Augustine argued that Pelagius did not account for the corrupting nature of sin. Nor did Pelagius, Augustine argued, have any answer for the frustration of creation Paul speaks of in Romans 8. Paul, himself, was torn by his own guilt as well as his own inability to avoid sin. "What I don't want to do, I do," Paul wrote. "What I desire to do, I cannot" (Rom. 7:13–24). Augustine also felt, in himself, this inner turmoil and powerlessness before sin. Augustine could not avoid sin. Even Paul could not avoid sin. Some greater power was at work.

Augustine would ultimately argue that the root of the problem lay in a form of inherited defect. Adam's sin resulted in an impaired will; this defective will was passed on to his descendants. Prior to his sin, Adam's will was perfect: he could decide to obey or to rebel. After Adam's sin, his will became defective. He and his progeny, all of humanity, could not choose to be good, only evil. This will was regenerated by faith and baptism. Yet, Augustine insisted, the sin itself was not imparted – merely the degenerated human will. Since Jesus was sinless (2 Cor. 5:21), he must, though human, have avoided this degeneration. Augustine then turned to Matthew and Luke and claims of Jesus' virgin birth; Jesus had no human father. Therefore, the inherited degenerate will must be inherited from one's father. Since a sure sign of the consuming power of sin was the overwhelming power of sexual desire, Augustine reasoned that this was the human will seeking to perpetuate further degeneration by the production of other beings with degenerate will. Lust was the surest proof of imperfect human will.

Augustine next turned to the question of salvation by grace (election). Returning to the question of God's foreknowledge, he reasoned, as before, that God still elected those who would be faithful, who would not reject God. But, humans, with their defective wills, were unable to accept God. God, then, offered the gift of faith to those whom God had elected. These received the free gift of faith which allowed them to will God's will and obey God's commands (and, thus, be open to the Spirit's regeneration). At the end of time, humans would be fully restored in their will and would serve God in peace.

The debate between Pelagius and Augustine was as complex as it was intense. In many ways, what I've just presented is a gross oversimplification. Notably, though, the reasoning of both individuals was rooted in the language of Paul. For Augustine, Romans 5–7 was the central, pivotal text. Again, Augustine assumes that Romans reflects a fairly standard and static view of Paul's teaching and thought. Especially important for Augustine, Paul's autobiographical moments – his admission of his own constant and persistent battle against sin even as he served as an apostle – were central to his understanding of the perniciousness of sin and were evidence for the devastation of human will. Augustine framed his own autobiography very much in the same terms as this Pauline autobiography. The real experience of sin, temptation, and lust, the real experience of self-defeat and discouragement, were as foundational for Augustine's arguments as any text or rational principle.

Pseudo-Dionysius the Areopagite

In Eastern traditions theologians and scholars focused more on Paul as mystic, exploring passages which called for "imitating Christ," understood by some as *apotheosis*, a transforming of the human spirit into something more God-like via the Holy Spirit. When Paul spoke about being "crucified with Christ" yet still living, many Eastern Christians found a focus for their own spiritual journey of transformation. Eastern soteriologies are often more mystic and more frequently involve monastic and ascetic practices. Pauline texts are key for such doctrines. Believers mystically participate in Jesus and become mystically one with him. Many later Eastern Orthodox theologies would assert that when a believer changed states through various rituals – when they were saved, for example, or ordained into the clergy – they became "ontologically different." In simpler terms, encounters with the sacred transformed a person's fundamental essence. They were, literally, a different kind (or species) of human. Jesus, as God incarnate, remade and restored humanity by being the perfect human. Via the Holy Spirit, modern believers can also grow into that nature. In other words, Jesus "resets" corrupted humanity, making a life of fidelity to God possible. Redeemed believers are no longer "of this world," but have begun a process of becoming God-like. Mystical and ascetic practices can speed this growth.

Paul (2 Thess. 2:15; 2 Tim. 3) also articulates the orthodox yearning for traditional consistency (and for the authority of confessions which arise as a result). Orthodox theology, however, is not rooted in intellectual ideas, but in mystic transformations and in therapy – in healing and restoring of the essential "human" quality via participation in Christ. It is too much to say Eastern thought is all emotion and tradition and Western is all hierarchy and analytical reason. Yet, these stereotypes exist for a reason. It is also too much to say that these theological elements were created by readings of Paul. They do, however, participate in a reciprocal system of both creation and reinscription of values.

They most certainly also craft a biography of Paul. Paul was the model for ascetic self-denial. Paul lived as a single man, eschewed (according to the doctrine of the church) sex, denied himself the comforts of rich living, and at times even lived in deprivation (Phil. 4:10–14; 2 Cor. 11). He endured all these things so that he would be a more effective servant of God. As we saw in a previous chapter, many extra-biblical accounts of Paul's life and many pseudepigraphic Pauline texts emphasized Paul's self-denial. In some texts, like the Acts of Paul, Paul's gospel message is little more than a call for asceticism. Nearly all of these texts were written in Greek. They remained available to Christians, both ordained and lay, scholar and non-scholar. Figures such as

Theckla remained very vivid in popular memory. She appears often in Eastern iconography, suggesting her story (and, indirectly, a story about Paul) continued to flourish in the East. In nearly all these texts, as well, Paul as an ascetic is a central theme.

A series of engaging documents purporting to be the writings of a student of Paul began to appear in the East in the first half of the sixth century CE. Acts of the Apostles 17:16–34 describes a trip by Paul to the city of Athens. Athens was famous for its schools, universities, and intellectual life. In Acts 17, Paul is shown teaching in the synagogues and disputing with Jews over Jesus. Overheard by some Athenian philosophers, he is accused of preaching a new deity and taken to the Areopagus. The Areopagus (literally the "high place" of the city) was a center of temples, gymnasia (which in the ancient world contained libraries and lecture halls), and other cultural facilities. Preaching a new or foreign deity in Athens was illegal; Paul's presentation is a combination of a "guest lecture" and a trial. Acts shows Paul giving a speech that first connects to preconceived ideas and practices among the Greeks and then turns to a message about Jesus.

In Acts, most of the Athenian intellectuals dismiss Paul, but a few find his ideas persuasive. Two are named in 17:34–5: Dionysius and a woman named Damaris. In the sixth century CE, a series of documents purporting to be written by Dionysius the Areopagite appeared in the Eastern empire. They were wildly popular. In these documents, written in Greek, the author assumes the identity of Paul's philosopher convert. He claims to have particular and exclusive access to Paul's teachings, particularly to his philosophically based mystic and esoteric ideas. In the later Middle Ages, these documents were assumed to be authentic, written by a first-generation student of Paul. According to legend, Dionysius, after conversion, traveled to Gaul (modern-day France) and began a career as a scholar-evangelist. He is remembered as "St. Denis," the patron saint of France. Most scholars today believe that "Dionysius" (called, today, "Pseudo-Dionysius") was a sixth-century monk and ascetic, most likely from the region of Syria. He was heavily influenced by Neoplatonism and had, as an agenda, the synchronization of Pauline thought and Greek philosophy. The documents feign a sense of verisimilitude, claiming Paul as a source, referring to events contemporary with Paul, and quoting only from the Hebrew Bible and texts that the author believed had been written in Paul's lifetime. In addition to some letters, Pseudo-Dionysius was the author of four major works: *The Divine Names, Mystical Theology, Celestial Hierarchy*, and *Ecclesiastical Hierarchy*.

In *Divine Names*, Pseudo-Dionysius reflected on the names used for God in the Hebrew text. Each name reveals some attribute of God (but also limits thinking about God and, so, must be transcended). In *Mystical Theology* he works out his notion of knowing God. He argued that any language or concept for God was inadequate. Human knowledge and experience could not explain or encompass the complexity of God. At best, we can only articulate what God is not or see where God has been but is no longer. A major metaphor for Pseudo-Dionysius is the "passing by" or tangential revelation of God found in various Bible passages such as Exodus 33:12–23 and John 1:8. All we, as humans, can know of God is that everything we think we know about God is, in a significant way, wrong or incomplete.

The *Celestial Hierarchy* and *Ecclesiastical Hierarchy* are two works that explore the order and organization of beings on earth and in heaven. Loosely interconnected, they explore the "rank" of beings in heaven, examining all the terms used in the Bible for celestial or angelic beings, describing the exact task for each, and paralleling these angelic beings with church clergy and sacraments. The material realm explains and displays the reality of heavenly beings.

The writings of Pseudo-Dionysius present these various ideas as the revelation of Paul to one of his elite, personal students. Paul is referred to with particular reverence, and Pseudo-Dionysius presents himself as the inheritor of secret, esoteric mysteries. Paul did not share most of these ideas with a general audience. Their mystical power (and risk) were too much for the average believer. Much of the material, particularly the ideas regarding the heavenly beings and order, is presented as the unique revelation given to Paul on his own mystical trip through the "third heavens."

In 2 Corinthians 12:1–10, Paul describes a journey into the "third heaven." Many in the ancient world believed in multiple tiers of the cosmos – "heavens"/"skies" – that were found above our terrestrial world. Normally, there were believed to be seven. The third, identified by Paul as "Paradise," was, roughly, halfway between humanity and God. During the period between the composition of the Hebrew Bible and the time of the New Testament, there were several Jewish writings about mystical journeys into the realms of the heavens. Some of the more famous celestial travelers were Adam and Enoch. Astute Bible readers may recall that Enoch, according to Genesis 5:23–4, was a righteous man who did not die but was, instead, "taken to be with the Lord." Paul begins this vision talking about "a certain man," suggesting that he was writing about some other person. Paul has been (and will continue through chapter 12) chiding the Corinthians for boasting over their spiritual accomplishments. He is most likely trying to quiet their boasts by suggesting something *really* worth boasting about – a heavenly vision – has occurred. By verses 7 and 8, Paul has switched from using third-person pronouns ("he") to the first person ("I"). Most readers, ancient and modern, have concluded that he is talking about one of his own visionary experiences but, to allay boasting and to remain humble, introduces the story as if it were about someone else (a "certain man").

The experience Paul describes was as dangerous as it was illuminating. He reports that, as a result of his vision, God allowed Satan to give him a "thorn in the flesh," some sort of physical torment (some scholars suggest this refers to his numerous illnesses or, perhaps, his difficulty in seeing). The torments were to produce humility; presumably, a heavenly vision would result in an elevated sense of one's own spiritual and mystical achievement. The physical torment was a constant reminder of limits, however, and was intended to check any sense of "boasting." Mysticism and visions were dangerous experiences, even as they were powerful spiritual achievements. Paul does not here, or elsewhere, reveal the contents of his vision – what was seen or heard on his journey into paradise.

A Christian text from the third century was not so coy. Titled the Apocalypse (or "Revelation") of (or "to") Paul, the work is a narrative report, told in the first person, of visions shown to Paul by a heavenly messenger. In his journey, Paul sees the ultimate fate of the dead – both the righteous and the sinful. Each receives reward or punishment according to his actions in life. Unfaithful bishops have devils harass them at the legs. Unfaithful readers of scripture have their tongues and lips cut with razors. Those who harmed widows and orphans are eaten by worms. The catalog of torments is graphic and extensive. A distressed Paul cries out for mercy for the damned. After rebukes (for thinking himself more merciful than God), he is eventually heeded. Jesus comes and stills the torments for a day (Easter).

Pseudo-Dionysius claimed to have been privy to special teachings and insights from Paul's mystical journey. His information about heavenly hierarchies comes directly from these esoteric teachings. Further, Pseudo-Dionysius' warnings about the inability of human language to describe God (or mystical encounters) arise from a long mystic tradition that argued that revelations always came at physical and spiritual risk. The visionary could become too proud, or could become confused or overconfident, and so descend into heresy. Mystical revelation, as Paul demonstrates in 2 Corinthians 12, could often come at a terrible cost. Pseudo-Dionysius argues, however, that mystical experience – becoming "at one" with God through visionary experience – also brought powerful insight and, to the properly disciplined and cultivated, could serve as a proof of God's goodness. It is obvious, as well, that Pseudo-Dionysius roots these ideas and arguments directly in a reconstructed Pauline biography. There is, after all, no clear indication or language in the text that requires a reader to conclude that Paul is describing his own experience in 2 Corinthians 12 or that the experience corresponds with what Pseudo-Dionysius calls "mysticism."

Much of the Western tradition, which emphasized Paul's rhetoric, use of autobiography, logic, and biblical scholarship, was based upon an Augustinian construction of Paul. Paul was, above all, a writer of ideas. These ideas were complex, admittedly, but knowledge of God was found by the rational, interpretive, exegetical encounter with Paul's written word. This written word produced a sense of a personality, an autobiography, which not only served as a model for imitation but also demonstrated and actualized Pauline theology.

Other traditions, such as those from the East (exemplified by Pseudo-Dionysius) emphasized the mystical elements of Paul's experiences. Paul spoke in tongues. Paul saw visions and had divinely inspired dreams. Paul performed miracles. Paul saw the resurrected Jesus. Paul, somehow mystically, could reveal Jesus in his own body. Paul made celestial journeys into paradise itself (and suffered physically as a result). Paul was spiritually transformed by all these mystical moments. Far from being tied by the limits of rationality, argument, and biblical interpretation, this mystical Paul "demonstrated Christ" in his own body; he was transformed and empowered by spiritual, mystical encounters.

Notably, each picture of Paul is represented within his own letters and in Acts. Yet the selection of texts and the locus of emphasis make all the difference to what "kind" of Paul emerges. In very general terms, some (particularly those influenced by Augustine) tended to emphasize Paul's intellect and created a "Paul" to be heeded, studied, considered. True, he was to be imitated as well, but imitated as the ultimate Christian intellect. For others (as we see in Pseudo-Dionysius), Paul was a visionary giant and the ultimate Christian mystic. He was to be "experienced." Imitating Paul meant being open to God's spirit as it transformed the believer into something beyond the mere limited human. Both images of Paul remained prominent into the Middle Ages, but, in general terms, the Western tradition of Christian intellectualism tended to follow an Augustinian model; the Eastern traditions of esoteric and mystical Christian experience and transformation tended to follow models similar to Pseudo-Dionysius.

Our next chapter will explore the conventions of the West, particularly into the era of the Middle Ages. Much of what we will find is that Paul is the principal text for those not satisfied with the status quo. Many interesting intersections between the mystic and the clergy in the Middle Ages are conjunctions of Dionysian and Augustinian ideas of Paul.

Chapter 4

The Medieval Paul(s)

Many introductory surveys of Western literature and culture focus heavily upon Greco-Roman materials, then closely on late antiquity. Other eras, such as the Renaissance, the Enlightenment, the Romantic period, and modernity, also get close readings The Middle Ages, a period from the eighth to the fourteenth centuries, is often treated only in summary. The result often reminds me of some grotesque "bobble-head" doll or tourist-stop caricature drawing. The lower body is well developed, the head has so much detail it becomes a gross exaggeration, but the trunk and neck are ludicrously underdeveloped. In many ways, I'm about to produce yet another of these creatures in this book. The vagaries of space, length, and audience are often the source of these distortions.

I hope, though, to avoid two false impressions such a caricature can create. One common mistake would be to assume that "not much interesting happened" in terms of medieval reading of the Bible. Students can be forgiven for concluding that, apart from some "high-water" moments, such as Ambrose, Anselm, the scholastics and a few others, the Middle Ages were rather static and not engaged in innovative biblical scholarship, but nothing could be further from the truth. A second mistake is to assume that the ideology of the Middle Ages was monolithic and fixed – that the Roman Catholic Church and her theology so dominated the intellectual landscape that no other variations were present. Again, this is a gross misreading.

Paul and the Bible in the Middle Ages

Paul plays a vibrant role in how biblical thinkers engaged Christian doctrine in the Reformation and later periods. Luther's notion of "sola scriptura" – that the basis for Christian belief and practice lay solely in the (properly interpreted) biblical text – forms the basis for post-medieval theology and doctrine. This does not, however, mean that the Bible was not a central text in the medieval period, nor that the majority of believers (and certainly this extends to the professional interpreters) were biblically illiterate.

Many of these encounters were via visual representations (icons, artwork, statuary, plays, and so on). Such representations, arguably, emphasize story rather than the letter of the text, but by emphasizing story, these traditions and techniques draw out characterization in even more vivid strokes. Artistic depictions of biblical texts are, themselves, a form of interpretation. How one chooses to portray a biblical scene (or, more accurately, how its characters are conventionally portrayed) reflects what one thinks is of interest in the story, and assumptions about what is important in it, about what the story "means."

In iconography, there are two main conventions for images of Paul. The first (reflecting an ancient Christian, non-canonical tradition) is the depiction of him as short, bald (or balding), hawk-nosed, stern, and often bow-legged. Second, and more significant, he is often shown holding a sword in one hand and a book in the other. The weighty tome is often held as if it were a shield. Both accessories are, most likely, allusions to Ephesians 6 and the famous "armor of God" described there. That metaphor refers to the "sword of the spirit" and the "shield of faith." These two accouterments suggest dual emphases in Pauline characterization. First, by his use of the sword, Paul is clearly being portrayed as a pugnacious champion of "Truth." Such, indeed, is readily apparent in many of the Pauline writings. He is also, of course, a famous author of the New Testament. 2 Timothy 3 (a letter assigned to Paul) asserts that "all Scripture is inspired." Paul refers to Jewish law as an "old covenant" which has been replaced by a "new covenant" under Jesus (2 Corinthians 3, note 3:14). "Covenant" is another word for "testament." Many

Christians refer to the Hebrew scriptures as the "Old Testament." To many medieval Christians, Paul not only declared the inspiration of the Bible, but also coined the terms Christians used to describe its various parts.

Paul's iconographic association with a book recalls his role in the construction of the Christian Bible itself. His writings, in a major way, *are* the Bible. Since the Bible is held up for display in a way that resembles a shield, the Bible is also an iconographic cipher for "faith." The Spirit, according to Paul, is the ultimate source of the Bible. Sword and Bible, then, conjoin to create an image of Paul as literary advocate for the "true" doctrine, protected by the Word of God even as he uses that Spirit-filled Word to advance on all challengers. This image is an interpretation of the biblical text; it is also evidence of popular knowledge of and interest in the Bible, and a strong statement about Paul's role in both. Not only was medieval scholarship biblically literate, the Bible and its images formed the central matrix for all medieval scholarship – ironically, to a much greater degree than the Bible factored into scholarly and public discourses in the later ages. Paul, as defender and author of that Bible, is a close second in importance.

Diversity of Thought in the Middle Ages

A second mistaken view of the Middle Ages that we should avoid is the assumption that the ideology, particularly the biblical and religious landscape, espoused in the period was uniform. The sway of the Roman Catholic Church was not universal, even in Europe. Outside Europe, a wide array of Christian doctrines flourished. Certainly, many of these were affected by the rise of Islam in the seventh century, but many small communities survived in pockets all over the Middle East and Turkey. Within Europe, Rome's greatest influence was limited to the Western nations, particularly France, Italy, northern Spain and what is now southern Germany. In the eastern areas, there was a vibrant community of the Orthodox Church, along with several other dissenting communities located in North Africa (particularly Egypt), northern Europe, southern Spain and southern Turkey, and Mesopotamia. Sweden and northern Germany were centers for large dissenter and "mystic" communities of believers.

For many of these communities, Paul was a central figure. But, unlike those which emphasized Paul the scholar, the "Paul of the mind," many of these traditions focused upon a mystic Paul. Paul was also popular because he was a model for faithful defiance of "false doctrines" and "illegitimate" authorities. Drawing on key passages such as 2 Corinthians 12 (where Paul describes a "mystic journey" up to the "seventh heavens" where he is shown wonders) and 1 Corinthians 14 (where Paul grants his own tendency to ecstatic speech), as well as many other minor passages, many found support for arguments for a direct engagement between the Holy Spirit and the average believer. The church, for these groups, was not needed as a mediator between the believer and God. Many saw passages such as Romans 8 (particularly verse 7) as supporting their position. Central Germany was, at times, placed under papal ban; priests of the church were not allowed to celebrate Mass or administer the sacraments. Drawing, in part, on texts such as the pastorals and Romans, many communities appointed their own leaders and conducted such services on their own. Key documents such as the *Theologica Germanica* defended such acts and rooted their defense in quasi-mystical readings of Paul and his views of the Holy Spirit. Many of the mystics also celebrated the asceticism they found in Paul, which we surveyed in the last chapter. Constructions of Paul, for some, formed the basis for a mystic Paul popular among dissident spiritualist groups and reticent monks.

The Middle Ages was a time of developing doctrine and practice; the intellectual life of the church may well have severed prior engagement with Greco-Roman literature (and, in that sense, have descended into "dark ages"), but it was hardly intellectually stagnant. The Bible played a key role in the construction of doctrine, the practice of faith, and the mind of the believer. The Bible permeated art and literature. Reconstructions of biblical characters and events shaped the way humans viewed themselves and their world. Thinking in the Middle Ages was not uniform nor without difference and dissent. While variation and diversity were discouraged by the authorities in many parts of central and eastern Europe, difference did occur and was particularly rampant in other parts of the "Christian world."

For the balance of this chapter, I would like to sketch two general images of Paul from the medieval period. The first, reflecting the iconography of Paul, is Paul the scholar. This view celebrates Paul as an advocate of "sound doctrine" (1 Tim. 4:1–9, 6:3–13), an advocate for truth (1 Tim. 6:11–16; 2 Tim. 3:1–7), and an intellectual giant of "God's wisdom" (1 Cor. 3:19). The second is rooted in the medieval fascination with Paul as a mystic and ascetic. In many ways, it is the Paul of ritual and mystical praxis.

Paul as the Scholar

The genre and rhetoric of Paul's letters became models for argument and exegesis in the Middle Ages. I do not mean to suggest that Paul, alone, was the model for these changes. Yet he certainly did play a central role in bringing these elements into Christian discourse. Paul was a critical model for the rhetorical style and argument of such notable medieval scholars and clerics as Hilduin, Erigena, Hugh of St. Victor, Thomas Aquinas, Anselm, Bonaventure, Albert the Great, Meister Eckhart, and Johannes Tauler. Many of these scholars wrote commentaries, sermons, or treatises on Paul's letters or Acts. Others used these texts extensively in their writing.

The literary genres of the encyclical as well as the "public epistle of the wise teacher" were ultimately adapted from the Pauline corpus (particularly the pastorals). They often include Pauline prayers, blessings, and benedictions in their address and conclusion. Many elements in Paul, such as the "public epistle" as a genre, had their roots in the non-Christian writing and practice of Paul's day. Seneca, for example, wrote and collected his letters to any of a number of correspondents. Paul's use of this letter-writing tradition would have been the medieval reader's primary encounter with such a form. Further, many of these medieval treatises make explicit use of Pauline language as almost an opening or benedictory formula. The Pauline corpus also carries a variety of epistolary styles, with examples of "thanks," "instruction," "exhortation," and "rebuke" written to both private individuals and communities. Paul also models the standard "opening" convention of blessing before God (as well as the closing benediction). Again, these are not elements unique to Paul's writing, but were adapted from pagan convention. Still, Paul would have provided the major moment of contact between medieval writers and these tropes.

Paul's letters (particularly Romans) use a style of argument made popular by an ancient Greek philosophical school, the Stoics. The letters frequently engage in an imaginary debate, where Paul takes on the voice of the reader to offer challenges to his own argument, and then uses these challenges to clarify his position, for example in Romans 3:1-2 or 3:9. Again, Paul does not, himself, invent this idea; but the medieval scholastics encountered this rhetorical style from Paul. For many medieval scholars, Paul was the gateway to Greek Stoic and Platonic philosophy. His use of deductive logic and dialectic were particular favorites of the scholastics. In Paul's day, classical rhetoric celebrated the use of various "voices" or orientations to rhetoric (the literature of persuasion). Principal "canons" of rhetoric were appeals to reason, appeals to history, appeals to emotion, and appeals to "delight." Relying heavily on Paul's use of these rhetorical devices, these methods were expanded and explained by the early Christian writer Augustine. Augustine, in turn, was instrumental in establishing the rhetoric of the medieval period.

Finally, Paul's techniques of biblical interpretation were imitated in medieval exegesis. Paul uses a very literalistic approach to texts, often stressing the importance of one particular word (indeed, even its tense, voice, and mood). But he also mixes in other methods of allegory and typology. In allegory, the "literal" meaning of a text (often problematical because it is too explicit or at odds with conventional thought) is, in a way, subverted or ignored. Instead, a "mystical" or a spiritual approach was taken. In typology readers of the Old Testament (the Hebrew Bible) find multiple examples of how biblical stories "prefigure" or symbolically "point toward" Jesus in the flesh.

Again, I am not arguing that these elements were generated by Paul or even that Paul is their sole source. Indeed, the opposite is very much the case. Paul was using standard forms, structures, and arguments of his day (such was the basis for any hope of persuasion; if Paul had been too individualistic in his approach, no one would have found his arguments convincing). Other writers used the same techniques. What I am suggesting, however, is that Pauline writings formed a principal "delivery vehicle" for these structures and ideas to enter into medieval philosophical and theological literature. Further, since Paul formed a unique collecting place for these various elements (since he exhibits so many of them), he became, de facto, a paradigm or pattern-setting figure for the author of sacred philosophy in the Middle Ages.

Paul and Medieval Cosmology and Anthropology

Paul was particularly critical for medieval doctrinal development. Theologians such as Abelard and Anselm and Aquinas developed their anthropologies (doctrines about the nature and state of humanity) as well as their cosmologies (systems and doctrines about the nature of the universe) from Pauline literature. More accurately, perhaps, they developed these doctrines from their readings of Augustine's reading of Paul. Paul writes that "all have sinned" and are separated from God. Further, Jesus unmakes the sinful state and reverses the curse of death imparted by Adam's sin. Following Augustine, medieval theologians argued that creation was essentially good, but was flawed by human sin which was perpetuated by Adam but inherited from each generation, normally via the "seed" of Adam. This inherited sin was a psychic/spiritual force that fatally flawed creation and was precipitated by a human quest for knowledge. Genesis 3 shows Eve tempted by promises that she, after eating the fruit of the Tree of the Knowledge of Good and Evil, will have her "eyes opened" and that she and Adam will "become like God." Following the assessment of this event in 1 Timothy 1, many medieval theologians also argued that Eve's "deception" was a basis for the exclusion of women from any official ministry in the church. The desire for forbidden knowledge was sinful. Deception, however, was a worse condition. In medieval thinking the central issue was not desire for knowledge or the practice of scholarship per se, but scholarship that was on any topic or program which was not explicitly theological in theme and submissive to God. Unless an inquiry were undertaken explicitly in order to draw closer to God, it was sinful. Theology was understood as the queen of the sciences, and intellectual life (particularly science, cosmology, history, and philosophy) were all forced into a theological frame.

This Pauline cosmology/anthropology was understood to be the product of sober abstract reflection on Paul's part. There was no awareness of Pauline disputes shaping his thought or of a progressive sense of his intellectual development. Paul was the basis for medieval notions of revelation and knowledge. In Romans, Paul notes that humans traded the "natural" for the "unnatural" as they turned from God, failing to note the reality of God in the universe. Nature itself offered an essay on God. To study the cosmos was to reflect on God. More exactly, reflection on God was study of the cosmos. The Enlightenment would shift this emphasis and understand the pursuit of science as an inquiry into God's mind. All creation, Paul writes, was participating in the eager expectation of Jesus' salvation (Rom. 8:18–25); to contemplate God was to contemplate creation itself. The surest proof of God, Anselm would argue in his famous ontological argument, is the existence of nature. Anselm argued that everything in nature happened as the result of some cause. Chasing this line of causation backward, one soon realized that there must be a "first cause," beyond which there was no other cause. This first cause, Anselm asserted, was God. To quote from Paul's speech on the Athenian Areopagus (a favorite text for the scholastics), God was that in which all the universe "lived and moved and found being."

Paul and the Doctrine of Transubstantiation

In many ways, the most distinctive doctrine to emerge from the Middle Ages was the belief in the transubstantiation of the dedicated Host during Eucharist. Eucharist (from the Greek for "to give thanks/thanksgiving") is the central ritual of what is now the

Roman Catholic Mass. It commemorates Jesus' last meal with his elite 12 disciples eaten on the last Thursday evening of his life. It is also called the Lord's Supper or Communion by most modern Protestants.

In many ways the Protestant and Catholic forms of the ritual are similar. Each tradition affirms it as a significant action of both confession (to the world) and renewal (with God). Each is a ritual reenactment of Jesus' last meal. The gospels found in the New Testament affirm that Jesus died on or around the first day of the Jewish festival of Passover. Passover, a week-long celebration of Jewish deliverance from slavery in Egypt, begins with a ceremonial meal. Two main components of this meal are unleavened bread (bread made without yeast) and wine. According to the gospels of Matthew, Mark, and Luke, during this last meal Jesus took a portion of the unleavened bread and passed it to his 12 apostles, enjoining them to "take and eat this bread, which is my body broken for you." He also circulated a cup of wine and instructed the apostles to drink saying "this is the cup of the new covenant of my blood poured out for you" (1 Cor. 11:24–5). Christians today celebrate this same ritual by prayers of blessing and circulating bread and wine; Paul, in 1 Corinthians 11:23–31, reports that he "received this tradition" and "passed it on" to the believers at Corinth, apparently serving as a link in the chain of teachings about Jesus, but also enjoining the practice on all later believers. Paul writes that "as often as you eat this bread and drink this cup, you proclaim Christ's death until he comes again" (1 Cor. 11:26). Catholics and Protestants would agree that by reenacting the meal via their ritual (Eucharist or Lord's Supper), they are participating in this communal Christian activity. Paul plays a critical role in the transmission of this ritual. Indeed, were it not for his letter to the Corinthians, there would be very little direct material in the New Testament to indicate that the earliest Christians understood that Jesus intended anyone other than the apostles to participate in the ritual.

Despite these similarities, however, some key differences remain. For Roman Catholics (and a few other groups), the observance of the ritual is considered a "sacrament." The term "sacrament" was first used by Tertullian. A sacrament is a ritual established by Jesus himself that is "an outward sign of an invisible grace." The Roman Catholic Church identifies seven sacraments. Paul writes, explicitly, about six of them. He does not directly discuss extreme unction (last rites). Eastern Orthodox Christians acknowledge these seven, but leave the definition of sacrament more open and flexible. For them, there are at least seven, whereas Roman Catholics bind the definition more carefully. Luther (whom we will address in the next chapter) accepted the "outward sign of an invisible grace," but, according to his readings of the gospels, Jesus only established two rituals (baptism and the Eucharist). So Episcopalians and mainline Protestants still use the language of sacrament but do not believe that the bread and wine are literally the body and blood of Jesus. Lutherans believe in a "real presence," which could, perhaps, be understood as a mediating position between transubstantiation and a more radical reformer position of symbolic reenactment and remembrance of Jesus' final night.

In more common terms, a sacramental idea of the ritual asserts that, if properly engaged in (supervised by ordained clergy, undertaken by knowledgeable believers), it imparts a particular spiritual "power" or sustenance. For these believers, sharing in the ritual is a way of sharing in God's power. For many Protestants, however, the ritual has a deep symbolic meaning, but not necessarily any particular "power." They view the ritual as an "ordinance," something done because Jesus commanded it, but not with any special power beyond its deep and very meaningful symbolism.

At the core of these differences lies a belief about the very nature of the bread (called the Host). Key thinkers and writers in the Middle Ages, reasoning out the nuances of biblical language, pondering the (somewhat unusual) statements of Jesus about eating his own "body" and "blood," and rooting both notions in a very real sense of genuine spiritual powers in the world (powers moderns might refer to as "supernatural"), began to argue that consuming the eucharistic Host was a sacrament precisely because the Host was transformed into the literal body and blood of Jesus. The priest enables this transformation, and has the (exclusive) power to do so through his own ordination (also a sacrament) and regardless of his own intention, spiritual state, or sinfulness. It is still God's body, the sacrament is still efficacious, regardless of the spiritual state of either the giver or the receiver. This transformation is technically known as "transubstantiation" (the "substance" of the bread is altered, *trans*posed into something new). Improper consumption of the Host (taking it while in a state of sin) compounds one's sinful state.

Key theologians who were instrumental in the development of the doctrine of transubstantiation, Ratramnus and Radbertus, developed their thinking often in direct dialog with Paul. Notably, Paul writes in 1 Corinthians 11:32 that incorrect consumption of the Host (eating the bread while one still has a guilty conscience or is in a state of sin) can cause people to become "weak and ill" or perhaps even "die." To many modern people, events in the world are caused by "natural" or "supernatural" forces. To the medieval mind, there was no "supernatural," because there was no "natural" as we moderns know it. *Everything* in the world was influenced by some spiritual agency. The debates between Ratramnus and Radbertus, where the doctrine of transubstantiation was fundamentally worked through, employ a typological reading of the bread/Host as allegory but also as a spiritual reality manifested in physical symbol. They engage 1 Corinthians 11 in detail, along with 2 Corinthians 4. They focus intently on 1 Corinthians 11:27–32.

In doctrines of transubstantiation, the bread and wine become the body and blood of Jesus. In a very real sense, then, the messiah is, once again, offered as a sacrifice for the community. "Mass" means sacrifice, and it is performed on an "altar" not a "table." Believers, again, experience the flesh-and-blood Jesus. The language of the Mass is taken from the Temple. For other believers, who hold to the Lord's Supper as an ordinance, the metaphorical spirit of the meal becomes paramount. It is overseen by the community, not by a special intercessory priest. It is an invitation to Christ's table, not a participation in Christ's sacrifice on an altar.

In this one example, we see both aspects of the "medieval mind" at work – a mind, I argue, that was both rooted in readings of Paul *and* shaped the way in which Paul was read and understood.

On the one hand, we have meticulous reasoning and argument. In this, the intellectual rigor of the "life of the mind" is well on display. Yet, on the other hand, we have a real and immediate belief in transformational "supernatural" powers. The mysticism and "otherworldliness" of Paul are also on display. The doctrine of transubstantiation, then, is not only one of the most distinct theological positions to emerge from the Middle Ages, it is, in key ways, a remarkable exemplar of the dual foci of the medieval mind. This doctrine would later mark a substantial difference among the later reformers, dividing the communities who would follow Luther from those following Calvin. Though it derives primarily from the gospels, the Christian theology of the Eucharist is also dependent upon particular readings of Paul.

Social and Civil Order

Paul famously concludes in Romans 13 that "government does not bear the sword in vain." More aggressively, he argues that God is actually the authority behind all forms of governance. Medieval linkage of the head of state with the divinely appointed ruler draws on several biblical sources, but the social order of a divine state imposing God's rule is articulated (and defended) largely on the basis of Pauline texts such as Romans. In addition to chapter 13's bold assertion, chapters 1–3 of Romans indicate that all of humanity is under God's rule. Failing to concede God's authority is a violation of nature (Rom. 1:18–19).

Within the governance of the Western church, the centralization of the authority of God in one figure is largely defensible from the gospels. In Matthew 16:13–20 Jesus asks his inner circle of followers "Who are people saying that I am?" The answer is varied: "Some say Elijah, some say John the Baptist, some say a prophet." Jesus then asks, "Who do you think I am?" One of the 12, Simon Peter, immediately answers: "You are the Christ, the son of the living God." Jesus then praises Peter and promises "upon this rock I will build my church ... whatever you enjoin on earth is enjoined in heaven; whatever you negate on earth. will be negated in heaven." Modern Protestants recognize the "rock" in this quotation to be a reference to the confession of Jesus as Christ. Catholics, however, recognize that the name "Peter" means "rock." They then assert that Peter, for his confession, was given the authority by Jesus to succeed Jesus after his ascension. Whatever Peter enjoined or negated on earth became divine law. Peter became the successor to Jesus, authorized to appoint, or design a system for appointing, his own successor. Peter, in other words, became the first pope. Others succeeded him according to various means. The doctrine of papal authority, then, is rooted in the Synoptic Gospels as well as the sacrament of confession.

Church hierarchy demands church order. The church offices of deacon and overseer/bishop are found largely in the New Testament mostly in the Pauline portions. The offices are mentioned in Acts. The pastorals, however, are the only place in the New Testament that discusses the qualifications of those who are to hold these offices. 1 Timothy 3 and Titus 1 are the only two locations. 1 and 2 Timothy and Titus also stress the importance of following the bishop; bishops have the final responsibility, and authority, for the maintenance of "sound doctrine." Bishops establish order and discipline for the entire community. Deacons execute the instructions of the bishop. It is not clear if, in the first century, Christian communities were governed by a board of bishops or a single official. Two words, "overseer" and "elder," seem to be used interchangeably. Most likely, there was a mix of practices. The medieval Roman church, however, interpreted these passages to mean a single individual who administrated (or governed) the entire community. Priests were the authority for a given congregation. Groups of congregations in a particular region were governed by bishops. Bishops were the "priests" for "priests." Bishops, in turn, answered (and confessed) to cardinals. Cardinals answered to the pope. Much of this hierarchy was defended through citation of Pauline traditions. Pseudo-Dionysius, as we saw earlier, wrote an extensive treatise on the hierarchy of the church which included sacraments and ordinances. Curiously, Paul asserts in 1 Timothy 3 that bishops are to be "the husband of one wife." The medieval church, in the West, insisted bishops be celibate. The Eastern church (and later Protestants) allowed clergy to marry. The medieval West, however, argued for celibacy based upon Paul's assertion that single people were more flexible in the service of God. Later writers argued that bishops were married to the church. The medieval church also argued that Paul's remarks in 1 Timothy clearly indicated that women, single or married, were unfit for clerical ordination. Peter was the source of papal authority; Paul articulated ecclesiastical structure. If Peter was the foundation for the church, Paul was the architect.

Papal authority, however, could easily become a "paper tiger." For it to have real power, the church must have a means of enforcement. Those who rebel against the pope must face some consequence. In one of Paul's letters to the Corinthian believers, he identified an individual (not by name but by description of action) whom he deemed immoral. In this case, a man was cohabiting with his "father's wife," presumably his stepmother. Paul commands that the community warn the individual to stop this behavior. If the sinner did not repent, Paul commanded the Corinthians to "expel the immoral brother" and "hand him over to Satan." In 1 Corinthians 11, Paul also asserts that those not properly prepared should not take (should not be allowed to take?) the Lord's Supper.

Paul assumes that baptism unites believers with Jesus, and is a mystic participation in Jesus' death and resurrection (Romans, Corinthians). He also assumes that sexual continence (marriage) creates a unique spiritual bond between partners. He suggests that there are supernatural, mystic properties associated with transforming states (such as dedication to a cause, sex, death, etc.). These transformations are mediated by belief and through the believing community. They are also essential for the reconciliation of the believer with God. Yet Paul also insists that repeated and flagrant moral violation should result in expulsion from the believing community. The fusion of these policies culminates in the doctrines of church-controlled sacrament and ecclesiastical excommunication which is, in essence, the refusal by the church to recognize a member and allow him or her to participate in Mass/Holy Communion or to benefit from the sacraments. When these ideas are integrated into Pauline systems of government and, more precisely, when the mediating officers – the administration and leadership of the church – are given military and political power, the result is very much like the church–state fusion found in the medieval period.

Obviously, this fusion was founded on other elements (spiritual – other parts of the biblical tradition; material – political, economic, and social realities) which influenced their development and illustration. As well, these passages from Paul frequently float independent of obvious allusion to Pauline biography. They become "proof text" bases for faith and practice and doctrine – in some ways relating to the mind of Paul independent of *any* biographical context. Indeed, many would argue that these passages are taken out of historical and biographical context to form abstract doctrine without real regard for or bearing on Paul's original intention.

However, they very much do impinge on biographical reconstructions of Paul. They assume he was actually inspired and that he was authorized to administer his congregations and advise them even though he himself was apparently never a bishop/elder; his words were (or at least should have been) heeded. As we saw in chapter 1, all of these are assumptions. Further, they all participate in an image of Paul as a distant but involved theological mind. Much like the senior clerics, monastics, and administrative clergy themselves in the medieval period, there is a pervasive image of Paul as a (cloistered?) theological expert, issuing principled and dogmatic missives to outlying congregations. Paul is Anselm. The implied biography of Paul *is* (in part) papal. This biographical construction pervades the treatment of his texts and is readily reflected in iconography of him, cloistered, dutifully writing his encyclicals about church practice and faith.

While the overlap between an implicit Pauline biography and medieval scholasticism is clearly present, it is difficult to identify which makes which. Did medieval clerics construct their image of a life of the cloistered spiritual mind as a result of their construction of Pauline biography? Or did they draw out a biography of Paul based upon their readings of his letters in their own cloistered contexts? Ultimately, the answer is elusive because, ultimately, the answer to both questions is "Yes."

Paul and Medieval Anti-Judaism

Before leaving this portion of our chapter a few observations are in order regarding the anti-Semitic implications of the biography of Paul we have just traced. In many ways, this image of Paul is dependent upon and requires a significant Pauline "Other" for Paul's conflicts. Paul, in his letters, is frequently engaged in intense conflict. To medieval clerics, it was unthinkable to have him in conflict with others who were authentically Christian. Certainly, it couldn't be an ongoing conflict with Peter. If Paul was regarded without question as a leading voice in the church – deferred to and heeded by all – who were his various opponents? His doctrinal letters from a cloistered study were directed against some heretic. Through most of the medieval period, the "heretics" in question were understood to be observant Jews or Jews who would not fully embrace Jesus. Jews faced horrid persecutions in the Middle Ages. In addition to ongoing ghettoization and social persecution (laws restricting where Jews could live, whom they could marry, what careers they could engage in, what property they could own, etc.), Jews faced episodes of city- or state-wide physical persecution (ranging from exile to murder). The Fourth Lateran Council even forced them to wear distinctive hats when in public.

Paul is certainly not the sole source for Christian anti-Semitism, nor were Pauline texts and biography the sole (or even major) means by which these ideas were communicated across Europe. Once again, much of the responsibility lies within the gospels (particularly John). Jesus is frequently shown in conflict with "the Jews," seemingly all of them. Even the Synoptic Gospels of Matthew, Mark, and Luke were more nuanced in their portrayal of Jesus in conflict with specific individuals or parties of Jews – the Pharisees or the scribes and priests, or the Sadducees. All four perpetuate images of Jesus' death at the hands of the Temple authorities and "all Jerusalem" rather than the response of Roman colonizers, perhaps in league with some collaborating members of the Jerusalem aristocracy. One need look no further than the (in)famous medieval Passion plays, where every effort is taken to portray Jews as "Christ killers." All the blame for Jesus' death was laid at the feet of the Jews. The Romans are absolved. In some traditions, even Pilate is sainted. Doubtless, these wildly popular events were the basis for more than a little popular anti-Semitism. The iconography of the Middle Ages also heightens the problem. Jews are depicted with bestial facial features, demonic attributes, pointed ears, tails, horns, and as always groveling and plotting. A widespread trope in central Europe was a Jew bent over eating pig excrement as the pig defecates.

Paul is not the sole source of medieval anti-Judaism, but passages such as 1 Thessalonians 2:14–16 certainly didn't help. There, the text asserts that Jews "killed both the Lord Jesus and the prophets and drove us out" and that "God's wrath has come upon them at last." Many modern scholars who study the ancient copies of the New Testament feel these verses were added by a later hand, but medieval scholars embraced them. Paul's letters were interpreted in a way that substantially participated in anti-Jewish caricatures and drove some even further toward virulent anti-Judaism. Hebrews asserts that the former ways of engaging with God via Jewish law ("covenant") are now superseded. In 2 Corinthians, Paul flatly describes them as "Old Covenant." In Galatians, Paul asserts that Jewish ritual laws and practices were of value only as "schoolmasters" training humanity to the point where it was able to receive Jesus' revelation about righteousness. In 2 Corinthians 4, Jews viewed God only from "behind a veil." God had "hardened their hearts" and caused them to reject Jesus (Rom. 11:25). Oddly, though, Paul's bold assertion that "all Israel shall be saved" and that the "promises and call of God are irrevocable" in Romans 11:33 were often ignored. When read, they were interpreted to refer to the "spiritual Israel." Despite the fact that such a reading requires taking the same word, "Israel," as literal in the first half of the sentence but suddenly "spiritual" in the second, medieval readers nearly unanimously interpreted it to mean that Christians were the true Israel. This authorized them to lay claim to virtually every promise of God in the Bible.

These texts, as I've noted, establish Jews as the paradigmatic heretics, particularly given the reconstruction of Pauline biography we have just seen. The cloistered Paul was articulating theological truths which were seen as devastating to Judaism's existence. Even more, though, is what the implied biography ignores: Paul himself *and nearly all the first followers of Jesus* were Jews. The debates in the Pauline corpus are between one messianic Jew and another set of (possibly also messianic) Jews about the teachings of Jesus, another Jew. The arguments are all "in-house" theological debates. In many ways, Pauline biographies could be drawn which fully concede a literal and simple reading of the passages I've just outlined, yet still do not see Paul as rejecting Jews or "Judaism." Perhaps, one could see Paul as a voice of one community of Jews debating another – much like, in modern terms, Conservative Jews debating Reform Jews on Sabbath observance. While all sides argue vigorously, none denies the other's status as Jews. My point is not to lay all the evils of medieval anti-Semitism at Paul's door. Nor am I arguing (at this juncture) for or against a particular reading of Paul's views on Jews and Judaism and the biographical context such a reading creates. What I am arguing is that reconstructed Pauline biography lies beneath these readings from medieval exegesis.

The method of medieval interpretation, its exegesis, polemic, doctrine of church, church order, sacraments, rhetoric, logic, and understanding of the Bible, as well as the way such interpretations were written down for dissemination, can *all* be rooted in Pauline character, text, and biography. In most other instances, this rooting is implicit. In either case, it is foundational and it is intrinsically (and inseparably) tied to Pauline biography.

Paul the Ascetic and Mystic

It is tempting to assert that individuals in the Middle Ages were more superstitious and had a greater credulity regarding the "supernatural." Certainly, examples from witch hunts to belief in Satan-accelerated plagues to "wonder" cures of illnesses by contact with the bones of a saint can be readily produced. These seem sharply at odds with modern science because they are. However, calling these "superstition," or belief in a "supernatural" power, is to misspeak. For a medieval mind, these were not "superstition." They were the fabric of an empirically derived, logically examined view of the universe. It is easy, after all, for a modern person schooled in physics and astronomy to overlook how much "common sense" is inherent in a belief that the earth does not move. In addition, the "supernatural" was simply understood as the "natural." Beings with particular powers and influences were as readily assumed in taxonomy and cosmology as are unusually miraculous creatures in the world today (how, indeed, can one rationally approach something as mysterious as a jellyfish or platypus?).

Medieval exegetes focused much more on the spiritual or "supernatural" elements of Paul's letters than moderns might, and, we must concede, they had textual bases for doing so. Paul believed he was taught his "Gospel" directly from the lips of a dead man. He spoke in tongues and believed devoutly in prophecy. He likely believed in divinely ordained dreams and omens. He conceded, as we have already seen, that improper consumption of the Communion Host could produce disease or death, that sex produced a mystical union, that baptism was a direct and mystical participation in the death and resurrection of Christ. He had visions and miraculous, out-of-body, tours of heaven. He believed that Satan himself sent physical torments. In short, he lived in a world that many moderns would call "superstitious" or "supernatural." These elements seem troublesome to a "rational" mind precisely because they are not, themselves, rational. They are pre-/post-/a-rational experiences. They are the substance of mysticism.

Mysticism is the belief in one's ability to unite with some supernatural, sacred force or personality. It is often associated with intuition and inspiration. A mystic yearns for the loss of self and for the loss of reason (something that Paul himself celebrated). Instead, the mystic revels in the impartation of arcane and obscure "knowledge" arising from the experience of divine/spiritual encounter. Paul was, to the core, a mystic.

Many mystics achieve their spiritual highs by diminishment of the body. Most practice some form of asceticism – the denial of some luxury or bodily need in order to focus one's thoughts on a particular end. Many mystics (and many others) would bifurcate body and soul. The "real" world (the material world) is understood as a hindrance to those who would achieve a "spiritual" (immaterial) truth or reality. Hunger, pleasure, sexuality – physicality in general – distract one's spirit from pursuit of the truth. To quiet these desires, one needs to focus on spiritual ends, but also to deprive the body of its distractions.

Paul exhibits many of these tendencies in his letters. Much of this arises from his missionary travels and what appears to be an intense belief that the world was soon to end. Paul does not disparage marriage, but he clearly advocates the "single life," since it allows one to be flexible in serving God (1 Cor. 7). While not opposed to marriage (or sexuality), Paul clearly saw these drives as secondary (at best) to his spiritual calling. He celebrates his own privations. Again, these were the result of his mission orientation (and Paul seems to offer them as proof of his own dedication). He endured privation, hunger and danger for the sake of his mission. As he writes, "I batter my body, daily, for the cause of Christ" (1 Cor. 9:27). Indeed, he was bold about his own sufferings. He would assert, "I display the sufferings of Christ in my own body" and "I filled up the sufferings of Christ in my own body for your sake" (Gal. 6:27; Col. 1:24).

As we have noted, for Paul these seemed to be privations for his own mission. But as we've also noted, the medieval readers of Paul didn't emphasize his missionary aspect. Instead, they tended to see Paul as an exemplar of ascetic or monastic living. The development of monasticism in Christianity is complex. In part, it began at a very early stage. In the early fourth century, Constantine the Great became emperor of the Roman empire. Constantine, though not himself baptized until he was on his deathbed, was highly sympathetic to Christianity. His mother, Helena, was an active and devout Christian. Constantine had taken the throne after a particularly bitter time for Christians in Roman history. One of his predecessors (and rivals) was Justinian. The emperor Justinian had made Christianity illegal and had subjected Christians to the harshest possible punishments. After Constantine's accession, the empire went from being rabidly hostile to Christianity to treating Christianity as a protected religion (indeed, one could argue, as *the* religion of the empire). Many who had never suffered persecution now rushed into the local church. Many came for political or economic reasons. As a result, many of the devout found "the church" had become too worldly and too interconnected with politics. They left the main community and retreated into deserted places for spiritual reflection, enduring intense privation and suffering to stoke their spiritual fires. This practice lasted well on through late antiquity into the Middle Ages. Such devout followers were either solitary (anchorite) or lived in highly disciplined communities (cenobite). Adherents of both approaches forcibly "incarcerated" their bodies away from mainstream culture, living in spiritual "cells" as monks and nuns.

In point of fact, the Middle Ages, in many ways, made such privation mainstream. Benedict, Francis, and dozens of others formalized themselves into specific groups or "orders" of monastic communities, organized around strict rules regarding times of prayer, diet, worship schedule, study, and reflection. These groups considered themselves to be in the front line of the war against Satan. As "advanced positions" they drew Satan's most intense temptations. Their prayers and steadfast commitment also, vicariously, made the entire world more "holy" before God.

Many of these groups organized around Pauline notions of "body buffeting." All were celibate. In part, this is a reflection of the current readings about the life and example of Jesus (Jesus does not appear to ever have been married). Many, however, rooted this privation in the words of the apostle. The holiest course was the life that allowed the most time for dedication to God. As Paul enjoined, a higher spiritual gift of celibacy was given to some for the advancement of the gospel. As a result, many prized celibacy for monks as well as for clergy.

These moments of privation also provided times for reflection on doctrine (an activity rooted in their view of Paul) as well as enhancing one's chances of a mystical encounter with God. Visions abounded among the desert monks and nuns and other cloistered individuals. These visions often provided critical insights into God's desires and plans for humanity as well as into key articles of Christian doctrine. As I have argued in this chapter, the privations of Paul, in the Pauline biography of the Middle Ages, were, by and large, separated from his mission work. In it's place was a notion of Paul as paradigmatic monk. Isolated, he encountered God in mystic visions facilitated by his isolation and privation, which resulted in insights written to debunk heretics. For many medieval writers, this was an overwhelmingly seductive model. As before, the aggregate elements of these models were not solely derived from Pauline biographies, but they were clearly present in Pauline models, particularly in composite forms.

A particularly influential motif was Paul's vision of the "third heaven." As we noted earlier, in 2 Corinthians, Paul reports he paid a terrible price for these divine revelations. Lest he become too proud, Satan put a "thorn in the flesh" that would torment him. Paul seems to readily equate divine revelation with torturous cost. Motifs of the "journey" literature associated with Paul spread through the Middle Ages. These motifs were elaborated upon and expanded. Many were also joined with the graphic images of judgment and hell found throughout medieval literature and art. Paul's visions not only provided the basis for medieval cosmology, but also served as the test case for substantial and significant mystic engagement with God. Paul's "circles" or substructures of heaven and hell provided the base for Pseudo-Dionysius' speculations. These, in turn, provided the basis for medieval mystics and other traditions. Among others, Paul the mystic was influential on Heinrich Suso, John Ruysbroeck, Nicholas of Cusa, Denis the Carthusian, John Colet, and John of the Cross. Finally, these provided fodder for other, more literary, speculations, such as those of Dante (in his *Divine Comedy*) and, later, Milton.

For many of these communities, the opponents mentioned in Paul's writings – the "Pauline opponents" – were understood as those who proposed a "secularized" faith. This would either be those who sought to live the Christian faith within the context of general medieval society or those who sought to further merge Christian faith and secular political power, a long-standing concern of many Christian mystics. These communities tended to equate the opponents of Paul with the established religious authorities. In many ways, however, this heightened the anti-Semitism involved. The opponents of Paul were reduced to "the Jews." Opponents of the mystical initiates (or the scholastic intellectuals) were also "the Jews." In other words, "the Jews" became anyone someone considered anti-spiritual. The effects of this transformation would prove deadly.

Paul, and a particular type of Pauline biography, played a central role in medieval interpretation of the Bible. Paul as the traveling missionary was downplayed. Paul the mystic and ascetic was centralized. When this was added to Paul the theologian and Paul the letter-writer, a model of the medieval, cloistered ascetic was established. For many in the "Paul as mystic" community, "Paul as the contentious rebel" was central. In time, one individual would wed the notions of Paul the mystic and Paul the theologian. These two models would be betrothed in a context of "Paul the contentious theologian" resisting (Jewish) heresy. This culmination would erupt, aggressively, in the writings of the late medieval monk, scholar, and clergyman Martin Luther.

Chapter 5

Paul and the Rise of
Protestant Christianity

Luther's Challenge

On the morning of October 31, 1517, the Augustinian monk
Martin Luther nailed a list of 96 theses to the door of the church
at Wittenberg, Germany. He had earlier made a trip to Rome
which had shaken his confidence in the hierarchy and doctrine of
the church he had sworn to give his life to serve. He surely paused
a moment with his hand smoothing the paper against the hard,
wet oak before turning to leave, orange and yellow leaves in the
gutters of the damp stairs, his cloak cinched against himself to
ward off the autumn chill.

   The action was a definite call to discussion and, historically,
would prove dramatically decisive. Within five years, Luther
would be excommunicated and his teaching banned at the Diet of
Worms. He would face eventual exile from his homeland. In its
immediate moment, however, though decisive, his action was,
perhaps, much less dramatic. Luther was following a fairly staid
practice of the publication of a lecture or seminar series. This was
something much more akin to a modern "call for papers" circulated among academics – a specific group a university invites to
contribute to an academic conference on a given topic – calling on
those interested to submit papers or abstracts of papers to be read
and discussed at the conference. Luther was being bold by announc-
ing a new list of topics, on what were often considered closed
subjects, reconsidering basic elements of church practice and faith.

The nailing of the theses (his own positions) was designed to generate discussion and elicit either "Yes, and" or "No, because" responses. The content of his arguments, on the surface, seemed more a reaction against excessive policies than calls for systemic, wholesale reform, a call for redecoration or remolding, not radical full renovation and reconstruction.

Still, the content of Luther's 96 theses had explosive significance. Luther was arguing, by implication, for radically new ways of viewing the nature and role of the clergy. He challenged whether or not the separation of some into the category of "clergy" radically remade (in technical terms, "ontologically transformed") them such that they were, in themselves, authorized to forgive sin. Further, he argued that there had been numerous abuses within the hierarchy of the established clerical bodies (culminating in a corrupt papacy) and there was a need for a wholesale reform. Eventually, Luther would oppose celibacy for members of the clergy.

More, Luther was reimaging the very structures of Christian salvation. His theology of salvation (formally known as "soteriology") recognized two stages: justification (being redeemed by God and placed in the category of "saved") and sanctification (being transformed into the likeness of God, brought into compliance with God's will, more in imitation of Jesus, whom Luther saw as the exemplar of God's will incarnate). Luther was combating theological systems that continued to emphasize the work of the believer in redemption of sin and sanctification. Luther argued that the Christian was immediately, fully, and suddenly transitioned into a state of justification on the possession of faith. Faith and faith alone redeemed the believer. No action – not baptism, not confession, not attending Mass, not penance – added one iota to the state of justification. Baptism and Mass were merely the outward signs of this otherwise unseen grace. They could instill assurance, but they did not effect salvation. Sanctification, further, was a transformative act which, though more the result of the individual believer's works, was largely empowered by God's Holy Spirit. Faith alone, not any work, saved humans. Luther coined the Latin expression *sola fide* for this concept. In time, it would become apparent that Luther's principal authority for these assertions was Paul.

Sola Scriptura

Luther was, in essence, challenging church teachings via his readings of the Bible. He was asserting that the highest authority was not the church, but the Bible. When the teaching of the church – any teaching – diverged from the "plain sense" of the Bible, the church was wrong. As we have seen, prior to Luther, the church (in the West) had argued for a notion of progressive revelation. In the Gospel of Matthew, Jesus seems to bestow authority on the apostle Peter to "bind and loosen" (to enjoin or to exonerate) doctrinal matters on earth. Such authority, it was argued, was transferred by Peter in limited ways to other early first-generation believers, and in full to Peter's successor. According to the church, the roots of papal authority sprang from this bestowal to Peter. Each pope ruled with Petrine authority, the current manifestation of an unbroken line of apostolic succession and ordination. The writings of Paul provided the structure for church order and discipline. In sympathy, the teachings of the church as governed by the papacy, particularly when articulated in papally endorsed bulls and creeds, established the full force of Christian theology. Authority was located in the leadership. Though based on the language of the Bible, it was theology as mediated by authorized interpreters and doctors of the church.

Luther, instead, argued that the location of authority was solely in scripture. The Bible, and the Bible alone, was the basis for Christian theology and teaching. The church, only in so far as it was in compliance with biblical mandate, held authority. The role of the church was to mediate and clarify authority; it could not, of itself, construct it. Each individual believer could (conceivably) embrace that truth for him or herself. Luther, however, stopped short of full egalitarianism and wide-ranging authority. The Bible must still be interpreted "correctly," in other words, with "proper" training and sincerity. Further, ordination did invest the clergy with unique spiritual aides and assistance in interpretation and, as a result, clerical readings were generally more valid than those of the laity. Still, for Luther, if biblical text seemed at all to be at odds with church doctrine, church doctrine needed modification.

It may surprise many modern readers, accustomed as many of us are to ideas avowing an individual's right to private interpretation and belief, how radical Luther's ideas were. Perhaps even more surprising to some would be the absence of any translations of the Bible from Latin into vernacular tongues. The church, indeed, often vigorously opposed any attempt at translation of the Bible, condemning those who engaged in the practice as heretics and martyring many. There was concern that, reading for themselves, the laity would become less reliant on and less compliant to clergy. Luther produced a very popular, vernacular, German translation of the Bible.

Luther was reacting against many clergy abuses and other church ideas that he found objectionable. He called for a renewed piety and emphasis on character among the clergy. He felt (perhaps rightly) that many high-ranking clerics were simply sons of the wealthy who had been awarded church offices not so much on the basis of individual qualification as on that of "generosity of soul" (i.e., giving large amounts of money to the church coffers). They had no real intention of living piously and little to no training in theological matters. Further, the church practice of selling indulgences infuriated him. Often, as penance for sin, individuals were charged with making contributions to the church. Anticipating sins, many contributed in advance of the act, effectively purchasing the right to an indulgence. The poor, however, were condemned to brutal acts of penance in order to remain within the fellowship of the church. Not able to pay fines, they often paid with their bodies, doing bloody acts of service or giving grotesque displays of piety (such as crawling up the steps of local cathedrals over and over again, leaving bloody trails from broken knees).

Notably, Luther arrived at his ideas while serving as Professor of Biblical Exegesis at Wittenberg. In some ways, to the specialist in hammers, every problem is a nail. Luther upholds this tradition. For him, the solution to the need for reform lies in a proper understanding of biblical text, notably using his own methods, derived from new "objective" and "precise" modes of biblical interpretation. An essential component of his methodology was to avoid allegorical or mystical interpretations of obscure (or simply fecund) biblical passages. Instead, Luther rooted his readings in careful grammatical analysis and reconstruction of the historical setting. He searched for the author's original intention. A passage could not mean what Paul did not intend.

Luther's method has subtle implications for Pauline biography. First, Luther suggests that authentic readings of a biblical text are singular. Variant readings must, of necessity, be in conflict and if two conflict, one must be harmonized to agree with the other, or one must be ignored. Second, Luther's reading is dependent upon the reconstruction of grammatical and historical analysis. Both of these are in turn dependent upon data. New data revises readings (at the minimum, by nuance). This also implies that those with the most language skills and historical knowledge are the most authentic or accurate interpreters. Luther opened up the potential for biblical interpretation to be undertaken by the average believer, but his methodology restricted the pragmatic possibilities and emphasized the role of the trained interpreter. The remarks found in 2 Timothy 3 are the absolute foundation for any such views. For this system to work, one must have a very elevated view of an inspired text. The Bible must be "God breathed" in a unique way. 2 Timothy 3 also asserts that the Bible can equip a sincere reader with everything needed for knowledge of God, good works, and the correction of error. Luther also tied this view of scripture to arguments found in Hebrews that argued that Jesus alone was the intercessor and mediator between humanity and God. The church, if it assumed such a role, was usurping Jesus' authority. Apostolic succession and the hierarchical authority of the church, as we saw earlier, were founded on the "rock" of Peter's confession. Allegiance to *sola scriptura* is founded on 2 Timothy 3. Structures of church order based on Pauline texts were being challenged by doctrines of scripture which were also based on Pauline texts.

This leaves an opening for a subtle problem: how should the Bible be interpreted? The seemingly endless array of doctrinal positions found in Protestantism largely arise from conflicting answers to this question. Many may argue that reading the Bible in historical context – limiting the range of possible meanings for a biblical text to what the author most likely intended to express – is the solution. Yet, as we have seen, historical reading is fraught with a background of uncertainty. Indeed, it is very true that we are hindered from reading the full sense of Paul's letters by centuries – millennia – of cultural difference, not to mention language. We have no hope, unless we learn Greek or read a translation. Even learning Greek requires some form of mediation – a teacher or grammar is required. Next, we must select the correct text. There can be no unfiltered access to the language of Paul. As we have discussed earlier, there are real limits to our modern ability to relive or realize the cultural and historical setting of Paul's letters. The village idiot of Corinth was more culturally savvy regarding the Roman world than the entire classics department at Cambridge. Unable to understand Paul because of our culture and language gaps, we must learn about antiquity, seeking out whatever sources and contemporary writers we may find.

Yet, as we also saw, if we cannot fully understand Paul because of this cultural and linguistic gap, how can we understand the other classical and ancient writers well enough to hope to reconstruct an image of that culture? If we cannot read Paul without reconstructing his cultural world, how can we read Seneca to reconstruct that world? Despite how clear-eyed historical and literal approaches may seem, there is no objective platform from which to read. Scholars do not have value-neutral facts to assemble. Another concern is the problem of the historical setting of Paul's letters. In short, one must ask, which one of many possible contexts is *the* relevant context for Pauline letters? We know so little of Paul's chronology. How can we confidently identify which cultural moment and location we need to reconstruct to interpret the letters (particularly since we can only know anything about any potential candidates for Paul's world from first reading the letters)? We must locate Paul's letters in their historical context in order to read and interpret them. But we must read and interpret the letters in order to identify any candidate historical contexts. Finally, in many ways, ironically, the focus on authorial intention violates the strict letter of 2 Timothy 3. The text asserts that all *scripture* is God-breathed. The Bible does not, in this passage, assert that the *author* or *the author's intention* are God-breathed. In a very real way, a strictly literal reading of 2 Timothy 3 could be compatible with an argument that non-literal readings of biblical text, so long as they are readings of biblical *text*, could presumably still honor and participate in the God-breathed, inspired nature of scripture. The only "test" 2 Timothy offers is that the reading be "useful" for "reproof, for correction, and for training in righteousness so that the person of God may be complete and equipped for any good deeds." In other words, the only "test" for a "valid" reading of the Bible that 2 Timothy 3 requires is that the reading is ethical.

The Science of Biblical Interpretation

Luther argued that passages which were difficult or unclear were best interpreted in light of more transparent language elsewhere in the Bible. This somewhat circular strategy practically guarantees that a consistent and uniform sense of early Christian theology will emerge. Any rough edges will be shorn off. Luther famously, for example, regarded James' admonition to demonstrate one's faith by one's works as being in conflict with the more exact (and more often written) language in Paul about justification "by grace through faith not by works." Certainly, Paul's idea is more prevalent in the New Testament; Paul wrote far more than the author of James (or, at least, more of Paul's material is preserved). But does that mean his ideas were the more prevalent in the first centuries? Further, is Luther even reading James correctly? Might James be saying "How I act demonstrates what I value?" Even if not, might, as well, there have been a real divergence of thought among early believers? Luther's readings disregard such variation. Yet, more perniciously, they also guarantee a consistent picture of Paul across his career (and when compared with Acts). Paul's remarks to the Galatians regarding circumcision (written early in his work and in the midst of hot-tempered conflict) are taken as the interpretive rule for his remarks in Romans 9–11 (a letter written much later and, apparently, beyond the immediate tensions of argument). Would a mature Paul, not in conflict, have been as aggressive as the younger Paul fighting for credibility in Galatians? Even if the letters reflect a much shorter time span, the contextual variations (different audiences, needs, and circumstances) would prohibit "flat" readings of Paul that see no nuance or change in his letters. All of this, once again, reveals the real problems regarding the possibility of reconstructing the historical setting of Paul's letters.

Luther is, most certainly, one of the most important biblical interpreters of the late Middle Ages/Renaissance and his work is vital for the history of Pauline biography. Still, his interest in biblical text, and his confidence in the existence of a single, controllable method of interpretation are rooted in earlier scholarship. Luther did not, himself, develop many of the key elements of his methodology. Instead, he is one of the more prominent (and prolific) proponents of a long line of thought.

One of the first in that line is the Dutch critic Hugo de Groot. De Groot argued that the Bible would be best read if it were treated in the same way as any other book from antiquity. His ideas led him to inquire what would change about biblical texts if we read them as we did, say, the writings of Homer. What resulted was a subtle but significant shift in the authority of the Bible. Instead of being a book that was largely just mystically or spiritually "true," the text was subject to "normal" rules of history. In time, de Groot's ideas would suggest that the normal rules of evaluating historical verisimilitude be applied to biblical texts. Prior to de Groot, biblical accounts set the standard for history and science. If Joshua 14 reported that the sun had stood still, then (a) it had stood still, and (b) it must move around the earth. The implication of de Groot is that if the Bible (just like any other ancient text) reported such an event, then the Bible was, at best, being metaphorical (or accommodating human language); at worst, it was simply in error.

Another scholar, Erasmus, agreed in principle with de Groot. Erasmus also engaged in a long, meticulous process of textual reconstruction. Many modern people remain startled to learn that there are no original copies of the Bible in existence. Indeed, there are not even full texts of the copies that remain of its constituent books. Further, the hundreds of fragmentary (and late) copies which have survived have slightly different wordings. No two copies completely agree. Erasmus began a process of reconstruction of the biblical text to reveal the "most probable" original content. Such, by implication, prefers and prejudices "original intent" of the author and begins the process of meticulous translation and language study.

This tradition of scholarship prior to Luther (and there are many other figures) still assumed a fairly uniform Bible as a whole, but also emphasized the reading of the Bible with a particular method. What is radical in this idea is not that the Bible is read in conjunction with another body of literature or ideology. The church had long argued that this was necessary. But the Bible also needed to be read in correlation with various rules or approaches. Augustine suggested the "rule of love." Only those interpretations that fostered love of God and fellow humans could be reasonable interpretations of the Bible. The church had also argued for the rule of faith (*regula fide*), where the confessions of the church and church doctrine – inherently argued to be consistent – guided the reader safely through rough straits of biblical text. The radical element now being proposed, however, was that *existing thought and doctrine* could – indeed must – be modified by what was found in biblical text. With a new "science" of interpretation (though that term was not yet in vogue), right – even singularly right – interpretation of the Bible was thought possible.

In passing, one might also note that Luther was not the originator of "Protestant" thought. There had been numerous dissident theologians and thinkers prior to Luther. Some called for reform (as Luther did). Others called for full separation from the existing church (for example, the Swiss reformer Zwingli). Many of the modern Protestants (for example, modern Baptists) trace their lineage through these reformers; Luther's reforms are not only not the origin of "Protestantism," they are not even in the ancestry of all modern Protestants. These primitivist movements were quite common; they are called "primitivists" because they often rooted themselves in ancient (often first-century or biblical-era) Christian thought. Many argued that a primal Christian teaching and theology had been corrupted or ignored by the later church.

Luther's ideas flow directly from this conversation. His confidence in correcting church practice and doctrine arose from his confidence in his own exegetical method. It is an error to attach too much credit (or blame, depending on one's orientation) to Luther.

Yet a subtle and pernicious idea also begins to take root, and Luther was among the most prominent in advancing and developing it. Arguing that the Bible can be interpreted systematically suggests that there is only one correct interpretation, and that this interpretation arises *naturally* from the biblical text itself. And the text was to be interpreted in appropriate historical contexts. Every sincere (and properly trained and informed) person would reach the same (or similar) conclusion regarding biblical meaning. Variations indicated a lack of intelligence, lack of training, or lack of sincerity. Finally, biblical meanings were locked and singular (and reliant, entirely, upon the information available to the interpreter).

Luther's Reading of Paul's View of the Jews

In many ways, Luther read his own life into Paul's letters, casting himself as the ideologically driven iconoclast. Luther often saw himself marginalized (as Paul had been) by opponents attacking his ordination and credibility. He was challenged for bringing a "new" or innovative gospel. To the contrary, Luther argued, he was one of the lone voices for the original, unmolested and unadulterated "gospel."

Luther saw much of his work as an opposition to the type of legalism he saw in the church around him. Strictly, "legalism" is the belief that one earns salvation by good works. God is obligated to respond. Further, any slight deviation from the set pattern or program results in damnation. What one intends (or believes) does not matter; one is saved or damned only upon the exact rule of one's compliance with a system of rules. Luther saw Paul's opposition to the binding of Jewish law, indeed even Paul's whole view of Jewish law, as anti-legalism. Luther saw Paul opposing any idea that individuals are saved by works of law (or damned by violation of a minor element of it). Such a view diminished the glory and grace of God. For Luther, God is more glorious for saving we humans, who are totally depraved and totally incapable of doing good or keeping the law. Luther, then, sees the core tension in Paul as a tension between salvation by grace or salvation by works.

Luther was reacting against structures in the church of his day which seemed far more concerned with the mechanics of action and obligation than with any real sense of devotion. Individuals were "damned" by the church or assigned heavy penance for minor violations of church law, even if they were ignorant of these proscriptions or had intended something different. Other individuals remained within the church's good graces because they acted in compliance with the strict letter of church law, even though they could not care less about any real devotion. For Luther, this was a tacit violation of what he read in Paul's letters regarding justification by grace.

Yet the problem Luther saw in his day may not have been even close to the situation described by Paul. Luther saw a Judaism laden with "law," and "Judaism" was a figure, for Luther, of "Catholicism" or the parts of "Catholicism" he disagreed with. True enough, Jewish halakhic and kosher codes are intense and extensive. Yet Jews today (and Jews in Paul's day too, by every indication) have no notion that they are "saved" by keeping these laws. To begin, within Judaism, there is nothing quite like the Christian notion of "damnation." By being out of compliance with law, one is an outlier vis-à-vis the larger Jewish community (both present and past) and one is not preserving the distinct nature and role that God bestowed on the Jews in making them an "elect" people. While violations of Jewish law mean one is not observant or not taking one's Judaism seriously, it is not itself a basis for damnation or exclusion from God. In the Hebrew Bible, the only "sin" that intrudes between God and humanity is idolatry. Eating pork would violate God's commands and would, in part, put a barrier between oneself and God, but this is only because it is a failure to live up to the distinct call of God in setting apart Jews as the "elect of God."

Judaism, however, does not assume humans – Jew or gentile – are depraved. Doing good works is not earning back merit. It is, instead, the acquisition of even more blessings. All humans,

Jew and non-Jew alike, are blessed by God; even existing in this world is a blessing from God. God has, in Judaism, selected a particular people and given them a law. Keeping this law *adds blessings*. Violation of Sabbath rules does not result in damnation. It does, however, inhibit one from receiving and enjoying the full blessing of the Sabbath. It does have a cost, but it does not result in damnation.

Luther's notion of total depravity and the impossibility of humans being good added to his concerns about "legalism" in the church of his day colored his reading of Paul. Indeed, Luther retrojects many of these ideas into his interpretation of Paul's letters. Luther sees Paul's rejection of law as a rejection of legalistic notions of merit-based salvation. Paul, however, very likely never even heard of such an idea. Indeed, Luther constructs a theology where one is saved by simply believing, regardless of any success (or, in extreme, even attempt) to keep the rule of the law. Notably, Paul condemns exactly this idea in Romans 3. In that chapter, he suggests that the person who simply relies on being a Jew and does nothing to recognize this or to remain within the community is not accepted by God. In other words, the person who relies *solely* on having been elected (through grace) by God and *makes no attempt to do what God asks* is *condemned* by Paul (in language that seems to suggest that everyone else of his day would condemn them as well).

Unfortunately, a substantial element of that voice sounded anti-Jewish tones. To be sure, Luther would argue that his opposition to Judaism was rooted in biblical text itself (and independent of his own preferences or ideas). Remember, central to Luther's confidence in a systematic method of reading is that it is disinterested in the sense that the reader simply observes what the text instructs without any direct participation. Luther would argue that his own preferences were very much *not* involved in his discovery of meaning in the text (he would likely deny that he "constructed" meaning).

And Luther certainly has some language in Paul to work with. In Galatians, Paul insists that there is no basis for salvation for the circumcised (Gal. 5:4); to accept the Jewish law is to deny the power of Jesus and to embrace "another gospel" (Gal. 1:6–9).

Jews who observe the law are "under a curse" (Gal. 3:10). The law is merely an elementary schoolteacher, preparing her student for later success, or a slave master, enforcing his capricious rule (Gal. 3–4). Romans 3, under Luther's reading, savaged Jews who imposed law on others but didn't keep it themselves. When Luther applies his values of a uniform message and interpreting the "unknown" by the "known" across scripture, the picture grows even more clear. There is little question that the Johannine writings pit the faith of Jesus against "the Jews" and Jewish law. The epistle to the Hebrews roots out the furthest corners of the idea that Christianity replaces Judaism (and that Judaism was defective). Hebrews, as we have seen, was vital for Luther's views that Jesus alone was the mediator between humanity and God (Heb. 4:14–5:10, 8:1–9:22).

Yet Luther's reading ignores other elements. We have already noted some of his weaknesses regarding Romans 3. In Romans 9–11, Paul argues that Jews, though not accepting Jesus, are still essential for faith in Christ to exist. Any gentiles who are Christians, Paul argues, are like wild grapes grafted onto another root. Notably, the root remains intact; if the root dies, the whole plant does. Paul argues in Romans 9–11 that Jews of his day did not, wholesale, accept Jesus because a (temporary?) resistance to the idea had been placed upon them by God. This had been done so that Jesus would be killed (according to the scriptures, Paul would add) which would enable resurrection and a display of God's fidelity and power. The hardening was for a purpose and limited (either in scope or duration, the text is not clear which Paul thinks). Yet the Jews have not "stumbled so as to fall." Instead, Paul asserts that "the promises of God are irrevocable." God had promised Abraham that God would never forsake God's chosen people. Accordingly, Paul asserts, "all Israel shall be saved."

Luther has to circumvent the "plain sense" of this language. Moreover, he never attends to the polemic context of Galatians (or reads Galatians as a very early letter whose language is made extreme by the bitterness of the conflict and ameliorated by later reflection). He also tends to oversimplify Paul's language on "law." Luther, for example, reads nearly every reference to "law" in Paul as a reference to "*the* Law," or the Mosaic covenant. In the Greek of Romans, however, Paul studiously avoids the use of a definite article. Paul is also very positive about a "Law of Christ" and the "Law of Spirit." When Paul refers to the "Law of Sin and Death" there is much more contextual evidence to suggest he views sin itself as an enslaving power (and is not making a condemnatory remark about Judaism). Finally, as I have already mentioned, a notion that anyone is "saved" by keeping the law is not in Judaism. When Paul argued that salvation was extended by God's election and grace, every indication is that Jews of his day would have agreed. Paul may not be countering a specific charge to the contrary; instead, he may be drawing upon a common value. In other words, Paul would be saying, "No one is saved just by works, right?" expecting agreement from his audience. Paul continues "So, then, what's the basis for having any barriers remain between Jew and gentile?", hopefully drawing his audience into an agreeable, "None, I guess."

My point here is not to argue Pauline exegesis, per se. I merely want to bring to the surface how multiple readings of Luther's "simple truths" are possible depending on the tone one recognizes and the historical context one creates, not to mention how one incorporates or excludes other New Testament texts and Christian doctrines. In other words, the interpretation is not, as Luther suggests, disinvested or uninvolved; the interpreter is making choices. In the eyes of some scholars, Luther errs in his own method, but he errs precisely because this method itself has inconsistencies. If we grant this, then the overall views of the interpreter are critically important to note.

We have already discussed how Luther's opposition to "legalism" very likely reflects his experience with his own church. It certainly isn't rooted in a recognizable Jewish theology. Luther also seems to identify with Paul. Luther faced issues in his own life (outside detractors, law-based theology – particularly vis-à-vis sanctification, marginalized voice) that emerge in Paul's writings. Like Paul, Luther felt opposed and slandered. Like Paul, he felt that his credentials were questioned and challenged by "super apostles." Like Paul, he felt dismissed (unfairly) by the churches. Like Paul, he experienced this through the deeper and more painful filter of feeling compelled to speak out for truth as he knew it.

Like Paul, Luther casts himself as the honest iconoclast, wrongfully despised and persecuted for having the integrity to speak out openly for the truth.

In part, Luther also may well be layering his own context onto Jews. He is in some ways using accusations of "Jewishness" as a form of insult to his opponents. There is little doubt that, by modern standards, sixteenth-century Germany was a highly anti-Semitic culture. Jews faced regular and open social and popular hostility. They were often considered less human. Tainted forever as "Christ killers," many Christians argued that any abuse or misfortune Jews endured was at least tolerable (if not justifiable) as fitting punishment by God. Jews were regarded as greedy, lazy, filthy, and traitorous. In art and iconography, they were depicted as bestial and subhuman. Local pogroms and mob attacks could erupt without provocation.

It is virtually impossible to imagine Luther could have been untouched by this context. His vitriolic (and, frankly, profane and juvenile) joy in berating the church officials who opposed him in anti-Jewish terms is often palpable. In a sense, his imposition of "Jewish" ideology and identity onto his opponents matches his self-identification with the character of the rejected but righteously honest iconoclast. Not only does this identification solidify (and reinforce) Luther's self-image, it diminishes his opponents by likening them to "stubborn Jews."

Many scholars would mitigate this last point. Luther's entire context, as we've seen, was anti-Jewish. Is it fair, some would ask, to hold him accountable? Certainly, it is not fair to hold him *uniquely* accountable. That does not mean, however, that we can factor out such influences. Few Jews today, for example, would be consoled by apologies for lukewarm Nazis that observe that they were simply "people of their day" and part of a larger anti-Jewish culture. Even fewer would find "Well, she wasn't as bad as Goebbels" much comfort.

A more serious objection is that, while Luther was unquestionably influenced by the anti-Judaism of his times, in his early career he was outspoken in support of many Jewish issues and Jewish culture. He often and openly acknowledged that the substance of his beloved biblical text was grounded in Judaism. He asserted, along with Paul, that the Jews had "much in every way" to celebrate regarding God's blessings and election. Luther also wrote against the killing of Jews for simply being Jews and wrote a treatise on the Jewishness of Jesus. He did not, however, aggressively advocate against mob attacks (and presumably did not rule out any potentially justifiable killing – or dismissal – of Jews).

Luther's most extensive direct treatment of Judaism is his notorious *The Jews and their Lies*. The treatise is, on one level, an assertion of Christian doctrines (particularly regarding the identity of Jesus as the Jewish messiah) vis-à-vis Jewish theology and exegesis of the Hebrew Bible. Though some would argue that such positions are inherently supersessionist, asserting that Jesus is the promised messiah (according to the Scriptures) and, as messiah, initiated a new age and new way of relating to God, was fairly standard Christian theological fare. Luther moves on, however, to assert that the Jews concealed the reality of Jesus from their scriptures and that rabbinic practice and faith are (willful?) distortions of biblical truth. For Luther, when Jews disagree that Jesus is the messiah of God and establishes a new form of faith, they are "lying." They are not merely ignorant; they are duplicitous. Luther unfurls a stream of invective and anti-Jewish tirades and often undergirds these with citations of Acts and Paul's letters.

It is true that Luther wrote this treatise in response to reports that he had received regarding some Jewish proselytizers and opponents of Christianity. Certainly, this added to his aggression, but this really isn't sufficient defense for his vitriol. It may be *why* Luther was angry, but his anger is still anti-Jewish and bigoted. What, after all, is ultimately wrong with Jews not believing in Jesus and openly discussing their faith and religious practices with others? Still, one wonders if Luther's images of Jews and Judaism do not show through quite clearly. Certainly, he did not find the accusations of Jewish "lies" prima facie implausible. He felt no need to investigate; he simply accepted that such arguments had been made. Further, though doubtless himself offended by what he perceived as an attack on his own values, Luther's aggression was unabated and unqualified. One can not help wondering if some of his own, latent issues emerged in this. Certainly, they do in his treatment of Galatians.

What we see, then, is a developing irony. Luther argued most forcefully for a return to the biblical text. This would seem a very positive move for the possibility of a return of a "historical Paul." Further, Luther argued for a systematic approach to the interpretation of the Bible. One might well expect that a rigorous methodology would circumvent many of the problems of the biographical construction of Paul. In other words, there is good reason to imagine that Luther's ideas would establish a credible, defensible, historical Paul.

Yet Luther's system certainly has the potential of masking the interpreter's own experiences, limitations, and biases under the veneer of "objective" methodology. His ideas tend to flatten out the diversity of early Christian thought. He tends to simplify Pauline complexity and ambiguity. He is led more by constructions (canonical and otherwise) of Pauline thought than rude and rigid conformity to the bare minimum of what text projects. All this is caped with a gloss of inevitability; Luther's reading, schooled in methodology and presented as "objective," seems insurmountable.

Yet, as we have seen, Luther's own immediate conflicts, his understanding of Judaism, his own prejudices, and his own experience and personal struggles clearly permeate his reconstructions of Pauline thought and biography. More disconcerting, Luther also is the key figure for constructions of Paul in the early Reformation. Indeed, his program is largely responsible for the central location of Pauline thought in modern Protestant theology. One wonders, as well, if any latent (or overt) anti-Judaism or anti-Semitism also sprouted from the seeds of those 96 theses.

Chapter 6

Paul in the Age of Colonization

Biblical scholarship of the nineteenth century produced two very different readings of the Acts of the Apostles. One strand (what were known as the "higher critics" of Germany and the Netherlands) took a radical view against the historicity of Acts. Another, largely affiliated with English and American evangelicalism and missionary societies, fiercely resisted such skepticism. For these scholars, Paul, as presented in Acts, was the paradigm for Christian missions and evangelism; the historicity of Acts' presentation of Paul was zealously defended. This chapter will explore Pauline scholarship in the era of European colonization. I will contrast two readings of the historicity of Paul and Acts with particular attention to the political and colonial aspects and implications of each. My final review will be an examination of nineteenth-century readings of Philemon. As we will see, views of the various opinions regarding the historicity of the Bible often dovetail with the needs and social location of the scholars involved.

The Rise of European Colonization

The eighteenth and nineteenth centuries are typically thought of as eras of European cultural (and imperial) expansion and of the rise of Romanticism and Naturalism. These factors are related. The end of the Renaissance brought an age of exploration and expansion; Europe was growing increasingly aware of a world not bordered by the Mediterranean or North Atlantic. Much as the (re)discovery of Eastern and Asian lands had led Europe to encounter an influx of new ideas and materials, the age of colonial expansion increased the wealth of European nations but also offered a context for the expansion and promulgation of European modes of government, religion and philosophical and intellectual development. After the general age of exploration of new worlds, a remarkable period of European colonization occurred. The first wave was generally around "unclaimed" (by any other European sovereignty, at any rate) "new" lands and territories mostly in the Americas. This surge in territorial expansion soon led to the acquisition of other sovereign areas such as India, by the British, and Southeast Asia, by the French and Dutch.

One aspect of colonization is intellectual and cultural hegemony. "Hegemony" describes the cultural and intellectual rule of one people or culture by another, more dominant, group. In colonization, there is also an attendant process of cultural control. For example, British control of India resulted in the transformation of the official, legal language to English, along with the construction of British-style schools, civic processes, courts, and industry. Along with secular, civil transformation, colonialism also introduced religious transformations. Often, these were imposed as a set: English literacy was often produced by training students to read the Bible. A key participant in this process of religious colonization were the missionary programs of large societies such as the para-church groups, the American Bible Society and the British Bible Society.

These organized "Bible Societies" were rooted in Protestant ideologies of *sola scriptura*. The Bible alone (and only the Bible) produced the essence of Christianity. Accordingly, these societies focused on spreading the availability of "the word." The societies spreading the influence of the Bible relied on several key components of Pauline reconstructions. First, there was the emphasis on word (and word alone) as the means of salvation. This was directly rooted in a Lutheran/Protestant infatuation with scripture (which is in turn, as we have seen, rooted in Pauline argument). Second, Paul is, of course, the missionary par excellence in the New Testament. Indeed, many of these missionary societies and Bible societies directly based their model for work in the Pauline characterization found in Acts. A particular nexus for both elements (the emphasis on the word and upon Paul the missionary) occurs in the pastoral letters. In these letters, Paul is presented as active in the mission field. He also advises his protégés on missionary expansion. Perhaps most famously, 2 Timothy 3:14–17 presents the *sine qua non* argument for scriptural authority. It is little surprise, then, that as Pauline metaphors, character, reconstruction, and exegesis became central for missionary expansions, insistence on the historical reliability of these Pauline writings also became central.

The Rise of Christian Missions

According to the *Oxford English Dictionary*, common use of the words "mission" or "missionary" as terms primarily indicating Christian proselytism dates to the late sixteenth and early seventeenth centuries. The "era of modern missions" is often said to have begun with the work of William Carey in 1793, particularly his notable sermon "An Inquiry into the Obligation of Christians to Use Means for the Conversion of the Heathens." The sermon, based on Isaiah 54:2–3, was reprinted as an 87-page tract and permeated with images from Acts of the Apostles, particularly Paul's three "missionary journeys" as fulfillments of Jesus' commanded expansion in Acts 1:8. Carey's summons was answered. Within the next century, translation of the Bible exploded (from 50 translations to 250), and the number of missionary societies – professional, parachurch groups designed to vet, train, finance, and monitor missionaries abroad – increased from virtually none to over 100.

Among the first missionaries sent from North America (some argue *the* first) was Adoniram Judson. He and his wife Ann focused their energies on Burma. Judson was educated at Andover Theological Seminary and, as a student, had forged his zealous plans for his work among a student group called "the Brethren" (the normal term for believers in Acts). Acts and Pauline materials also provided other critical elements of his vocabulary. In his reports, Judson denied that his plan to win the Burmese interior for Christ was unreasonable; he repeatedly appealed to God's greater wisdom (echoing 1 Corinthians 2). He called his first, pivotal, converts "apostles."

The Yorkshire-born Hudson Taylor spent 51 years of his life, most of the latter nineteenth century, undertaking missions in inland China. His work included more than 18,000 conversions, the construction of well over 100 schools, and the importation of over 800 fellow missionaries. He was founder of the China Inland Missions. This success was not without cost. Taylor's wife, Maria, died in childbirth while in the mission field; Taylor responded in overt biblical language, echoing Paul's assertions about the hope of the resurrection found in 1 Corinthians. Taylor's ambitions imitated those of Paul, a fact not lost on Ruth Tucker, a scholar of the history of Christian missions. She argues boldly, in *From Jerusalem to Irian Jaya*, that Taylor's organization, territory, and system were matched by those of no other Christian missionary except Paul, whom Taylor used as his model. Taylor was particularly adept at learning indigenous languages and cultures, affecting local cultural norms even to the detail of his dress. His rationale was Paul's own assertion that he had "become all things to all men so that he might, by any means, win some" (1 Cor. 9:22). His strategy became the model for many Christian missionaries after him.

The nineteenth century was also a time for blossoming Bible societies. Among the first of these was the British and Foreign Bible Society. This organization was founded in 1804, largely from the work and advocacy of Thomas Charles. Charles was a Bible-seller in Wales. He reports the story of a young woman, Mary (Jacob) Jones, who, at the age of 16, saved her meager income for six years to purchase a Bible translated into her native Welsh. To purchase the text, she had to walk more than 20 miles (barefoot) to the Reverend Charles' shop. According to one version of the tale, when she arrived, she found that all copies were sold out or promised away, so she waited an additional two days. Reverend Charles was deeply moved (though, apparently, not enough to simply give her a copy, appropriate one of the reserved copies for her, or even offer her a ride back home), and founded the Religious Tract Society, whose primary purpose was to disseminate Bibles in indigenous dialects and languages.

Charles' program eventually became the British and Foreign Bible Society. Its mission was to disseminate Bibles, free of charge, in indigenous languages, throughout the world. No other campaign of evangelism was to be undertaken. No additional doctrinal materials were to be circulated. The reason for the proscriptions was twofold: (1) they ensured that monies and participation could be drawn from various, divergent Protestant groups; (2) most all of these Protestant groups deeply believed that a legible Bible was all that was needed to bring the sincere seeker to a saving faith. Despite their differences, nearly every denomination was united in the belief that sincere seekers, if left alone to simply read the Bible, would believe "correctly."

By 1808 similar societies were being founded in the US (the earliest being the Pennsylvania Bible Society). These societies were organized into the American Bible Society in 1816 (their home offices are still in Manhattan). Other societies rapidly developed. The Edinburgh and Glasgow societies were founded (they merged in 1825 into the Scottish Bible Society). The Australian Bible Society was formed in 1817. The Bible Society of New South Wales began in 1817, and societies began in Scotland (1809), Columbia (1825), and New Zealand (1846). The multiple societies often found themselves at cross purposes, doubly covering some regions and territories while neglecting others. In time, these societies came to be collected under the auspices of the United Bible Societies, an organization that currently gives away tens of millions of Bibles per year and publishes the standard scholarly texts for the Bible in Greek and Hebrew.

Pauline ideology and theology directly and indirectly permeate the Bible societies. They are expressly rooted in Protestantism. Notably the Scottish Bible Society formed because the British and Foreign Bible Society began to circulate Bibles containing the Apocrypha, 14 additional Old Testament books found in ancient Greek translations. Roman Catholics recognize these texts, though they see them as subordinate to the main canon; Protestants deny them any status at all. The tensions were felt on both sides of the Catholic/Protestant divide. Pope Gregory XIV issued an encyclical in 1844 (*Inter Praecipias*) that condemned the widespread dissemination of the vernacular Bible.

Bible societies' insistence on the power of *sola scriptura* is rooted in Lutheran notions, which, as we have seen, were rooted in Pauline notions. The central role of the Bible is, of course, established by 2 Timothy 3. According to nineteenth-century Protestants, and more than a few modern Bible readers, these verses indicated that the Bible was the inspired (and, many argued, inerrant) word of God. Such status made its circulation not only critical, but paramount. No other action was as important or required. Indeed, for many, any further action was dangerously close to the introduction of "human doctrines."

Another controversy among Bible societies surrounded translation. Several groups refused to simply transliterate Greek and Hebrew words into their target languages during translation. One of the most contentious areas was the treatment of the Greek word *baptizomai*. *Baptizomai* may mean "wash" or "immerse." For many Christians, this was a point of contention, since the word also describes the initiatory rite for believers as described in Acts. Should new members be "washed" or must they be fully immersed in water? Translations which used "immerse" were taken by many to be express violations of the Bible Society charters that nothing but the simple word of God – no human doctrine or creed – was to be disseminated. Responding, the Baptist theologian W. H. Wyckoff wrote an impassioned plea: *The American Bible Society and the Baptists, the Question Discussed, Shall the Whole Word of God be Given to the Heathen*? (1842). Wyckoff's title echoes Acts 20:21 and 18:11 (where both passages are connected to Paul and Pauline missions), reflecting how deeply the notion of spreading the written word of Christian texts was associated with the Pauline mission. Dissension over what constitutes "canon" boundaries, or when and how translation itself becomes interpretation, demonstrates many of the limits of such thinking. The pinnacle of rigor regarding scholarship that reinforces arguments of historicity of Acts is very likely the work of William Ramsay.

Debating Biblical Historicity

Ramsay himself outlines his own life history in very "Pauline" terms. He self-identifies as a classicist and atheist who began his inquiry into the New Testament with the desire to disprove the historicity of Acts. He was looking to undermine the credibility of Luke as a historian. In short: he failed. His inquiry actually reinforced his confidence in the historicity of Acts: he concluded that Acts was a valid and valuable historical source which should be trusted. He then spun out work after work defending Pauline authorship and Acts' historicity. His books are still mainstays in Pauline scholarship. Encyclopedic in scope, virtually no element was too minor for their gaze. In a very real way, Ramsay (and others like him – George Foot Moore, George Lightfoot, and more) were defending biblical historicity in such a way that it preserved biblical literacy. Ramsay was also, in his work, directly challenging several other scholars with far less confidence in the biblical text.

The historicity of the Bible was under direct challenge by a second major component/community in the nineteenth century. In 1827, Ferdinand Christian Baur was appointed to the faculty of the University of Tübingen. Baur, as professor of New Testament and ancient Christianity, began to develop a search for some "universal" element of Christian "identity" which was not rooted in traditional textuality. Indeed, Baur, drawing on earlier work that insisted the Bible could (perhaps "should") be read according to the standards of any other book, began asking hard questions about the historical reliability of the texts.

Such questions were hardly new or unique. Much study, for example, had already been done regarding the historical context of Jesus of Nazareth. The extant materials, the gospels, were clearly written some time after the death of Jesus, and (as John 20:21 overtly notes) were written by believers, for believers, in order to create (or reinforce) new believers. In other words, the writings had a clear theologically motivated tendency (Baur's word) and ideological agenda. Such an agenda, many argued, clouded the historicity of the works, obscuring any objective history which was emerging.

Baur turned these questions to the broader issues of the canonization of New Testament writings and the career of Paul. Paul had seemed a more "historically stable" figure. After all, 13 letters of the New Testament explicitly identify Paul as their author (several stress they are written or signed in Paul's own handwriting). Jesus left no direct historical witness, but Paul left an abundance. Even more, in Paul's letters, he frequently describes personal encounters, inner thoughts, and specific events and people. Finally, there is the narrative of Acts which can serve as a good frame for understanding his work and travels. Certainly, it would seem that a historian has much more to work with in Paul than with Jesus.

Baur began by critiquing the process of manuscript preservation and collection. Certainly, from a historical perspective, it is reasonable to ask if other documents related to first-century Christianity that didn't survive were simply lost or, perhaps were even suppressed or destroyed for theological reasons. It is also possible that some documents may have been altered or forged to either create a "document trail" for one ideology or to silence critics. Baur, then, began his work without any assumptions that the New Testament collection was complete, was generated in the form in which it currently exists, or that it represented all the views of the first century. Further, Baur did not assume that Acts represented Paul's real career. All of these questions, Baur argued, must be proven or discarded.

Baur began to doubt the authenticity of several of Paul's writings. In time, he would only concede Pauline authorship of Romans, 1 Corinthians, Galatians, and Philippians. He argued that several of Paul's letters had been altered. By comparison of Paul's letters with Acts, Baur also deduced that Acts was written well after Paul's death as an attempt to soften and redeem his reputation. Baur noted Paul's letters bespoke a context of aggressive conflict and controversy over how to understand the role of Jesus as messiah (hardly an original observation). For Baur, the central conflict was between Paul and the "Judaizers." Paul wanted the messianic age to mean that gentiles, as gentiles, were included in the "elect of God." Others wanted gentiles to convert to Judaism. Paul's opponents were centered in Jerusalem and led by James, Jesus' brother, and Peter, Jesus' lead disciple. Paul's letters refer to both by name. Paul found himself in deep conflict with the "party of James and Peter." Paul's letters, Baur argued, flatly refuted their positions.

What happened, in time, was that Paul's party won part of the argument (the inclusion of gentiles) but lost parts of other arguments.

The compromise that resulted formed second-century Christian theology. This newly hybridized system would, in time, become the voice of orthodoxy. They first altered, then forged, letters in the names of both Paul and Peter to achieve a sense of reconciliation and to gloss over the initial conflicts. Next, they wrote Acts of the Apostles, which presented this hybridized harmony (stressing the unity of early believers) and foisting all the conflict onto "the Jews." Finally, they omitted or erased (either actively by suppression or passively by non-preservation) documents which presented the conflict in terms that were too sharp.

Baur awakened significant debates regarding the "center" of Paul's argument (his main issue), Paul's opponents, and the potential for variations within ancient Christianity. Implicitly, he also awakened debates about who bears the "burden of proof" behind claims of the New Testament and ancient Christian history. Must the New Testament be taken at face value as a historical work, assuming it presents a reasonably accurate picture of ancient Christianity, or must that picture itself be defended? In short, Baur (and those students who followed after him, a group later known as the Tübingen school) awakened a host of questions about the reliability of Acts and of the picture left behind by Paul's letters. Once the debate was begun, the reconstruction (or potential reconstructions) of early Christianity via Paul was well under way and not likely to reach a "compromisable" position.

As one might imagine, the Tubingen school's reconstructions, if correct, would have a devastating effect on missionary ideologies dependent upon Pauline models and doctrines. To put the matter simply, if Paul's letters were both altered and/or stripped of a proper context, they could no longer be reliably used to construct the Pauline ideology central to the Bible societies. Further, they would no longer serve as central texts for missiology. Missions and proselytism, at minimum, require confident certainty about one's central ideology.

Detaching Paul from Acts (by rendering Acts a historically spurious document) also had devastating effects on conventional reconstructions of Pauline biography. The very center of Pauline theology, as asserted by missionary societies and more than a few forms of Protestant Christianity, was now under debate.

The founding figure of Christian missions was now shrouded in historical mist. The very ground of Christian missions, if the Tübingen school was correct, was rendered an unstable foundation of sand. And Baur and his followers were building their arguments largely atop biblical text. Granted, one could argue (and many did) that they were imposing too much conjecture and that they were cynically predisposed to mistrust the Bible's veracity. Baur and his cohort, however, could counter that they were only noting discrepancies found in the Bible itself, and deriving solutions that were the simplest rational possibility. No one could really argue that their readings were prima facie impossible. Baur countered that his opponents had their own biases toward faith as well.

In many ways, this conflict defined the "sides" of major debates within biblical criticism for the next 200 years. Not surprisingly, those who continued to advocate Christian missions and the Bible as the core text for Christian teaching responded vigorously to Baur's challenge. Those who affirmed that the Bible was the inspired, inerrant word of God were particularly exercised by Baur's assertion that 2 Timothy was a forgery. Those who advocated Christian missions and biblical theology had a deep and highly invested interest in sustaining a "historical" Paul and the potential for these documents to lead to reliable historical data. Those who did not (most often those who desired the "essence" or "idea" of Christian "philosophy") had a deep interest in rooting out the senselessness of positivist assertions. In many ways the divergence of views on historicity set against these attendant desires for evangelism still remain.

The Letter to Philemon and Debates over Slavery

It is important to note that Paul (and the Pauline writings) played still another major role in the colonial period. Before leaving any discussion of Paul in the nineteenth century, and particularly when we've framed our remarks so far in the context of colonial expansion of the West, some attention should be paid to the scholarship on Paul's letter to Philemon.

Philemon has been a notoriously difficult letter for scholarship. On first review it seems, deceptively, to be a simple document. Philemon is less than a chapter in length, somewhere around 300 words. Not only is it brief, it also seems remarkably specific. The letter presents itself as being written to a single individual, Philemon, and addresses one particular issue: some concerns surrounding an individual, Onesimus, and his relationship with Philemon. For such a short letter there are a remarkable number of references to specific individuals; indeed, the density of proper names, per word count, is the highest in the entire Pauline canon. Philemon mentions (in addition to references to Jesus) Timothy, Philemon, Apphia, Archippus, Onesimus, Epaphras, Mark, Aristarchus, Demas, and Luke. Paul asserts (v. 19) that he is writing the letter in his "own hand." He refers to imprisonment. Several of these names correspond to Paul's other letters and Acts. In short, there is a great deal of specific data in this brief letter which addresses one particular person about one general concern, all written from a clearly established setting. It would seem, then, to be one of the few letters of Paul where scholars could really find a concrete setting and context (and would have but one issue to unravel to determine the meaning).

Indeed, the "meaning" seems to come readily. Paul, imprisoned (and thus most likely toward the end of his life), is recommending a man named Onesimus who is returning to Philemon after some dispute. Paul argues that both men are believers in Jesus and therefore "brothers" in Christ. Philemon, who owes some moral debt to Paul, is being asked to receive Onesimus in love. Paul promises to repay any debts incurred or to make good any damage done (out of what funds, given that Paul is in prison, we cannot know) by Onesimus. Paul's rhetoric (his style of argument) is cautious and ornate, but he clearly has an idea in mind of at least the spirit he wants Philemon to display.

But, beyond this, the letter becomes phantasmagoric. The specific cause of the harm done to Philemon is never declared, nor is the exact identity of Onesimus. To be sure, there are hints. Paul is encouraging Philemon to "receive back" Onesimus. The name Onesimus itself may be a clue. Strictly, it means "useful" or "beneficial." Paul puns on the name in verse 11. It is hardly a proper name; more likely, it is the name of a slave. In the Roman empire, slavery was well known and widely practiced. Slaves who were slaves from birth were not considered full "people"; they didn't need "real" names, much in the way that moderns might name a working animal. Slavery in the Roman empire could entail household management or a personal secretary. It could also entail a lifetime of back-breaking labor or even forced involvement in the sex industry. In any case, a slave's life was not his or her own. Slaves were bred, bought, and sold at the owner's whim. Their children could also be bought or sold. They were treated in whatever way their owner desired and had no legal right of appeal.

Many scholars, following early traditions, argued that Philemon had once owned a slave Onesimus. Onesimus escaped, an offense that could result in a severe beating, maiming, or even his death if Philemon desired. The escaped Onesimus, many suggest, somehow encountered Paul while Paul was a prisoner (perhaps in Rome). The incarcerated Paul preached to Onesimus and converted him to following Jesus. Now, Paul is sending Onesimus back to Philemon, Onesimus' former master and Paul's own close friend, indeed, even Paul's convert. Paul has written his letter to encourage Philemon to accept Onesimus back without punishment, hinting that Philemon should go further and set Onesimus free. Paul's language must be artful, since he is interfering with a delicate matter of Philemon's household management and is cautious about undue disruption. Indeed, a cagey Paul addresses the letter to Philemon's whole household (tradition holds that Aphia is his wife and Archippus his son) as well as to the whole church community (led by, tradition asserts, Philemon).

Further reflection, however, reveals that some mysteries remain. To begin, how would a fugitive slave have encountered an imprisoned Paul? One obvious answer would be that Onesimus was captured and incarcerated along with Paul, yet this would certainly be a coincidence that strains credulity. Further, if this scenario were true, Paul, in sending Onesimus back, would be in direct violation of Deuteronomy 23:15–16, which forbids the return of a runaway slave. The letter never openly asserts that Onesimus is a slave. It never really identifies anyone's relationships (the family portrait that scholarship has sometimes drawn from verse 1 is entirely conjecture). Verse 22 seems to suggest that Paul either expects freedom or already has some latitude regarding his travel and lodging. Several contemporary scholars have constructed serious readings of Philemon that begin with quite different assumptions. For example, Onesimus the slave may have been sent by Philemon to care for Paul during Paul's incarceration. Paul is, in effect, refusing the gift but being cautious about his language so that he neither offends Philemon nor seems to be displeased with Onesimus. Other scholars have explored possibilities for the identities of Aphia and Archippus. Reading closely, it may be that Aphia is the matron for a house church and has no relationship to Philemon at all; the only real reason to assume otherwise is a preconceived notion that women would not normally be leaders of congregations despite the reference's in Paul's other letters to Phoebe and Chloe.

Behind all these reasons looms the largest problem: if Onesimus is a slave, Paul is upholding the institution of slavery in sending Onesimus home. Such a reading is consistent with other parts of the Pauline canon. Despite passages such as Galatians 3:28 (which declares that there is no "slave or free" in Christ), Paul writes in 1 Corinthians 7 that slaves are to "remain as you are" and not be obsessed with achieving freedom. In the disputed letters, Paul insists in Colossians and Ephesians that slaves are to obey their masters. He uses "slave" as a metaphor for his own service to the cause of Jesus (Rom. 7:24) and even as a metaphor to describe Jesus' submission to God's will (Phil. 2:7).

Some scholars have rightly noted that, according to biblical texts, Judaism had a different ethic of slavery. According to Exodus 21, fellow Jews who were sold as slaves could not be owned for life (and must also, according to Exodus 20:10, be allowed to observe the Sabbath rest); in effect, they were indentured servants. One may well ask if this law was ever actually enforced. Even if it was, one must note that this was not the norm in Greco-Roman culture and does not even apply to Jews who might own non-Jews. Others have argued that slavery in the Roman world was much less egregious than was slavery in the American nineteenth century. I, for one, doubt this. Of course, some slaves in the Roman world were highly skilled administrators; others may well have developed a genuine affection for their masters, but this would hardly have been universal. Prostitutes (male and female) were often slaves. Other slaves worked in agriculture, in ships' galleys, in construction, stone quarries (a highly dangerous occupation), salt mines, and a host of other difficult, painful, and deadly environments. Further, I cannot imagine how one could ever compare the lot of the American slave with that of the average slave (whatever that was) in the Roman world; there is simply not enough data. Finally, I very much doubt if slaves in the ancient world would take comfort from knowing "it could be worse." And if they did not, they would be justified. Saying that one could be treated worse does not amend the reality that one is currently being treated inhumanely.

In our modern world, we know very clearly that owning another human being is simply, totally, completely and fundamentally immoral. Even if one intends to not be harsh, it is immoral. We acknowledge that it was once an economic and social reality. Yet this does not make it less immoral.

Some contemporary scholars have insisted that Paul was struggling with a cultural norm that was simply too large to correct. Paul, concerned with spreading the gospel of Jesus, was not going to jeopardize his larger spiritual mission by becoming embroiled in secondary social matters. Yet this argument is, on its very face, immoral. Slavery is not a secondary social matter. It is at least as important as marriage, sexual choice, sexual expression, management of finances, diet, and education. Paul speaks to all these issues. To ignore the moral elements of owning another human by relegating that ownership to "secondary" social status is immoral. Complying with social mores regarding dress and hair length is not the same as remaining complicit in slavery. Other scholars have argued that if slavery and slave ownership were practiced as Paul intended, while they might, *de jure*, continue, they would, *de facto*, cease. Indeed, they see hints that Paul is pushing Philemon to release Onesimus in verse 21. But why does Paul stop short of commanding this? It seems that the only real answer is that Paul was very much a man of his own age. In short, while he might (and this is not certain) have found slavery unsavory (and might particularly have opposed harsh or sexual treatment of slaves), he was unwilling to make the moral violation of owning another human being a basis for condemnation.

This, most assuredly, is at least uncomfortable (if not a vital problem) for modern interpreters. It was an even more acute tension in the nineteenth century, which saw increasing argument against slavery as an institution. Since many of those engaged in the argument were Christian, the New Testament, specifically Philemon, was pivotal in the debate. Many contemporary Christians have never closely read nor debated Philemon; this was most certainly not the case 175 years ago. Philemon was hotly debated. Our contemporary idea that slavery is always already immoral – that it cannot be conducted in any moral way – is largely a product of these arguments.

Several writers argued that slavery was permissible (if unpalatable to some) because the New Testament does not explicitly condemn the institution. They argued that some ways of treating slaves may be immoral, but the institution itself was not condemned. This implied, they argued, that there was, at least philosophically, a moral way to own a slave. Some argued this because they were, themselves, slave owners. In the American South, many individuals who were devout in their dedication to Christianity roundly attacked those advocates for the abolition of slavery as adding to (or sitting in moral judgment over) the Bible. Reading the Bible literally, they took the absence of condemnation as tacit endorsement. If such arguments were less than convincing, they turned to Philemon. Paul not only does not condemn slavery, he sends Onesimus – a convert – back into servitude. This, they argued, was as good as a clear statement by Paul that slavery, as an institution, was perfectly permissible.

A noteworthy advocate of this position was Moses Stuart, a venerated professor of theology at Asbury Seminary. Stuart, who wrote extensively that he himself found slavery distasteful, examined Philemon in close detail, poring over its Greek text. Stuart wrote that he was forced to conclude that Philemon tacitly endorsed slavery. The key issue for interpreters was the absence of any specific language in Philemon that openly asserted that Onesimus was an escaped slave owned by Philemon. Philemon 15–16 reads "Perhaps this is why [Onesimus] was parted from you for a while, that you might have him back forever, no longer as a slave but more than a slave, as a beloved brother, especially to me but how much more to you, both in the flesh and in the Lord." Abolitionists argued that Paul's use of "slave" was a metaphor; his use of both "brother" and "in the flesh" indicated that Onesimus and Philemon were siblings – physical brothers parted by some domestic dispute. Paul was reconciling this dispute and, given that it was a matter between such close kin, was being very careful in his language.

Stuart argued that any sense of the Greek of Philemon was devastating to this argument. Though he admitted that the phrase "in the flesh" was difficult, the most natural way to read the passage was to assume "slave" was to be taken literally while "brother" was metaphorical (or spiritual: brothers in faith). "In the flesh," Stuart argued, was best understood as a reference to Onesimus' impending physical return to Philemon. Stuart was hardly alone in this reading. He went on to develop his thoughts in later publications, citing the uniform received traditions regarding the biographical context of Philemon (that Onesimus, the escaped slave, had met Paul and been converted to Christ). This biography was taken as "obvious" and necessary (despite many of the places we have already noted where interpreters are "reading into" and "behind" the actual text). Regard for the reliability and authority of the Bible, he argued, simply forced one to admit that Paul endorsed slavery. More troubling for the context of the antebellum South, Paul was also endorsing the return of escaped slaves. A contemporary scholar, H. Sheldon Smith, asserted that supporters of slavery felt more theologically centered in Paul's letters and were more familiar with the nuances of their contents than with the teachings of Jesus.

Paul's writings, particularly Philemon, were among the most examined and debated writings in the New Testament during the first half of the nineteenth century in America. These writings, particularly Philemon, were examined closely side by side with reconstructions of Pauline biography. It is fair to refer to Philemon as one of the most important New Testament writings in the antebellum American South. Nat Turner was inspired, in part, by readings of Philemon. The famous case of Moses Roper (an escaped slave who later wrote a memoir) waged extensive and aggressive combat against readings of Onesimus as a slave; Roper argued forcefully that Onesimus was an estranged brother of Philemon.

The literature of the nineteenth century is replete with examples of abolitionist ridicule and horror in the face of such readings. Frederick Douglass famously (and frequently) savaged the morality of Christians who would use the text of the Bible (a text they presented as being infallible) for support of slavery. Even many defenders of biblical inerrancy today squirm a bit at the implications. Douglass centered his attacks on how readers were constructing hypothetical biographies of Philemon to produce arguments from silence that supported their immoral position, all the while arguing that they were "compelled" to do so by the text itself. Abolitionists told horror stories of slaves who sought refuge in local churches only to be handed over to slave-hunters by the very clergy who argued that biblical authority enjoined them to the act. One of the boldest in opposition was Harriet Beecher Stowe, who wrote extensively about the evils of slavery and the immorality of its perpetuation. She addressed, head on, the assertions that slavery was compatible with biblical revelation; she asserted that, if this were true, then the very Bible was itself immoral.

Once again, as with the struggles over the historicity of Pauline biography found in Acts and the support for missionary societies, larger social issues hinged around the interpretation of Paul. And, once again, these interpretations hinged around hypothetical reconstructions of Pauline biography. On the one side were defenders of an "orthodox" history of Paul (and supporters of a doggedly and dogmatically literal reading of scripture). These were "compelled" by biblical text read in light of conventional and received Pauline biographies to allow, if not outright defend, the institution of slavery. Many did so despite their own feelings that slavery was immoral. They were bound, they argued, by the "simple truth of the Bible."

Others, however, rejected these claims. A handful concluded that it did seem that Paul did not oppose slavery. This, however, was a moral failure on Paul's part. Paul need no longer be consulted on the matter. Though some went so far as to reject biblical authority, most continued to wrestle with the text. Their struggle was to find a more plastic means of interpreting the Bible. They attempted this via a rewriting of Pauline biography. Most certainly, they were correct to point out that supporters of slavery could only argue with biblical text *after* they had created a hypothetical biographical context in which to frame the biblical text. The book of Philemon itself, if kept strictly to the content of its own text, is vague, at best. But equally certain, those who sought to reconstruct an alternate Pauline biography and context for Philemon were themselves led by a firm assertion that slavery was wrong. The Bible could not be endorsing slavery, a position that, though unsavory, must be conceded as a very possible – if not likely – reading of Paul's text.

The debate could not have been more polemical nor more important. Human lives were at stake. Yet the debate could also have not been more theoretical. It hinged around Pauline biography; the arguments both pro and con rose and fell based on the reliability of this reconstructed biography. As we have seen, this is not the first time that this has been so. Nor is it the first time that human lives have been altered (or ended) based on interpretations of Paul which were, in their own turn, based upon Pauline biography. Sadly, horribly, it would also not be the last.

Chapter 7

Paul in the Twentieth Century

Caroline Walker Bynum, a brilliant medievalist, has written a particularly brilliant book titled *Fragmentation and Redemption*. It in no way deals with our subject (at least not at any length) – she is writing about images of the body and gender in the Middle Ages – but I am jealous of her title. On the one hand, it's simply an elegant phrase. But more, it would make a very effective title for a review of Paul in the twentieth century. If a single motif can be determined in Pauline studies in the twentieth century, it is that of fragmentation and attempts to redeem some positive value in Paul. The twentieth century saw an explosion of biographies and reconstructions of Paul. Each is defended vigorously and exclusively. Proponents of one Paul rarely concede that other views are informed or sincere. To disagree is to be doing Paul "wrong," ignorantly, or with an agenda of either faith or disintegration of faith. In many ways, the struggle over Paul's identity has outpaced research into Jesus. For example, the "reconstructed" historical images of Jesus are often varied by nuance or emphasis. Many still remain compatible. Reconstructed versions of Paul however, are often totally incompatible. There is a great deal more variety in them. In addition, there also seem to be more stringent limits on possible historical questions. For example, there has never really been a serious argument that Paul did not exist, though there have been a few radical suggestions that he invented Jesus.

Late Modernism and Postmodernism

The twentieth century was a century fraught with significant, and at times disastrous, developments in world history. Technology, a direct descendant of the developing ideas of science from the eighteenth and nineteenth centuries, conceived and gave birth to twins. One nursery cradled unlimited hope and potential for humanity. Vaccinations, energy resources for manufacturing, communications enhancements all seemed to awaken an unlimited potential for human ease and expansion. The blind were given sight, the lame walked, the poor were uplifted. Could any human problem remain? Yet, prosperity's evil twin remained: the twentieth century also left a staggering sense of alienation, vast disparities of wealth, environmental devastation, depletion of resources, war, and genocide.

In other words, the twentieth century marks both the highest moment and greatest optimism of modernism as well as the seeds of its demise. Modernism, amongst its other tenets, refers to the belief that humans, using objective scientific methods and reasoning, could unravel any problem, dissolve any conflict, and make tangible, measurable "progress" toward solving any dilemma. Indeed, tremendous strides were made. Yet the promises of modernity remained elusive. Scientists were not dispassionate. Technology could be turned to good or ill. Hatred and war persisted. The technologies of the twentieth century not only failed to end such rivalries, but there are serious arguments that they enabled genocide. Genocide – mass extermination of an entire ethnicity – needs technology to become possible. Indeed, one of the most heinous forms of genocide in the entire century – the Nazi attempt to eradicate Judaism – had its origins in "modernist" notions of race and genetics. More than a few Nazis felt that it was their dispassionate, scientific "duty" to remove "lesser" races or genetic "defects" in order for progress to advance, and genocide would never have happened without the technology and the bureaucracy of the modern state.

In response to the problems posed (or left remaining) by modernity, the twentieth century saw, in its latter years, the rise of an intellectual movement called "postmodernity." At the risk of oversimplifying, postmodernity can be defined (quoting Lyotard's *The Postmodern Condition*) as "suspicion of all grand narratives" or "metanarratives." Any idea or system purporting to be an overarching explanation or organizing system is a "metanarrative." Postmodernism challenges the objectivity of any form of knowledge, from history to science, from textual interpretation to theology. Humans are always already invested in the process, often operating under hidden "metanarratives" and preconceived systems of bias and intellectual programs.

Postmodernity swept through the intellectual systems of the Western world. As could be expected, theology and biblical studies (and, for our interests, Pauline studies) were not immune to or aloof from the raging debates. The nineteenth century saw central debates over the historical setting of Paul, the reliability of tradition, and the central location of Pauline writings for Christian theology (particularly missions and evangelism). The twentieth century saw these debates increase. It added, however, debates over the consistency of Pauline thought, the contribution of Pauline ideology to the horrors of anti-Semitism, and other central issues about the location of the interpreter. Within the broader field of religious and cultural studies, new voices (often from previously "marginalized" communities) began to insist upon being heard. In a similar way, these debates entered into Pauline theology. Paul's contribution to gender identity, feminist thought (or its suppression), and racial/colonial controls became a central theme.

Many of these debates are related (and often very similar in tone and theme). Perhaps the most central debates surround, in summation, the role of Pauline writings in the development of various aspects of identity (or "subjectivity"). How does Paul contribute to the early construction of a Western concept of "identity" (a concept that incorporates gender, race, class, and ideology)? Central, as well, is the stark question posed by the shocking images that emerged after World War II. To what extent did Nazi devastation of Jews in the Holocaust emerge from a general culture of anti-Semitism in Germany? Given, as well, the centrality of reformed (Lutheran) theology in Germany, and the centrality of Paul for Lutheran thought, to what extent did readings of *Paul* contribute to the anti-Semitism of central Europe? Reading and interpreting Paul took on a graphic and irreversible ethical tone.

Early Twentieth-Century Biblical Scholarship

As the twentieth century began, the polarizations in Christian scholarship that marked the nineteenth century were, in general, becoming more entrenched in opposition than engaged in a search for a compromise position. Some biblical scholars continued their examination of the historical accuracy of the Bible, concluding that the Bible was not a reliable history and accepting positions critical of biblical historicity (and claims of authority) as settled conclusions. For many, the debates over issues such as the Pauline authorship of the pastorals, for example, was settled and should be accepted as "received opinion." Paul was not the author. Scholars now turned to the development and defense of alternative arguments. Other scholars wrote extensive and precise essays refuting point for point arguments that they perceived as threats to biblical authority and inerrancy, often suggesting that critics of the Bible were not informed or had a hidden agenda to subvert biblical truth or simply jump on a bandwagon of popular scholarship. Still others were beginning to dismiss biblical scholarship altogether. Scholarly debates over fragmentary Greek inscriptions found carved into shards of pottery seemed so far removed from social debates about child labor, women's suffrage, sweeping epidemics of deadly disease, rising poverty, and escalating international tensions that, whatever the findings, they were irrelevant.

A few scholars made attempts at reconciliation. One was the German scholar Adolf von Harnack, a specialist in early Christian history interested in the rigorous reconstruction of the New Testament as a historical document. Notably, though, he was also keenly interested in applied ethics and the practice of Christian faith. Von Harnack was highly skeptical of the historical reliability of the New Testament. Though his focus was on writings associated with John, he also did extensive work on Greco-Roman religions, the Acts of the Apostles and the *Church History* of Eusebius.

Though von Harnack was skeptical, he still argued that the Bible had a role in the life of the believer. His solution was a modern Christianity that embraced the ideals of ancient believers but that was aware of the scholarly problems presented by the text, itself. He wanted to remove the "husks" of form to discern the kernel of truth in Christianity. Von Harnack was convinced that a modern Christian could not – indeed, *should* not view their faith as time-less and detached from the real vagaries of human experience and limitation. He felt a "sober-eyed" view of Christian history provided by "higher criticism" would establish such a distance. Yet, as the "husks" or chaff – the protective forms that had pre-served the seed of Christian idealism – they could be discarded without loss. Rituals, forms, and doctrines, however, all still held a motivating and reconciling power. They participated directly in the essence of Christianity; they were the "seed" or "kernel" of Christianity.

Von Harnack's ideas were taken up by Rudolf Karl Bultmann, professor of New Testament at the University of Marburg. Bultmann devoted a substantial amount of his career to the writ-ings of Paul and to studies of the life of Jesus. In both cases, Bultmann argued against reliance on the biblical material as his-torical. The real Jesus of history, he argued, was no longer recov-erable. This was not the critical loss it might first appear to be, however. Recovery of a "real Jesus of history" was not necessary for Christianity. Bultmann, taking some of his ideas from von Harnack, wanted to "demythologize" Christianity. For Bultmann, the modern mind could not be asked to accept what ancient, more credulous, peoples had regarding God and the miraculous. Bultmann was not using the word "myth" in its popular sense of "silly story believed by the credulous." At least not entirely. To be sure, he was convinced that any assertion that the Jesus of his-tory was a miracle-worker and exorcist who rose from the dead after three days was less than acutely critical and informed his-torically. Bultmann was using "myth" in a technical sense, as a description of a genre of religious writing, where "myth" is under-stood as "stories about the sacred." For Bultmann, the power of "myth" transcended the literal truth of the stories themselves. Christianity, he argued, had become too engrossed in the historical veracity of its narrative of faith. Modern science, he asserted, had proven that miracles did not, and could not, occur. Modern history, he continued, had silenced any expectations of a historically reliable text, layering their stories so thickly with confessions of faith and false attribution that the truth about what actually had happened was long lost. Modern believers could not be asked to sustain the same simple credulity of medieval believers; Christianity, if it was to be useful and expect to survive in the modern world, needed to be demythologized.

Counter-responses

Both von Harnack and Bultmann were attempting to save Christianity from its own Bible. Both were devoted to the highest standards of modern historiography. Ironically, the positions of both also effectively severed Christianity from its roots and cut it loose from its moorings of tradition and text. Critics challenged that the result was a deeper detachment of Christianity precisely because of a more intimate, but also more skeptical, linkage of Christianity to pragmatic, originary, history-of-religions historical roots.

One of the most outspoken critics of von Harnack and Bultmann was Karl Barth. Barth rejected the ideas of both his one-time professor (Harnack) and his close contemporary (Bultmann). In a book simply (and aptly) titled *NO!*, Barth argued for a historically rooted Christianity that affirmed without question Christian doctrine and saw the Bible as the only, legitimate revealed source for God and Jesus. Theology, if it was to be *Christian* theology, must be rooted in biblical theology. Though historical inquiry could help clarify parts of the Bible, Christian revelation was not to be criticized or corrected, certainly not "demythologized." Further, Christianity was not to be defended; it should be merely asserted and then understood.

Barth's famous connection to Pauline studies was his commentary on Romans. In many ways, the book is neither a commentary nor even obliquely connected to traditional historical analysis of Romans. Barth reads the text slowly, essentially producing theological "riffs" in response to Pauline phrases. The dissociation from "historical context," however, was part of Barth's point; he was chasing a permanent "idea" of Christian theology that transcended "history" and was also impervious to the radically skeptical historical reconstructions of other scholars such as Bultmann. What emerges is a synthetic theology, aloof from text while seemingly undergirded by it. Paul's writings provided one major Christian revelation, the life of Jesus provided the other. This revelation seems, in many ways, to be detached completely from a rigorous reconstruction of a historical Paul. In his commentary, Barth rarely (if at all) does anything further than comment on the intellectual and spiritual implications of Paul's ideas. A "historical Paul" or the "historical setting-in-life" of Romans seem outside Barth's interests. In essence, it is as if the actual historical context of Paul doesn't matter.

Yet Barth insists that it does. In fact, he frames his major theological structure on his construction of Paul (a construction implied and assumed more than it is articulated and defended). Barth argued for what he termed "dialectical theology." His organizing structure was a Hegelian dialectic. In simple terms, the philosopher Hegel argued that truth was located by taking one idea (thesis), contrasting it with an opposing idea (antithesis) and reconciling the two into a third option (synthesis). For Barth, the conflicting theses were grace and law. He sees the bulk of Pauline theology as an exploration of these two seemingly opposite ideas. His assumptions about biblical inspiration and authority were such that he freely asserted a consistent and constant theological core in all of the New Testament. Paul's later work agreed completely with Paul's earliest writings. Paul agreed completely with other New Testament writers such as John or Peter. Barth argued for an abandonment of traditional "higher criticism" as found in Baur or the later von Harnack and Bultmann. In its place, he sought a historically informed reading of the Bible in pursuit of a biblical theology.

Yet Barth did have a construction of a historical Paul. In general outline, Barth's Paul was Luther's with a few key modifications. Both Barth and Bultmann, then, perpetuate two devastatingly dangerous trends. First, Paul is seen to be engaging issues of law verses grace in a context outside of intramural Jewish messianic debates. Such a reading strips Paul from any reconstructed context of a Paul engaged in debates with other Jews about nuances of Jewish identity now altered in light of the Jewish messiah. One could easily argue Paul's assertions about life "in Christ" were automatically (and *in toto*) in contrast to Judaism and Jewish Covenant. Paul is, in Barthian theology, always and completely arguing for the superiority of Christ and setting a life of Christian faith against a legalistic Judaism. For Barth, Paul is released from his historical context(s), particularly his Judaism. The result was highly fecund for the construction of anti-Semitic Christianities. Judaism becomes entangled with "legalism" and, so, a "thesis" to be contrasted with an antithesis of "cheap grace" of a faith understood as mere intellectual assent to Jesus' lordship. Judaism, then, was to be superseded by the "synthesis" of Barth's theology.

Debates over the Bible and the Rise of Anti-Semitism

"Anti-Semitism" is more than just opposition to Jews or Judaism. In many ways, it is one of the byproducts of modernity, though it has roots in long-standing opposition to Jews in Western culture in general, and some forms of Christianity in particular. Much in Paul could be read as anti-Jewish, for example. Luther was most decidedly anti-Jewish. The term "anti-Semitism," however, was first coined in the nineteenth century as a term to articulate a "rational" and "scientific" basis for hatred of Jews as a racial group based on genetic inferiority. Luther, like most people prior to the late eighteenth century, did not understand "race" in terms of genetic difference that was manifested in unfavorable physical traits or genetically produced behaviors. Luther's notions of "race" involved ethnic distinction – food customs, language, worship, and religious affiliation. While Western culture from the earliest medieval era did, in fact, have a stereotyped image of how Jews "looked," Luther's opposition to Jews and Judaism did not, then, arise from notions of "race," but from the content of Jewish faith and practice. Such, however, is certainly different from modern notions of "racism" (here, anti-Semitism).

In many ways, Barth argued to return to Lutheran notions regarding race. In his commentary on Romans, he argued that the implications of Jesus' death for all humanity destroyed notions of race and nationalism. However, he failed, in many ways, to notice that Paul was arguing with Jews about issues of Judaism and not necessarily advocating a whole new form of religiosity. Because of this, Barth inadvertently constructed a system that still, effectively, denigrated Judaism. One was free to "be" a Jew (racially), but not to think or act like one. Barth argued that Paul's religious views were continuous with Judaism. But he also argued that Paul was arguing for a whole new way of relating to God. This new system was effected by grace via God's free election and the believer's faithful reception. To Barth, Paul was arguing that engaging with God via keeping Jewish law was no longer permissible. As we have seen, reading Paul as a figure within Judaism arguing for a Jewish messiah who brought liberation to the gentiles would see Paul arguing for systems of gentile "faith in Christ" operating *alongside* Jewish systems of law. Barth did not agree; there was but one way, after the resurrection of Jesus, to be justified before God. This reading arises directly from the way Barth reconstructed the historical Paul. Barth's arguments against nationalism or (embodied) race also complicated the equation. By disentangling the identity and origins of Christian books from Jewish contexts, all that was left were Jewish bodies, now regarded as, at best, irrelevant and immaterial. At worst, these Jewish bodies marked by circumcision and ritual observances were proof of a will in rebellion against God's revelation in Christ (and so were themselves heretical).

In very real ways the ideas of von Harnack and Bultmann weren't much better for Jews. Much of their work corrected longstanding prejudices against Jews found in biblical texts by restoring a historical awareness of the context and community that produced those texts. The backgrounds of both Jesus and Paul were carefully articulated, and the notion of an inerrant Bible, buoyant above cultural influences and human biases, was left listing in the water, if still afloat at all. Yet they also produced a Christianity which was severed from those origins. In many ways, Judaism was no longer needed. Christianity, without a sense of continuity, could be affirmed in a world without Judaism. The branch of Christianity had been cut from the root of Judaism. If the root were to be unearthed, Christianity could continue to flourish.

This displacement found its ultimate expression in the Holocaust. Barth, himself, opposed the rise of the German National Socialist Party, but he did so in large part because it interfered with the actions of the German church and because of his assertions against nationalism and race, both destroyed via the cross of Jesus. Yet his theological system, stripping Paul from a context of Judaism and relegating Jewish practice and Jewish bodies to the realms of the immaterial or superseded, did little to support arguments against anti-Semitism. In many ways, actually, Barth offered support for the anti-Semites: Jews who insisted on remaining actively Jewish in their religious practice were under the condemnation of God for rejecting God's messiah. They were worthy of damnation and hell. It is a short step from such assertions to arguments that Jews were "deserving" of public scorn and ostracism. In a context where others were vociferously arguing that Jews were less human, ideologies such as Barth's could readily do more harm than good. The Nazi programs for extermination of the Jews were not conducted in isolation. They occurred under the constant public gaze of German Christians, many of whom also directly participated in the exterminations. Barth lifted Paul from any specific historical locus because in many ways, for Barth, the location was immaterial. Paul's ideas mattered; his historical biography mattered much less. The whole Bible, Barth argued, presented a uniform and consistent theology. Paul's remarks about Jewish law in Galatians could not be understood in conflict with the image of Jewish law found in Hebrews, much less Deuteronomy. If Paul or Hebrews asserted that the law could not provide human redemption or forgiveness, this must be the case. Barth saw Paul's ideas as "free-floating" above Paul's cultural and historical context – eternal and fixed, inspired and constant. He argued this to counter what he felt was a radical skepticism in historians such as Bultmann. Yet Barth was very much constructing, without reflection (or place for correction), his own "historical Paul," and his intellectualization of Paul severed Paul from his

Jewishness at a catastrophically dangerous moment of history: Barth's own.

Barth did not, of course, completely reject either history or the need for an awareness of the contemporary implications of one's theology. He asserted continuity in Christian faith, used historical tools of grammar and contextual analysis, and famously argued that the Christian pastor should prepare sermons with a Bible in one hand and a newspaper in the other. Yet, as we have seen, the implications of his ideas – in what he does *not* assert – could have dire consequences. Insisting that historical contexts are secondary to the derivation of textual meaning is still, at its base, a historical argument. Further, Barth clearly had a historical Paul in mind in his reading: a Paul who "converted" away from Judaism to Christianity and saw Jewish law as insufficient to address the problem of human sin. Barth's historical reconstruction – being implied and assumed more than articulated and defended – was also impervious to critique or modification. What emerged was a system where the "meaning" of the text was "obvious" and above critique or alteration. It simply "was."

Bultmann was very concerned with contemporary events and ethics as well. His program of "demythology" was constructed to *save* Christianity and to preserve the very best of its ethical program. Bultmann was also a historian who was very much involved in reconstructing contexts for the ancient Paul and critiquing the New Testament text where appropriate. Yet when these two interests of demythologizing and historical revision were joined together, they effectively severed contemporary Christianity from its historical roots. Again, this dissociation came at exactly the wrong moment. Bultmann offered a way of being Christian which was consistent with the best advances in history and science that modernity had to provide. One could be completely "modern" and still retain the essence of Christian faith. But Christian faith could also survive in a world without Jews. Nazi ideology was, at its core, a celebration of "rational" and scientific achievements without regard to the limitations of sentimentality. Bultmann's approach was "clear-eyed" enough to be reasonable. Even better to a Nazi mind, it offered an argument for confidence that the best in Christianity could continue even if the Jews did not.

Redeeming Paul: Paul in the Later Twentieth Century

Jewish bodies as well as Jewish thinking and religion were graph-ically thrust back into the collective attention of the Christian West in the aftermath of the Holocaust. Many were asking how such horrors could have occurred in a nation that was so devoutly, overwhelmingly Christian. In the minds of some, the burden of Christian anti-Semitism belonged to Paul and Paul's remarks about Judaism. Nearly everyone, even an ardent defender of Paul, is aware, in the aftermath of the Holocaust, of the terrible poten-tial in 1 Thessalonians 2 and the letter to the Galatians. The images of death, emaciation, and savage treatment were sobering to the religious mind. The period following World War II saw the begin-ning of a general reevaluation of ethnicity and civil rights among the nations of the West. Religious studies (not to mention Christian theology and, in particular, Pauline studies) were not unaffected. One reason was that bitter and horrid anti-Semitism can readily be found in Christian literature and history. Unnervingly often, it is found in very close proximity to Paul. The list of scholars using Pauline texts to devalue or diminish some aspect of Judaism and Jewish religiosity is certainly long: Marcion, Tertullian, Jerome, Augustine, Cyril, Aquinas, Luther, Barth. At times it seems like the greatest riddle in Paul is not election and will, nor grace and law, nor even rationality and mysticism. At times it seems that the most elusive reading of Paul is one which affirms his views about Jesus without diminishing opinion about Judaism and Jewish religiosity in ways that would legitimate anti-Judaism.

In many ways Pauline scholarship of the twentieth century after World War II was an attempt to address pre-war scholarship and issues in light of the Holocaust. Many see Paul (or readings of Paul) as integrally responsible for the ideologies that led to, or at least allowed, the genocide to occur. For about 100 years prior to the war, scholarship had been debating the historicity of bibli-cal writings and struggling to articulate how a "Bible in history," a document that often revealed fissures, flaws, and complexity when examined under the microscope of historical reconstruc-tion, intersected with Christian doctrine. The Holocaust fore-grounded how a wide array of Western intellectual constructions intersected with political and cultural identity in ways that had real, immediate, and potentially deadly consequences. Ideas alter experience even as experience alters ideas. Much of the scholarship in the humanities post-World War II turned its attention to these problems. Scholarship on Paul was acutely interested in them. In biblical studies, particularly in Pauline studies, this attention became focused on the way biblical text shaped (and was shaped by) socio-political ideology both past and present.

Paul and Subjectivity

Post-World War II scholarship on Paul turned to two major questions. First, how do Paul's writings reflect historical location? Some attention turned toward articulating the "core" of Paul's ideas and teachings as derived from a close reading of all his letters. How did Paul, a diaspora Jew, experience Judaism and Greco-Roman culture, and what did he think of Judaism after he became a follower of Jesus? The second line of inquiry involves more generic questions surrounding the construction of "subjectivity" (or "identity"). What "personality" of Paul emerges from analysis of his work? How do Paul and the Pauline writings address gender, sexuality, and nationality?

One must admit that the two general questions I describe above are *huge* arcs; there is risk, I admit, that they are so broadly defined that they become functionally meaningless. Were this not enough, the twentieth century also saw generic shifts in the study of the humanities that questioned, in fundamental ways, how "meaning" could be produced in texts at all, what, if anything, a term like "history" might mean, and how, if at all, any large intellectual and cultural narrative could be told. Pauline studies were not immune to these questions. The late twentieth century produced a burgeoning program of reading surrounding questions of biography in Paul: Paul's own biography, the way he shaped the "biography" of Western intellectual culture, how he understood the key structures – gender, ethnicity, sexuality, religious affiliation – that make up a sense of "self" at its base. Scholars chased every possible nuance in hopes of finding a central core, or in hopes of demolishing any possibility of a central core. The resulting search for a "redemption" of Paul culminated in a heavily fragmented field.

The pivotal essay for understanding Pauline studies post-World War II is Krister Stendahl's "The Apostle Paul and the Introspective Consciousness of the West." Scholarship in the humanities in general made a turn toward exploration of "subjectivity" in the decades following World War II. "Subjectivity" is the construction of a "self" through rhetoric and engagement with culture. Many scholars were arguing that a self-conscious notion of "self" developed during the early centuries of the Roman empire. Of course, prior to this period, people thought of themselves as "people" with names, histories, occupations, and ideas. Yet the emphasis was more upon how one fit into groups and communities. Further, intense self-focus and self-consciousness manifested in something like "autobiography" was largely undeveloped in literature. For many scholars, the apostle Paul represented a key moment in this developing process. Augustine was understood as playing a key role in developing this Pauline practice of self-construction and is thought by many to be the first "autobiographer" in the modern sense of the term.

Stendahl's essay, in the largest part, was an exploration of Paul's role in the development of this "introspective consciousness" (subjectivity). Stendahl brought a wider-ranging conversation about what constituted a "self" and how people construct a sense of themselves into the nuanced discussion of biblical studies. For Stendahl, Paul does, indeed, play a critical role in the process. Paul adapts and adopts existing cultural forms and expressions into his own sense of self. This process was, in part, spurred on in Paul by his social and intellectual location as a man trapped between two expansive cultural "worlds" – Judaism and Greco-Roman culture. Paul understood Jesus as a means for fusing together the ideas, values, and practices of conflicting ideologies and experiences. He worked out many elements of his own religious and theological ideas via the life of Jesus and his own life. In other words, biography and autobiography were each a means for theological manifestation, expression, and insight, not simply locations for performance of ritual or allegiance. Biography and autobiography were not merely actualization and performance of ideology; they were the means for the construction and expression of ideology.

Along the way, Stendahl raised two other critical questions. First, central to his thesis is the argument that, for Paul, religious thinking and cultural context were neither separable nor at odds with one another. Stendahl argued that Paul was not a simple "homo religiosus" – a man whose arguments and actions were solely prompted by religious ideas. Paul's religious ideas did not develop in a psychological and cultural vacuum; they did not transcend either self or cultural context. Many of his religious ideas arose directly from his own psychological development and his cultural engagement. The results of this argument are pivotal.

For example, Paul argues that the rule of God transcends human government even as it is the ground for civil authority. Stendahl's thesis would suggest that this idea cannot be separated from Paul's personal context as a Roman citizen and a Jew, a member of a subordinate cultural class. Paul's political, intellectual, and personal desires shaped his theology even as they were shaped by it. Paul wanted a God-figure who transcended both human limitation (death) *and* cultural domination. Jesus, dying by crucifixion at the hands of Roman officials, could be seen as a victim of Roman political and military domination. Yet Jesus being raised from death by God was, as well, a divine displacement of these powers – a divine "overruling" of an unjust governmental action. Stendahl's argument would lead us to question if the latter implication – a resurrection that proves God transcends an unjust government that had been oppressive to Paul – could be casually separated from Paul's hunger for a biblically rooted engagement with the messiah. Paul engages issues of domestic management, wealth and poverty, slavery, marital status, and social interaction. Were all of his views shaped by an abstractly developed theology? Perhaps some of his theology was also shaped by his own cultural encounters.

A second implication of Stendahl's work is that Paul's use of broader cultural elements, such as religion, rhetoric, art, and entertainment became relevant. Scholars have long noted that Paul's metaphors appealed to commonly experienced social phenomena such as sporting events, Roman civil law, and popular literature. Many have suggested that Paul did this simply to facilitate communication of his spiritual ideas. Even more adventurous scholars have argued that Paul was not simply using metaphors to facilitate communication of his messianic ideas to gentiles but instead actively formed his doctrines by adopting (and sometimes adapting) elements from his broader religious and popular culture.

A third implication of Stendahl's essay is that many elements of "reality," even one's own sense of one's "self," are "plastic" (changeable). One's identity is never really "fixed" or static. In fact, it is largely a composite result of multiple communities, encounters, experiences, memories, and self-constructions. Identity can change. Indeed, it will do so with every change of circumstances and experiences. Further, every aspect of the "self" could be alterable. Later scholars would add that elements of conflict (when our sense of "self" is challenged by difference, experience, or disagreement) are the moments when we work hardest to establish a sense of "self." Such assertions will, in time, make the questions about gender, sexuality, memory, ethnicity, and conflict encountered in Paul's letters of critical importance.

Much of what follows Stendahl can be seen as responding to issues he raised. This is not to say that all subsequent scholarship is in direct discussion with Stendahl (though much is) or that scholars directly influenced by Stendahl are the norm in Pauline studies (though many Pauline scholars are so influenced). Nor do I mean that his essay is always directly cited or engaged (though, again, it often is). Rather, the issues raised by his essay anticipate many of the turns subsequent scholarship would take. Pauline scholarship post-World War II has, in a word, simply exploded in scope, variety, complexity, and volume. Doubtless, many lines of inquiry that currently seem vital will, with the perspective of time, prove to be insignificant. Also, we are far too close to the current work to really decide, with any accuracy, which work will turn out to be landmark. Any attempt to survey contemporary work will, of necessity, be focusing too much on some minor lines of discussion and not at all on some that will prove to be more pivotal. Those caveats aside, a quick "tour of the field" is useful.

The "New Perspective" on Paul (Paul and Judaism)

One scholar, influenced directly by Stendahl, has sparked an important conversation which has, perhaps, generated a larger response than any other in post-Stendahl scholarship. E. P. Sanders' monograph *Paul and Palestinian Judaism* was offered as a direct challenge to what he felt were insufficient readings of Paul. Sanders argued that Pauline scholarship had been too overwhelmed by Luther's readings and context. As such, it tended to the view that Paul was arguing that Christianity had replaced Judaism because Judaism was an inferior religion based on legalism and empty ritual. The central tensions in Paul's letters were election versus will and law versus grace. Pauline scholarship, Sanders argued, was presenting a superficial picture of Jewish doctrine and faith and passing that reading off as Paul's own. Sanders' monograph offered a withering critique of prior scholarship, bouncing current work off Paul's writings and contrasting commonly argued perspectives on Judaism against Jewish texts. Sanders argued that Paul would never have held such views. Further, Pauline scholars, recognizing that much of Paul's writing was produced in the context of conflict with divergent teachers, also argued it was a direct "mirror" of the opposition. In other words, scholars had assumed that whatever Paul asserted was the opposite of what his opponents argued. This reading strategy, Sanders argued, was far too simplistic (though it, not surprisingly, resulted in a Paul who was radically at odds with other teachers and produced a "Christianity" diametrically opposed to "Judaism").

Sanders argued for a "new perspective" on Paul, where Paul's Jewishness was foregrounded. Sanders asserted that Paul was seeking a new way of *remaining* Jewish (a way that would include gentiles) in light of the messiah. He challenged the dichotomies of law and grace, showing that Paul invoked both and did so as many other Jewish teachers and thinkers of his day would have done as well. For Sanders, the pivotal moment in Pauline thinking was his vision of the resurrected Jesus. After this event, Paul began trying to reason through a new image of God that recognized the messiah's arrival and found ways to spiritually (or metaphorically) deal with Hebrew Bible passages about the messianic age.

Sanders was challenged by J. D. G. Dunn (among others) on how the content of Paul's theology should be properly understood. While Dunn wanted more unique content to Pauline Christianity than Sanders had provided, he accepted the core of Sander's fundamental thesis: rigid readings of Paul that wrenched him from his Jewish context created arbitrary lines of difference. A similar, and in many ways related, line of inquiry developed around investigation of "the center of Pauline thought." J. C. Beker articulated a division of Pauline studies between "coherence" and "contingency." Each of Paul's letters was written to a particular, specific context (the situation at Corinth, the concerns at Galatia, etc.). Paul's remarks were aimed specifically at those contexts. At times, his views may seem to contradict one another. Beker argued that such moments were expressions of "contingent" thought in Paul. Paul's arguments and wording in each letter were subject to the context, and so were contingent upon that context. Beneath all Paul's letters, however, one could assume a "coherent" core of Pauline thought (though Beker was not optimistic that such a core could be located from our extant evidence). Readers need to separate the "coherent" from the "contingent," to find the underlying themes and beliefs of Paul and keep these distinct from context-specific instructions.

In some ways Beker's suggestion awakened a withering onslaught of study into the historical context of Paul's letters. A variety of "coherent" theologies, or "cores" to Pauline thought, have been suggested. Others worried aloud if, though certainly Beker's distinction was reasonable, any scholar (given the evidence) could separate the contingent from the coherent. If all we have are the letters, how can we determine, with any exactitude, what is the coherent core beyond a few key, broad structures? What parts of Paul's letter are "coherent" (constant, un-voided) and which apply only to a unique setting or issue? Such an approach, of course, makes a "historical Paul" radically central. Accordingly, quests for a Pauline core overlap greatly with studies of Paul's relationship to Judaism (the focus of the "new perspective" on Paul) and studies of Pauline (auto)biography. More recently, Daniel Boyarin has suggested that Paul's "coherent" center and "perspective" on Judaism arose from Paul's own cultural location as a diaspora Jew. Paul was, in Boyarin's terms Jewgreek/Greekjew. Paul the Jew wanted a way to affirm traditional Jewish texts, values, and hopes. Paul the Greco-Roman citizen wanted a way to affirm a basic "oneness" or unity among all peoples, Jew and gentile. He also wanted to be able to embrace what he regarded as the best in contemporary culture and philosophy. He found a way to unite these disparate interests in his teachings about Jesus as messiah. At present, scholars are still unable to reach a consensus on exactly what is at the core of Paul's thought or how to understand his views of Judaism.

Paul and Gender

When the twentieth century opened, women in the United States were not allowed to vote. None served in elected office. Women were not allowed to matriculate to most major universities. Women had little opportunity for gainful employment. In less than 100 years, not only were all these exclusions legally rectified, but many modern college students cannot even imagine someone being denied opportunities because of their sex. Women not only vote legally, but serve in both houses of the US Congress. The twentieth century saw a woman nominated for serious candidacy as Vice-President of the United States. Women were appointed to the Supreme Court. Women were allowed access to nearly every major university, and the federal government of the United States has written and enforced strict legislation making it illegal to discriminate, based on sex, in employment, compensation, advancement, and more. World-wide, the twentieth century saw women elected to the highest offices of government, some even as representatives of highly conservative political parties. At the dawn of the twentieth century, most ecclesiastical bodies in the United States would not ordain women or allow them to serve in high church office or as clergy. By the end of the twentieth century, most Christian denominations in the United States ordain women. Both those bodies who ordain women and those bodies who still refuse to do so use the writings of Paul as a biblical defense of their position.

Women have, historically, faced opposition to their service as clergy from readings of passages in Paul. Opponents of women's ordination have cited passages such as 1 Timothy 2:8–15 and 1 Corinthians 14:34–5. The prison epistles of Colossians and Ephesians also indicate that wives are to be subordinate to their husbands (Col. 3:18–25; Eph. 5:22–33). 1 Timothy 3:1–13, the qualification list for deacons and bishops, many argue, does not have language that would allow women. In Greek, the word for "woman" (*gyne*) is often used for "wife." Opponents of women's ordination argue that 1 Timothy 3:11 is speaking about the characteristics a deacon's wife should exhibit. Bishops are to be the "husband of one wife" (1 Tim. 3:2), which would exclude women. Few argue that Paul thought that women were, by nature, inferior to men; the difference between genders lies (these scholars argue) in their divinely given gender roles and their expression of (equal) faith and status.

Other scholars, however, have challenged these readings. Elisabeth Schüssler Fiorenza wrote a pivotal book, *In Memory of Her*, that opened the door for many subsequent feminist readings of the Bible. Schüssler Fiorenza's book drew attention to long-neglected references to women found in the Bible. What she found in Paul was a surprising presence of women as active partners in Paul's mission and ministry. Some significant figures whom we've already met in this book are Phoebe, Chloe, and Priscilla. In Romans 16, Paul sends personal greetings to people at Rome. Nearly half are women. Women are referred to as "fellow workers" (implying they engaged in ministry). One woman, Junia, is called "foremost among the Apostles." Schüssler Fiorenza argues that this phrase means that Paul is calling *Junia* an apostle. Paul argues in Galatians 3:28 that there is no difference between men and women. As we have already seen, he allows women to continue to pray and prophesy (publicly, though while wearing veils) in his letter to the Corinthians. Feminist scholars point out that there are good reasons to regard 1 Corinthians 14 as an altered text with an addition silencing women which was not present in the original text. The description of the deaconate in 1 Timothy 3 is more naturally read, they argue, as giving qualifications for women who serve as deacons, not as qualifications for a deacon's wife. After all, the office of overseer/bishop is *higher* than that of deacon. Why would there be no mention of qualifications for a bishop's wife (apart from number), but mention of qualities for the spouse of the lesser office of deacon?

In addition to these debates, several scholars have explored the cultural context of Paul's domestic codes and expectations. Others look at the implicit sex-based language in Paul's arguments and practice. The general sense is that Paul was more inclusive of women than many in his day. Bernadette Brooten and Ross Kraemer have made New Testament scholarship more aware of the active and vibrant role of women in the synagogues of the Jewish diaspora. Paul may have inherited some of his more egalitarian views from Judaism. Indeed, if the views of 1 Timothy 2 and 1 Corinthians 14 are taken as authentically Pauline, Paul would be far *less* inclusive than the Judaism of his day. Many scholars also question whether Paul's views pro or con women's ordination should be the final arbiter of modern church practice. His views, clearly, reflect his cultural location. Indeed, most modern scholars who argue that he does stop short of full egalitarianism suggest he did so because he did not want to violate the cultural norms of the Greco-Roman empire. Paul did not want to be so inclusive of women that he alienated the more socially conservative Romans. I doubt that this would have been the case. Yet even if it were, and this is, indeed, the rationale behind Paul's restrictions on women, then the spirit of the argument would suggest that, in our modern context, women *should* be ordained. In our modern world *not* ordaining women would become a cultural barrier. Finally, a few modern communities still follow centuries-old traditions that argue, based on 1 Timothy 2, women are not equal to men because of the sin of Eve (or because women are married). Few outside these churches regard this argument as compelling.

Scholars are also turning to examine Paul's use of gender identity and construction. The influential philosopher and cultural historian Michel Foucault began work on the composition of a multi-volume history of sexuality; he died with only the first three volumes completed. In volume 3, he explored how gender expectations in a culture – what it means to be a "man" or a "woman" – were constructed in the Roman world. Many of Foucault's ideas have been challenged, but nevertheless his work has inspired a host of scholars to begin working on gender descriptions and norms in the classical world and which are reflected in the New Testament, a product of that world. Scholars of gender and sexuality in the late twentieth century began to separate "gender" from "sexuality." "Sex" may be biologically determined, but "gender" – how one "should" act if one is male or female – is a cultural construct. Paul certainly has his own expectations. For example, he argues that "nature" indicates that men should have short hair (1 Cor. 11:14). In the same letter, he condemns men who act in an "effeminate" way, whatever that might entail (1 Cor. 6:9). Paul's instructions to husbands and wives very likely also engage his views of gender. Accordingly, scholars have turned to Paul's letters to see how he understood masculinity and femininity and where and how he invokes Greco-Roman or Jewish cultural norms.

Paul and Sexual Preference

Related to issues of gender are issues of sexual preference. The word "homosexuality" was first coined in nineteenth-century Germany as a medical diagnosis for what was then regarded as a sexual dysfunction – the desire for sexual encounter with another member of one's own biological sex. This definition depends on an idea scholars refer to as "heteronormativity," or the belief that humans are biologically oriented to desire sex only with partners of a different biological sex. The late twentieth century saw huge conflicts about the ordination of clergy who were gay. Arguments also surrounded whether or not homosexual encounters were sinful. Some even argued that homosexual desire itself was sinful. Same-sex couples were forbidden to marry, both by church doctrine and by several state governments in the United States.

Scholarship on sexual orientation expanded logarithmically in the late twentieth century. Many in the social sciences, humanities, and medical fields now no longer feel that there is a "normal" expression of human sexual preference apart from variety. Some argue that sexual preference is biologically determined, but not necessarily correlated to what reproductive organs one might possess; in other words, that someone may be born gay or bisexual. Others challenge this view as too essentialist. Sexual preference, they argue, is a cultural construct and personal expression. Much like other appetites, for example food preferences, sexual preferences may be culturally influenced, may be learned, or may vary at different points in one's life. Still others question precisely what "sex" entails and how that may interact with any of a range of human-to-human intimacies, desires, contacts, and encounters. The culmination of all these lines of inquiry is to very much unsettle what "normal" sexual desire or expression might mean.

The only writer in the New Testament to address same-sex sexual encounter is Paul. Paul uses the Greek word *arsenokoites* in 1 Corinthians 6:9 and 1 Timothy 1:10; in both uses, the action is condemned. Recall, however, that many scholars argue the latter was not written by Paul. The word is not found in any existing copies of Greek literature prior to Paul. Etymologically, some have argued that the word is best translated as "men who have sex with men." There are also strong scholarly reasons to remain cautious about what this word may mean beyond "sexually inappropriate behavior." Another, longer, more central and more direct passage is found in Romans 1:18–27. In that passage, Paul argues that humans, who apparently have an innate sense of God the creator, have turned from worship of God to worship of idols. Paul asserts, "they traded the truth about God for a lie, and worshiped the creation instead of the creator." As a result, "God gave them up" to their own passions. Humans became senseless, darkened, and foolish in their thinking. Romans 1 argues that this violation of worship first resulted in women trading "natural relations" with men for other female partners. Next, men also gave up "natural relations with women" and were "consumed with passion for one another ... committing shameless acts with men." So, Paul concludes, God's wrath is upon them.

Paul is one of a very few writers from antiquity to acknowledge and address (and condemn) female-to-female sexuality. Same-sex sexual practice, while not the norm, does not seem to have been rare in the Greco-Roman world, and those who engaged in it did not, as a rule, seem to be doing so in secret. The most common form of same-sex contact in Paul's day seems to have been between an adult man and an adolescent boy. There were particular conventions regarding the social status of the partners and what acts could, without censure, be performed upon what partners. In general, some consensus seems to be emerging that social status and gender hierarchies were to be observed. More passive partners were expected to be those who were of lower social status.

Scholars such as Dale Martin and Stephen D. Moore have observed that Paul's central concern in Romans 1 is not same-sex encounters per se, but the violation of "natural" forms of hierarchy and social organization. Humans replace God (creator) with idols (the created). They then become unthinking and driven by lusts or instincts. The human, which "by nature" is superior to the beast, is now bestial. Finally, they alter "normal" sexual practices. For Martin, then, Paul's chief concern is not sex at all but idolatry. Many Jews of Paul's day would, in fact, have seen Greco-Roman idolatry and physical/sexual excess as almost synonymous terms. Paul is arguing about "nature," and we have already seen that he would feel that hair length is also "natural." Moore argues that the problem that has Paul most upset in Romans 1 is violation of proper hierarchy. Humans, having resisted the divine hierarchy, are now left to live in complete chaos. Both are strong readings.

Many who read the Bible as opposing homosexuality may well grant either reading, but would still see Romans 1 as a condemnation. While Paul may very well be most alarmed at idolatry and the violation of nature that idolatry produces, he still, clearly, seems to be opposed to homosexuality. Others argue that Paul's opposition to homosexuality results from his culture and context and is not normative for modern believers. Still others argue that he cannot be addressing "homosexuality" at all. Paul, they argue, is not thinking of a long-term, monogamous, committed relationship between adults. One particularly intriguing reading sees Paul as opposing sex that violates one's "nature." If one is born with a same-sex orientation, to *suppress* that desire is a violation of nature. There is little consensus on any of these issues.

Paul and Politics and Ethnicity

As we have seen in this chapter, substantial work has been done by twentieth-century scholars on the ethnicity of Paul. Perhaps the single most extensive question in twentieth-century studies of Paul has been an inquiry into his relationship to his own Judaism and/or how Paul the Jew understood the Greco-Roman world in which he lived. As we saw in a previous chapter, Paul also played a role in the construction of the ideology of Western colonialism. So far, we have seen two examples of political and ethnic readings of Paul.

In the twentieth century several nations underwent political and social revolutions. It should not surprise any reader of this book to learn that these political and social changes also appear in scholarship on Paul. Several scholars have explored Paul's writings through the lens of Marxist political literature or, as one might expect, in resistance to these themes. Several other scholars have read Paul with an eye toward how his work would facilitate the liberation of oppressed peoples. Particularly popular within scholarship of South Africa and South America, Liberationist readings focus on Paul's language of inclusion. Marxist readings focus on his language of salvation as economic transfer, noting that his metaphors for sin and salvation are often metaphors of slavery or of manumission. Paul's language in Galatians 3:28 certainly offers a space for the empowerment of women. He asserts that "male or female" does not affect one's access to God. He also notes, however, that whether one is "slave or free" is equally immaterial. It does not take much interpretive energy to translate these concepts into a modern system of wealth and poverty.

In the late twentieth century a movement began in literary studies called "postcolonialism." Postcolonial criticism is the investigation of literature that was produced in the context of colonial encounter, and foregrounds issues of cultural hegemony, adaptation, and resistance. Postcolonial literature explores how both colonizing nations and colonized peoples are transformed by the mutual engagement of the two cultural systems, albeit an engagement on an uneven playing field. Such approaches have been most successfully employed to analyze how the Bible was used by colonizing nations of the West to inculturate colonized peoples. Paul, as we have already seen, provided a model for many such programs. Postcolonialism also explores how the colonized, often called the "subaltern," used the Bible to "write back" to their oppressors. A good example would be readings of Philemon that argued *against* slavery. Since postcolonial criticism foregrounds the process of cultural engagement of unequal powers, it has also been of interest to scholars of Paul's first-century context. After all, Paul himself is somewhat "hybrid" culturally, is a representative of a subaltern class in the Roman world, and conducted his work in the context of what was, in effect, the global empire of Rome. Scholars in the very late twentieth century began to use techniques of post-colonial criticism to analyze Paul's writings themselves.

During the twentieth century, several ethnic and economic minority groups in the United States gained access to universities, professional careers, and economic opportunity. This access often came as a result of intense struggles for legitimacy and opportunity. The Civil Rights movement in America during the 1950s and 1960s is but one example of a global phenomenon which ranged from India to South Africa to South America to the US and Europe and is, in many ways, still going on (and still to emerge in some nations). Many scholars began to read Paul's writings through the eyes of ethnic minorities. These readings highlighted the way that biblical text had been historically interpreted to protect and perpetuate the status and privilege of certain groups at the expense of others. Readings such as those in the work of Alan C. Callahan were innovative reimaginings of Pauline texts which reflected the interests of minority groups but which had long been rejected or ignored.

The Historicity of the Pauline Writings and Acts (again)

The twentieth century also saw renewed assertions among evangelical scholars of the literary integrity and Pauline authorship of all 13 epistles and vigorous evangelical defenses of the historicity of Acts. For many of these scholars, the various fragmentations of twentieth-century work on Paul had simply gone too far. The text was disintegrating from the solvent of too many ideologically driven readings. Notable New Testament scholars like Luke Timothy Johnson, Edwin Mounce, and Howard Marshall have argued for a reconstructed history of Paul that would include the pastorals as authentically Pauline. As liberals sought to root Paul in external context, evangelicals reasserted canonical contexts and, in many cases, returned to classics of Christian biblical interpretation from the early and medieval church. Many evangelicals feel that biblical studies since the onset of higher criticism has gone too far in their critique of historic Christian confession and in their challenge of biblical authority. Many evangelicals view modern Americans as too individualistic and too critical of authority. Challenges to the Bible and to church authority, they argue, are largely mounted from a self-interested desire to escape submission to God. The result is social disintegration.

Other scholars are returning their focus to the rhetoric of Paul (how he argued his points and attempted to persuade his audience). Still others (such as Gordon Fee) produced spine-breakingly thick, densely written examinations of every minute (Greek) expression of Paul. In some ways, this debate is intentionally "retro" in terms of historical assumptions and regard for the sovereignty of the Bible for Christian living. Yet another Stendahl-inspired line of inquiry surrounds investigation into the Greco-Roman setting of Paul's letters. Scholars of the historical context of Paul frequently pursue their work from two ends. For many, the only way to properly determine a text's "meaning" is to read the document in its historical and grammatical context. An ancient text cannot be understood to "mean" (or "intend to mean") something that the author (or, in some versions, the text's original audience) would not have intended. Modern readers are separated by a great many factors from an ancient Paul in terms of language, culture, and historical setting. Therefore, in addition to excruciatingly exact analysis of every word (and grammatical structure) in Paul, modern readers must struggle to reconstruct Paul's world and read the documents according to ancient politics, standards, metaphors, rhetoric, military history, geographical history, and more. Some (but certainly not all) scholars who are seeking to perform a "historical-grammatical" analysis of Paul do so because they regard the Bible as the highest revelation of God;

it must be interpreted correctly, and "correctly" is taken to mean in the ways the original author intended. Others see the text as much more human in its production, but still feel the most reasonable way to interpret a text, particularly a text that many people in the modern world regard as central for their own thinking and practice, is by reconstruction of its ancient setting. Many of these readers, though, approach the text with proper caution. They readily acknowledge that the Bible in general and Paul in particular have been used to support nefarious agendas and that much of the original meaning may well have been lost. Yet they are not ready to concede that the Bible is inherently "dangerous" to read or that the author's intention is completely obscured. Indeed, such a concession, many argue, results in a breakdown in authority, which is far more dangerous and unstable.

Still others are seeking to discover the influences of Paul's political and cultural world on the framing of his language and metaphors from the perspective of social sciences and intellectual and cultural history. Scholars such as Wayne Meeks, John Fitzgerald, Richard Horsely, Gerd Theissen, and others have identified numerous moments of resonance between Paul's writings and cultural changes and debates in the Roman world. In addition, multiple "biographies" of Paul have begun to emerge. In some ways, the current moment is infatuated with the "quest for the historical Paul." Some are searching for Paul's relationship to Judaism. Some are searching for Paul's coherent "core." Others are exploring how Paul reflects his ancient context (culturally and religiously), which, of course, presumes the reconstruction of that ancient context.

Paul and the Fragmentation of the Twentieth Century

In many ways, Pauline scholarship at present is focused on (re)constructions of Paul. A key interest is Pauline identity/biography, but also Pauline cultural responses. In part, this arises from a long-standing idea that a properly constructed "myth of origins" validates an idea. If one can show that a structure or practice existed in the past (even better: if one can construct an etiological myth where a cultural or ideological paradise existed prior to a barbarous intrusion of corrupting overlords) then that adds legitimating weight to desires and claims for the reconstruction of that past in the present. Any charge that one is arguing for an ideological "utopia," impossible to obtain (or sustain), is countered by a brisk point to history.

Two thoughts about this. First, I'm struck with how resonant it is across the history of reading Paul. Though for different motives, proponents of a variety of ideas have long sought legitimacy and/or validation in the past. Despite accusations of "revisionism" or "relativism," even highly postmodern modes of reading turn, at least when using Paul, toward referential forms of argumentation. Second, I am often struck with how wonderfully Pauline writings work for such arguments. In Paul, we have "first-century" documents in a first-person voice. They are records of that imagined, ideal past. But they are nothing if not ethereal remarks, ghosts in the library. As letters, their specific qualities can seem to root or anchor any number of ideas or reconstructions. But they remain floating above history and event; their ambiguity prevents a final, decisive argument as to origins.

Paul and Postmodernity

The word "postmodern" is used too often today. In many ways, it has become meaningless. The most basic definition is a way of viewing the world after the confidence of modernity had been shattered. More accurately, postmodernity is taken by most scholars of twentieth-century philosophical and literary movements to be, generally, a "suspicion of grand narratives." Among the "grand narratives" are beliefs in absolute truth and confidence that there is something uniquely human or "real" that transcends culture and language. Critics of postmodernism argue that it is little more than intellectual justification for believing that whatever one wants to be "true," is true. This is oversimplified. Postmodernists are often keenly aware that to argue that reality is an intellectual construct is madness. One stubbed and broken toe proves that rocks are real. Other critics of postmodernity are quick to point out that the rejection of grand narratives is, itself, a grand narrative. To say "we can know nothing for certain" is to claim to know at least one thing for certain. Again, good postmodern theory would agree, but would also quickly point out that they are not saying no grand narratives *could* exist or that *nothing* can be known for certain.

Careful postmodern thinking begins and ends with suspicion of authority systems and absolute fact. This does not mean that no facts exist. It does, however, mean that "large story arcs" – like, for example, the one I have used in this chapter – are much more about organizing our own claims to knowledge than they are about what "really" happened. Postmodernity is neither nihilist nor moral/intellectual relativism. Indeed, these, too, are grand narratives. Postmodernity is judicious cautiousness regarding truth claims, particularly those that are absolute. History and theology have been particularly critical battlefields over postmodern thought. Postmodern scholars are nearly allergic to claims about divine inspiration, universal truth, and absolute causation in history. Instead, they focus attention on how we tell our stories, who wins in the telling, and what is invested in the process. The best of postmodern scholarship reveals the limitations of argument by showing how our own rhetoric often betrays us or opens up the potential for meanings contradictory to those that seem to be intended. The particular technique of such demonstrations is often called "deconstruction." "Deconstruction" of a work does not mean to show that it is "wrong" or to reveal how its argument is being advanced. Instead, it reveals how the work's own (intended?) meaning is remarkably difficult to assert and how every "interpretation" opens possibilities for counter-readings. Though no longer widely accepted in detail, the general theories of Sigmund Freud certainly unveil for us how our own thoughts and plans often betray hidden meanings and are not, ultimately, static ideas, fixed and permanent. In many ways, deconstruction is "psychoanalysis" of the literary text, revealing how the text's own "subconscious" also occasionally intrudes into its text. The point is not to produce absolute "meanings." Indeed, the very point is to show how "absolute" meanings are elusive and to draw our attention to how much we, as interpreters or historians, create the meanings we "find."

Deconstructive readings of Paul have certainly been advanced. In many ways, this book itself is one. A postmodern reading of Paul would be highly suspicious of the possibility of an absolute history or biography of Paul. One of the more notable deconstructionists – the originator of the term, in fact – was Jacques Derrida. Derrida treats Paul's texts often, but often obliquely. His most sustained "interweaving" of his own readings, his developing philosophy of self, and his own notions of how biography and writing intersect is his work *Circumfessions*. Though rarely citing Paul directly, in this book Derrida uses Pauline structures of law, time, subjectivity, autobiography, and even Judaism as the "logic" beneath many of the turns and much of the structure of his argument.

Paul has also become very vogue in early twenty-first-century continental philosophy. The late German philosopher Jacob Taubes used a series of lectures on Romans 1 to explore his own work on the philosophy of politics and law. Taubes, himself Jewish, focused on how Paul negotiated the intersections of Jewishness and Romanness and paralleled this to the history of Jewish existence in twentieth-century Europe. The Italian philosopher Giorgio Agamben has used Paul to explore notions of "time" and reality, plotting out how Paul constructed notions of time and space in light of his messianic beliefs and (apocalyptic) agendas. Finally, the French philosopher Alain Badiou has written to challenge ideas of Paul that do not see him as part of a continuous line of early Roman imperial philosophers. For Badiou, Paul is more philosopher than religious innovator; Paul's central question was the development of subjectivity. Though none of them is a biblical scholar by training, in many ways the work of these three continental philosophers combines to address many of the questions that surrounded Paul in the twentieth century. Their work has only recently entered into discussions among biblical scholars. Time will tell what in what ways they move conversations forward.

Clearly, ideological lines are drawn, and Pauline texts often frame them. Again, in part these arise from the specific ambiguity of Paul, but, perhaps more than in any other era, the twentieth century revealed how much cultural and ideological needs shape the way interpreters read. The twentieth century also demonstrated that the stakes involved could not be higher.

Conclusion:
The Quest for the Historical Paul
or, What did we find if we couldn't find Paul?

(Auto)biography and Paul

A few months ago I was reading Jacob Taubes' *Political Theology of St. Paul* then 1 and 2 Corinthians. I was reading Taubes for a lecture in a seminar on Paul. I was reading Paul in advance of a lecture on the New Testament in general. I read for a few hours, jotting notes on the Greek, typing a bit on my computer, then turned to the television to watch coverage of the Republican National Convention nominating John McCain as its 2008 presidential candidate. The theme of the convention was "Country First." Former senator Fred Thompson (R Tennessee), himself a candidate for nomination earlier in the primary, introduced Senator McCain by reviewing his life story. He stressed (heavily) the time McCain had spent as a prisoner of war in Vietnam; he graphically described his torture and suffering at the hands of the Vietnamese. His conclusion was that this displayed McCain's "character" and potential as a leader. I was drawn almost immediately to 2 Corinthians 11:16–33. The tacit and facile way that suffering was equated to "character" and devotion and that suffering, almost alone, qualified one to lead, leapt out at me and struck me as unintelligible apart from a matrix of Pauline theology. Though Paul was not directly invoked, the image of Paul (the "maverick" willingly suffering to show his zeal and character) was very much in the room. References were repeatedly made to McCain's "maverick" status. I could not help but hear Paul's own assertions that his role as dissenting critic to both Greco-Roman culture and to the "super apostles" found throughout the beginning of 1 Corinthians and the ending of 2 Corinthians, was hiding beneath the rhetoric. There is no inherent, obvious virtue to dissent, yet it was lauded, without commentary, as a virtue. The very act of being a "maverick" and an iconoclast was presented as a quality for leadership and not as a sign of contrariness or idiosyncrasy or even, at its extreme, madness and foolishness (which calls to mind, of course, 1 Corinthians 2). The specter of Paul seemed to haunt nearly every remark.

And it continued. Subsequent speakers (Rudolph Giuliani, Mike Huckabee, and others) made references in their speeches to the "proven sacrifice" of McCain. Huckabee even ended his speech with an extensive parable about how all citizens owe their freedoms to war veterans, a parable with no immediate, exclusive connection to John McCain. More than once in the Convention, mention was made of McCain's ongoing physical maladies, how, for example, he cannot raise his arms any longer to salute the flag for which he fought or to take an oath of office. On later nights, Senator McCain's vice-presidential nominee, Governor Sarah Palin of Alaska, stressed how her "outsider" status was a virtue. One could hear the opposition to the "so-called super apostles" tectonically rumbling beneath the fissures of her rhetoric.

Theorist Max Weber wrote extensively on the integration of religious imagination and social organization. Even seemingly "secular" endeavors like economic theory are intimately tied to a culture's religious views (his is the phrase "Protestant work ethic"). Weber also described how cultures use religious language (among other strategies) to develop "ideal types" or consistent frames and categories of the "hero" or noble and virtuous ideas, standards, and personalities.

As has been elaborated at length, Christian Protestants (and evangelicals in particular) make up a substantial portion of the Republican Party in the US in the early twenty-first century. Clearly, many of the issues of this community (their views on women, gender identity, even perhaps the financial independence of the individual citizen – "if a man won't work, don't let him eat") are drawn from their readings of biblical text. Indeed, nearly all of these issues are found in the writings of Paul. It is little revelation to suggest that Paul and Pauline theology are central, perhaps pivotal, to Protestant and evangelical theology. The figure of Paul is a Protestant "ideal type." Though not directly quoted, he was most certainly, and most vividly, "cited" throughout the campaign. McCain's "straight talk" (opposed to the eloquence of Barak Obama) resonated throughout with echoes of Paul's own avoidance of "lofty words" and "human wisdom."

Nor could I help but note, from reading Taubes, that such constructions are not unique to our current moment in history. Taubes, a prominent Jewish continental philosopher of the twentieth century, was keenly interested in issues of hermeneutics, politics, and political theory. He was also a lecturer on Paul (particularly Corinthians) as well as Heidegger and Hobbes. He was particularly interested in how intellectual movements and philosophical literature of the nineteenth century (particularly in Germany) paved the way for the Holocaust and the destruction of 6 million Jews by the Nazis. In many ways, the writing of this book has been filled with similar moments – moments where I reflect upon the complex ways a "historical Paul" has been reconstructed (some beneficial, some benign, some pernicious) by scholars and used to undergird a particular reading, but also as a Weberian model of the "ideal."

Where Is Paul?

Given the contextual quality of most of his writings, reconstruction of the "historical Paul," though rarely described in such terms, certainly occupies a central role in Pauline scholarship. As scholars, we inquire into Paul's underlying, "coherent" theology, Paul's Jewishness, Paul's "Romanness," Paul's hybridity, and Paul's fundamental personality. Yet, as we've seen time and again in this survey, much like modern attempts to reconstruct the historical Jesus, scholarship has not only failed to produce a single defining image of Paul, but even failed to identify a reliable methodology. Also, reconstructed images of Paul (and his polemic) often reveal more about the interpreter's location than Paul's. And the fragmentation is, if anything, getting worse in the recent decades.

Unlike quests for the historical Jesus, however, in Pauline studies we do not have texts primarily about Paul, but texts arising (or purporting to arise) from Paul. Further, unlike Jesus research, which tends to produce historical "Jesuses" who differ primarily in emphasis but are not openly incompatible (Jesus the philosopher, the healer, the political rebel, the Torah sage), reconstructed images of Paul are often wildly divergent (Paul the anti-Semite, the good Jew, the homophobe, the closeted gay, the misogynist, the egalitarian, the convert from Judaism, the Roman, the Pharisee). Pauline pseudepigrapha and later traditions obviously present unique problems. This chapter will explore these issues, concentrating on how scholarship itself complicates the question. I will compare and contrast the alternate strategies and scholarship behind historical Jesus research and attempts to achieve Pauline coherence, noting how data from disputed Paulines both complicates the process and offers a glimpse into the first "quest for the historical Paul."

Questing

Perhaps we could return, again, to a scholar of Jesus whom we first met in the Introduction. In his 1915 monograph, *The Quest of the Historical Jesus,* Albert Schweitzer destabilizes any confidence modern scholars might have in reconstructing a "historical Jesus" via objective methods of historiography. He argues that historical reconstructions of Jesus actually turn out to be re-creations of the personality, culture, interests, and agendas of the questor more than they reflect a plausible Jesus from history (a point also demonstrated in postmodern/cultural studies criticism by Stephen D. Moore). Schweitzer famously concludes that any reliable, objective proof of Jesus, not to mention the more difficult task of unveiling Jesus of Nazareth in his full historical context, is impossible. Despite his late Victorian, fin-de-siècle dismantling of any reasonable hope for success, we are in what appears to be the later stages of a third "quest" for a historical Jesus. Volumes abound describing, with confident assurance, the "real" Jesus. We find works by Crossan, Sanders, Borg, Funk, Dunn, Witherington,

Meier, Horsley, and a legion of others each confidently assured that they have uncovered, finally, Jesus the mystic, Jesus the divine man, Jesus the healer, Jesus the cynic philosopher, Jesus the political revolutionary, Jesus the bandit, or Jesus, the "marginal Jew." We can hardly blame these moderns for not heeding Schweitzer; Schweitzer, himself, after careful inquiry that proved devastating to any true hope of success, offered – in the very same volume – a reconstructed Jesus of his own.

The multitude of historical Jesus figures, speaking over one another and clamoring in unison to present their credentials to authenticity like some bizarre re-creation of a 1960s game show, is certainly disconcerting to traditional Christian confession. Still, the utter breakdown of consensus also provokes unease among scholars (and, ironically, fuels confessional resistance to the merits of academic inquiry as well). Surely, however, John Dominic Crossan, in his book *The Historical Jesus*, is correct to note that the different Jesuses emerge from different reading methodologies. In part simply repeating Schweitzer, in part offering a very critical and subtle expansion, Crossan notes that it is the methodology of the reader that provokes such disparity. Still, these multiple Jesuses seem roughly compatible (or, at minimum, not wildly divergent); couldn't an itinerant cynic-style philosopher also have a reputation as a healer/mystic/exorcist, provoke civil rebellion, and be regarded by the Romans as a dissident or bandit? The differences seem more in emphasis than in basic essence.

Unfortunately, the same is hardly true of Paul. J. C. Beker's monumental *Paul the Apostle* introduced a strategy for understanding a veritable host of seeming contradictions in Paul. Beker, wisely noting that all of Paul's writings are contextually driven circumstantial correspondence and not systematic treatises, develops the dual levels of "coherence" and "contingency" in Paul, as we saw in Chapter 7. For Beker, it is critical to differentiate (in a reconstruction of the historical context of a given letter) what is a coherent, systematic Pauline thought from what is merely contingent to the particular circumstance of a given audience.

In attempts to reconstruct the "Paul" behind the Pauline letters and presumably to articulate their coherence (an attempt that would hopefully provide a base camp from which to strike for the more difficult summit of final biography), wildly different images of Paul have emerged.

The Ethics of Historical Reconstructions

But I don't want to leave the impression that these divergent reconstructions are merely scholarly curiosities or prizes in the collection of some biblical studies museum. They can have clear ethical implications in the real community of readers. Consider, for example the development of readings regarding one aspect of the historical Paul's biography – his understanding of his own Jewishness. Often framed as questions of "Paul's relationship to Jewish law," certainly Paul's prior views of Torah and its contributions to soteriological status and community description are critical not only to his understanding of anthropology in general, but also to his sense of his own Jewish self-image. One could scarcely imagine understanding "Judaism" without understanding both ethnic descent and Torah observance. The scholarship on Paul in our present moment is marked by fragmentation. This is, I would argue, a result of a growing awareness of the loss of historical moorings in a context of, as yet underdeveloped, systems of ethics for reading. We have not yet reflected enough on the issues this book's brief survey raises.

We might begin with Luther. In Luther's famous commentary on Galatians, to Paul the "law" is clearly insufficient for salvation. Luther read Paul's (admittedly sharp) polemic in Galatians as a repudiation of the entire body of Mosaic law and, by extension, Judaism. For example, he writes, on Galatians 3:24:

> Although a schoolmaster is very useful and really necessary for the education and training of boys, show me one boy or pupil who loves his schoolmaster! For example, did the Jews love Moses warmly and willingly do what he commanded? … [I]t is impossible for a pupil to love his schoolmaster. … How wonderful the pupil's righteousness is, that he obeys a threatening and harsh schoolmaster and even kisses his whip! Does he do this willingly and joyfully? When the schoolmaster is absent, he will break the

whip or throw it into the fire. And if he had authority over the schoolmaster, he would not let himself be beaten by the schoolmaster's whips but would order the schoolmaster to be whipped. Nevertheless, a schoolmaster is extremely necessary for a boy.

Reading such comments, I am struck by how clearly Luther's own experience shines through his remarks; one can scarcely escape an image of an adult Luther growing more and more rigid in his posture as he wrote, remembering past beatings. More ominously, one notes how he equates Jewish law with extreme, punitive harshness, something inherently unlovable. Further, any regard that might be present is servile docility, earned by the whip. In point of fact, however, Jews before, during, and after Luther's day clearly do love and regard the law very highly. The Torah and its commands are viewed as a blessing given by God from God's love and election. In rabbinic thought, honoring the law is a means of service to God and to humanity at large, a service predicated on pure faith (recall, there is no fully developed idea of "hell" in Judaism) that arises from the heart. Luther's image of law seems, like his views of schoolmasters, to be tied to his own experience of a religious system he deemed deeply abusive.

Luther's readings, as we saw, introduce a sharp division between Paul's conception of Judaism and his new concern with messianism (Luther, of course, simply equated the latter with Christianity). In other words, Luther, by introducing a level of division between the "old Paul" and the new, severs the connection of Jew and messianist, producing a Judaism that is, at best, vestigial, at worst, pernicious. For Luther, Jew is clearly separate from Christian, and Jew is now superseded.

F. C. Baur assumed the separation outlined by traditional Lutheran theologies. Baur, one of the most (in)famous of the German "higher critics," posited, again largely from Galatians (this time chapter 2), a sharp division between Pauline Christianity and Petrine/Jamesian groups. In his famous "Hebraists, Hellenists and Catholics," Baur suggests overtly that "the statements given in the Acts of the Apostles afford but a dim and confused picture of this early community of believers and yield little to the historian in the way of trustworthy or consistent materials." The

"Hebraists" (Jewish messianists led by James) were, in the first century, at critical theological odds with the "Hellenists" (Pauline, gentile Christians). These conflicting traditions were synchronized and harmonized by later orthodoxy ("the Catholics"). Baur, seeing contrasts within messianic movements, saw his radical historical revisions as necessary for the unveiling of original "history."

Baur faced extreme opposition from more conservative Christian scholars, who argued that his radical and revisionist views were designed to simply disrupt faith. He was viewed as intentionally antagonistic to orthodox Christian thought. Indeed, he seemed to revel in just that role and the conflicts it inspired. Still, Baur was no friend to Judaism. He understood a need (as, he would argue, Paul did as well) for a fundamental and necessary break between messianic/Christian communities and Judaism. He writes:

> Judaism is nothing more than the religion of the law in contradistinction to Christianity, which is religion of the spirit. Both its position in the world and its inner constitution declare that the function of Judaism is that of effecting a transition, of filling up interval.

"The law" and "faith" are in opposition, and Judaism is, at best, a "place-keeping" faith. Baur, of course, understood the origins of this tension as conflict between Pauline, gentile (faith)-oriented communities and Jamesian/Petrine communities which precisely avoided this separation and segregation. Pauline Hellenists, however, are Baur's ultimate interest. In his harsh historical rereadings of Paul he was not, per se, undermining Paul, but attempting to recover the original Pauline materials by stripping off the veneer that the fraudulent Acts and the disputed Pauline letters and pseudepigrapha (documents developing orthodox thought before Nicaea – discussed in our opening chapters) applied to the essence of the historical Paul. Adding to Luther's separation of Jew and Christian, Baur accelerates the bifurcation by observing that the two modes of faith are fundamentally and irreconcilably at odds with one another and have always been so. For Baur, Luther's separation of Jew from

Christian is assumed. Jew and Christian are now set in necessary (and hostile) tension.

Assuming, once again, a Lutheran separation of Pauline identity, Adolf von Harnack's work, as I have argued, also assumes at the minimum the elements of separation and opposition found in Luther and even in Baur. Von Harnack famously sought the "kernel" or center of religious sensibility beneath the husk or particularity of a given religious expression.

In his pivotal essay "The Founder of Christianity," Harnack identifies Paul as the bold and far-seeing "little Jew" who "delivered the Christian religion from Judaism." "What knowledge, what confidence," Harnack asks breathlessly, "what strength, was necessary to tear the new religion from its mother earth and plant it in an entirely new one!"

The thesis of von Harnack's *What Is Christianity?* (the larger work in which the final form of "The Founder of Christianity" was published), was that Jesus and Christianity offered a return to the essential religiosity and spirituality which had been lost in Judaism's aggressive interest in the particularities of religious performance. Von Harnack saw, in Paul, a like-minded ambition to define the essence of Jesus' teaching (salvation by faith) in opposition to his Judaizing opponents. Luther separates Paul from Judaism. Baur puts Paul in opposition to Judaism. Von Harnack offers a Paul that erases Judaism. Judaism has been "othered" and, ultimately, rendered expendable.

I need not articulate the devastating effects of this progression on German theology of the early twentieth century. I scarcely need to recall for the reader that we are in the late stages of a "new perspective" on Paul which reexamines his deep roots in Judaism and his presentation of the law. Following Beker's notions of contingency and coherence and Stendahl's refusal to separate Paul's ideas from his context, scholars are reevaluating claims that Paul was clearly at odds with all forms of Judaism or Greco-Roman thought and politics. Paul is now often read as a Jew arguing with other Jews about the halakhic status of gentile converts, not repudiating Judaism wholesale. Paul is seen as one of many cultural dissidents in the empire. Finally, I would hardly be the first scholar to note that this new sensitivity to Paul's

Judaism and social location is directly influenced by Christian responses to the Holocaust and our own modern concerns about political inclusivity and postcolonial politics.

My point, in this very brief survey, is to demonstrate how the definition of a single, central element of Pauline identity – Paul's view of (his own) Jewishness vis-à-vis the law and Jesus' messianism – has shaped the reading of the Pauline corpus as a whole and had clear, immediate public consequences. Further, I would also observe how, clearly, it is an attempt to deal with Paul's repeated presentation of himself in his letters as a person in opposition, often isolated, and struggling to define himself against larger, ambivalently described ideological forces. Notice, though, how each scholar above, Luther, Baur, and von Harnack, and our modern contemporaries, are themselves figures in conflict with larger religious communities. And notice how this process was mirrored in all those from before, be they Ante-Nicene, from late antiquity, or from the medieval or colonial periods. They (we) identify with Paul as the heroic dissident, much as they were themselves dissident in their own scholarly work. But they each also found in Paul a voice of reassurance. Both the permission to deviate *and* the reassurance to remain sleepily complacent can be consequential.

Clearly too, they, and we, associate with Paul and superimpose tensions and needs on any biographical reconstruction of him. For Luther, who identified himself as a lonely opponent to a legalistic and superficial church, Paul is also waging sole warfare with a similarly defined Judaism. Baur, chased and harried by the "orthodox," sees in Paul a radical rethinker of doctrine and courageous iconoclast against tradition. Von Harnack sees a Paul who, alone, has glimpsed the significance of the "essence" of Jesus' teachings. All this clearly seems to display a Schweitzerian practice of scholars who reconstruct a historical Paul according to their own needs and concerns. The Pauline faces they have described are familiar.

Comparing the Historical Data for Paul and for Jesus

Among scholars at present there is no uniform image or biography of Paul. I have suggested above that the existing array of "historical Pauls" is perhaps even more diverse and more fundamentally irreconcilable than the range of potential historical reconstructions of Jesus. Further, as I have also suggested, the role, community, and interests of the historian seem to attenuate their reconstruction of the past, much as we have found in historical Jesus research. Indeed, if any consensus has emerged from historical Jesus research, it is that the bias and methodology of the historian alters the content of the final reconstruction. Such a process must certainly be at play in any reconstruction of Paul, perhaps in ways that are even more acute than in historical Jesus inquiry. Beyond even questions of theological and cultural needs and concerns, beyond even assumptions about the reliability (or even final description) of received church opinion on Paul, how a scholar will view questions of authorship, redaction, or the historical reliability of the letters ascribed to Paul, how a historian reconstructs the contingent circumstances of any given Pauline writing, how a historian understands fundamental premises of Pauline chronology, how a historian describes or recognizes Pauline opponents, how a scholar views issues of "mirror-reading" to discover Pauline issues, how a scholar receives and/or reconciles any potential historical content from the Acts of the Apostles (or even the Acts of Paul) will, without question, shape the final biography of Paul which is composed.

A possible explanation for the divergent views of the historical Paul may arise from the seemingly infinite permutations and combinations of opinion on questions such as these. Indeed, a frequent explanation for divergent reconstructions of Paul often asserts just such idiosyncrasy or bias among scholars. Numerous scholars begin their biographies of Paul or their summaries of Pauline coherence/theology by assertions that they have forsaken the vagaries of Pauline commentary and returned to the simple texts (often read exclusively in Greek). A few even spend time addressing the exact question of how their modern reconstruction of Paul is accurate and all prior scholarship has been mistaken. Mistaken scholarship, it is asserted, has arisen from the bias of the scholars in question and is the reason behind any discrepancies in historical reconstruction. Certainly, that is, in part, true.

Yet my question is whether or not these biases, alone, account for the divergent images of Paul. Without doubt, there are as many (most likely more) epistemological, theological, and sociological intrusions on any attempt to reconstruct the historical Jesus. Further, as historical Jesus inquiry has shown us, it is impossible to either (a) extricate the historian from the historian's own social, religious, and political context or (b) identify or describe any standard for a "neutral" inquiry. Simply put, if we actually did discover the full picture of the historical Jesus, we wouldn't know it. Further, a "neutral" or "balanced" standard for inquiry, since there is no external measurement by which we may evaluate any one reading, is often little more than a coded reinscription of how a given author would reconstruct the figure in question. In other words, a "genuine" or authentic reconstruction of Paul is simply what any given historian would concede. The problem of the historian's own intrusion is insurmountable.

In a very interesting contrast, however, the data for a historical Paul would seem to be quite different in substance (and potential resolution) from the extant data for a historical Jesus. Regarding Jesus, we have only the second- (perhaps third- or fourth-) hand reports of anonymous authors who composed their gospels (gospels founded on oral tradition and redaction of non-extant sources) 30 to 60 years after Jesus' death. We have no data from Jesus' own "mouth" (or pen), unfiltered, of what Jesus taught. We have no reports, unfiltered, from Jesus himself regarding the particular details (including names and narratives) of his own mission travels, associates, or childhood, education, or values. We have no examples, unfiltered, from Jesus' own hand of the application of his teachings to specific issues and concerns of his community of later followers.

For Paul, of course, the situation is the exact opposite. While we have limited narratives about Paul (the book of Acts or the Acts of Paul), the abundance of our data comes from letters purportedly by Paul's own hand. We have extensive reports, by Paul, of his own life and ideology prior to his discovery of Jesus. We have extended and elaborate examples of Paul interpreting biblical texts, applying his theology to real ethical debates, summarizing his general theological concerns. We have moments when we see Paul perhaps quoting or accommodating pre-Pauline hymns or confessional statements into his own thought. We have a host of names, places, travel data, and narrative. We find achingly personal and private expressions of Paul's own regret for his past, his pain for his fellow Jews, his anxiety over his own stubborn tendency to sin, his personal anger, his own financial hardships, his sarcasm, in short, his full "humanness." Still, consensus on this historical Paul eludes us.

In part, this arises from the contingent, epistolary nature of the writings. We simply do not know as much about the audience and history behind Paul's letters as we would like. Instead, we can only observe that they are very much texts which are, to borrow from Erich Auerbach's *Mimesis*, "fraught with background." We can determine with certainty only that there is a rich context behind these writings which we will never know with certainty.

A deeper problem, and one which applies directly to the question of the disputed Paulines (or to the correlation of the letters themselves by Paul with the traditions by others about Paul), is not the amount of what we don't know; it is precisely the details that we do. Paul's letters often contain elements which seem to have fundamentally specific data upon which to build a reconstructed Paul. They describe names, places, and past events in specific detail. Yet they also often, by their very detail, awaken problems in resolution. Consider, for example the correlation of Galatians 2 and the book of Acts. The problem with the chronology of Paul's early career (and so the problem with the validity of either Galatians or Acts) is exactly a problem of facts. Did Paul or did Paul not go to Jerusalem soon after his vision of Jesus? Or, as another example, consider the problems of the pastoral letters (particularly Titus) and the reconstruction of Paul's late chronology. When was Paul in Crete? Was Paul or was Paul not released by the Romans and allowed to journey on to Spain before a second arrest? The strategies for reconciling these problems are legion. Notably, though, there is insufficient data to do much more than demonstrate possible lines of reconciliation; there is no way to conclusively settle the debates.

Seemingly specific and concrete, the details of Paul's biography become amazingly plastic. They can support an endless number of historical potentialities. It is their very specificity which is the problem; in many ways, they are too precise, offering concrete details that are difficult to reconcile or contextualize with other concrete details. They are, as I have elsewhere called them, examples of specific ambiguity.

This specific ambiguity becomes one of the central concerns when we turn to disputed Paulines, and, because of this, absolutely paramount to any reconstruction of the historical Paul. Indeed, one major reason for disputes over authenticity is that the specific data of some letters seems at odds with either the specific content of other letters or with the historical biography presented in Acts. If we move beyond the specific content of names and travel data to linguistic variation and theology, we discover the problem is even more acute. Were Paul less vivid, consistent, or distinct in his style and vocabulary, were Paul less coherent and consistent in his theology, there would be no problem. The difficult moments of theological tension are rarely those that are esoterically worded or mysterious (who, for example, doubts the Pauline injunction that women praying and prophesying in public should cover their heads "for the sake of the angels"?); instead, they are those moments that are worded with clarion precision ("all women should be silent in the assembly"). Ironically, were the Pauline corpus less specific (or shorter), less vivid or less consistent, we would have much less reason to debate or dispute Pauline authorship of any single text. We would also have much less diversity among confidently reconstructed "historical Pauls." Were it lacking in that specificity, however, we would have only the vaguest notion of any historical Paul at all; we would debate less, but that would be because consensus declared we could know virtually nothing for certain.

Implications: The Language of Paul

Comparison of the quests for the historical Paul and the historical Jesus could lead to new discoveries about the origins and contents of the writings ascribed to Paul. In the case of the disputed Paulines, for example, comparison of doublets and "synoptic" texts in Colossians and Ephesians or 1 Timothy and Titus might yield new possibilities for understanding the origins and interrelationships of these documents and the composition of epistles in general. There is a great deal of potential (as Dennis Ronald MacDonald has shown) in comparison of the oral legends about Paul and the specific ambiguity of the pastorals. A source-criticism modeled on the study of the synoptics can, of course, yield a great deal of insight into the epistles' incorporation and redaction of preexisting hymns, such as Colossians 1:15–16.

More striking to me, however, are the implications such comparisons awaken toward what we *can't* achieve in Pauline studies. Any construction of the historical Paul is limited by the bias and location of the investigating scholar. The recognition of the discrete categories of coherence and contingency only magnifies the complexity. Recognizing that Paul is not *homo religiosus* but is located in a particular cultural moment that influences his theology may make reconstructions of him more resonant with his culture, but they only do so by making the historical Paul dependent on the reconstruction of Roman imperial or Second Temple Jewish identity. Such contextual approaches only move the dilemmas backward one step; they do not eliminate the basic problem.

Further, and particularly acute for the discussion of the disputed Paulines, we are, from the nature of our texts, best able to articulate what or who Paul isn't. A fundamental question behind the debates over pseudepigraphic status is the comparison of what Paul could have said, or the language he "ordinarily" uses, against what he would *not* have said or composed. In terms of data about the historical Paul, we find the argument shifting toward what "Paul" is not. The process is one of scholarly exclusion.

The reconstructions of Paul take on the markers of lexicographic inquiry. Words do not have inherent "meaning" stored within them. Words only have meaning by their use, but every moment of discourse or use is distinct and context-driven. The meaning of a word is not static. Words do not carry fundamental meaning in and of themselves; words "mean" what they mean by the exclusion of other semantic possibilities. Words and language display nothing if not "specific ambiguity." We can only discover

"Paul" by his "context." We cannot clearly sift out or separate denotative and connotative elements of the final reconstruction. We cannot say who Paul "is"; we can only say what Paul (most likely) is not in a given reconstructed context. It should not surprise us, then, that, much as we cannot clearly and finally say what language "means" or how it functions, we also cannot reach consensus on the historical Paul.

Which, finally, brings us to questions of implications. If we acknowledge that language is neither static nor finite in application, nor precisely bounded in its implication, we realize that, ultimately, we must evaluate language by its effectiveness in use and its ethical potential. Clearly, we can see that there are ethical implications to any reconstruction of Paul. In our inquiry, I would suggest, we are wisest when we first concede what we cannot discover about Paul. Such an approach introduces the particular humility and plasticity of a reconstructed Paul that is both open to new scrutiny and attuned to ethical potentialities.

Further Reading

Since this book has been written for the non-specialist, the general reader, and the beginning (university) student, it seemed best to include an annotated guide for further reading and not the traditional list of "works cited." The following is, then, broken into two sections. Part I, General Reference, is an overview of some standard resources and reference works with material relevant to the study of Paul and the study of the history of Pauline scholarship. I have subdivided this portion into several parts and annotated most of the entries. I have limited this presentation to materials that are widely available to an English-speaking reader. Many of them can be found (or accessed) at a reasonable public library; most all of them could be found in any quality library at a university that offers courses in biblical studies. These lists are in no way comprehensive, but they will provide a good starting place for investigation.

Part II, Some Recommended Reading, is a list of titles that in my opinion are interesting and useful for the study of Paul. It is not a comprehensive list of works I used in the preparation of this volume. I have chosen to focus on books that are widely available. Many of these will, again, be found in local, well-stocked libraries. I have avoided listing books in German, French, Italian, or other languages of modern scholarship. I have been highly selective in my inclusion of journal articles, preferring those that are widely reprinted or anthologized. I have tried as much as possible to include books which are not overly technical or which assume substantial skill with biblical languages. Some have been selected because of their frequent citation in Pauline studies. Some have been chosen, quite frankly, because I find them unusually engaging. The major, relevant, books on Paul written by scholars that I discuss in this book are included in this list as well.

Arguably, I have omitted many of the items that are the lifeblood of serious biblical scholarship. Again, my intention is not to be exhaustive; I hope to be providing a map for independent exploration. I am confident that the works below will be an able gateway to the broader realm of biblical scholarship in general and Pauline studies in particular. I would hope for nothing more than that budding students of Paul would read their way beyond my listing here and learn enough to find the weaker spots in my own "brief history."

Translations of Bible passages, throughout, are my own, based on the Greek text of the United Bible Societies (4th edition) and the Hebrew text of the German Bible Society's *Biblia Hebraica Stuttgartensia*.

I General Reference

Internet resources

While there is an astonishing amount of useful material on the web, beginning students should always be cautious with using internet resources. Posters of these materials often do use standard practices of peer-evaluation in their content; they may not have any of the complex skills and specialized training of credentialed scholars. This is not to say that their work is "bad," merely that it should be used with caution. Beginning students, however, are those least equipped to evaluate content. The following three websites, however, are all produced by scholars and vetted by scholars. Even more valuable, they are veritable treasuretroves of links to other sites (which are, in turn, very often posted and vetted by scholars).

NT Gateway <www.ntgateway.com>. Maintained by Mark Goodacre of Duke University, this website is very much the "gold standard" for internet resources on the Bible. This is clearly an excellent first stop.

The Paul Page <www.thepaulpage.com>. Prepared by Mark M. Mattison, this is one of the longest and most exhaustive of websites that offer critical bibliographies of scholarship on Paul. It is an excellent site.

The Paul Project <http://thirdmill.org/paul/default.asp/category/paul>. A good survey of contemporary work on Paul.

Commentaries

Interpreting biblical text can be a very complicated task which often requires specialized skills in languages, culture, history, interpretive methodologies (hermeneutics), and more. Very few people are skilled enough to offer high-quality commentary on the whole Bible. The best commentaries are those where multiple authors are involved. Ideally, each author is selected for their particular book because of proven skill (via teaching and publication) with the relevant literature. Commentaries are sometimes written as regular, single-issue books. More commonly, they are produced in series edited by leading scholars in the field who have, again, proven consistent mettle by prior publication. The following is not comprehensive, but includes series that are commonly held in libraries and have stood the test of scholarly review.

The Anchor Bible Commentary. Edited by William Foxwell Albright and David Noel Freedman. (New York: Doubleday). Eclectic at times, but generally well respected. Technical at times, but widely available.

Hermeneia: A Critical and Historical Commentary on the Bible. Edited by Helmut Koester. (Philadelphia: Fortress Press). Again, highly eclectic. Most volumes represent European scholarship (many volumes are translations). Highly technical in places. Often skeptical of the historicity of the Bible.

The International Critical Commentary. Edited by J. A. Emerton and C. E. B. Cranfield. (Sheffield: T. & T. Clark). An "old standard" in many ways. Some volumes are highly technical. Some are very accessible. Many are dated. The series began at the turn of the prior century. Newer volumes have occasionally been commissioned to replace older, more dated volumes.

Interpretation: A Bible Commentary for Teaching and Preaching. Edited by James Luther Mays, Patrick D. Miller (OT), and Paul J. Achtemeier (NT). (Louisville, KY: John Knox Press). Overall this is balanced. Aimed at the general reader, pastor, or Bible teacher. Mainline Protestant. Not at all technical; deliberately accessible.

The New International Commentary on the New Testament. Edited by Ned B. Stonehouse, F. F. Bruce, and Gordon D. Fee. (Grand Rapids: Eerdmans). In general, evangelical. Thorough scholarship with copious annotation. Technical at times.

The New Testament Library. Edited by C. Clifton Black, John T. Carroll and Beverly Roberts Gaventa (Louisville: Westminster/John Knox). Generally well balanced and even. Tending toward mainline, Protestant theology (though mostly historical in approach). Again, at times technical.

Sacra Pagina. Edited by Daniel J. Harington, SJ (Collegeville, MN: Liturgical Press). Generally Roman Catholic. Very reasonable balance, however. Quality scholarship.

The Word Biblical Commentary. Edited by Bruce M. Metzger, David A. Hubbard, Glenn W. Barker, John D. W. Watts, and Ralph P. Martin (Nashville: Thomas Nelson). Generally conservative (evangelical). Thorough scholarship. Replete with bibliographies.

Dictionaries and general reference

Anchor Bible Dictionary. Edited by David N. Freedman. (New York: Doubleday). The former standard for biblical reference. Six volumes that include the work of several hundred scholars. Complete bibliographies. Though replaced by the *The New Interpreter's Bible Dictionary* (see below), it is still a remarkable resource (and widely available).

Dictionary of Paul and his Interpreters. Edited by Gerald F. Hawthorne, Ralph P. Martin, and Daniel G. Reid. (Downer's Grove: Intervarsity Press). A brilliant reference source for all things Paul. Most articles are accompanied by extensive bibliography. The volume trends toward evangelical scholarship but is, on the whole, very balanced.

The New Interpreter's Bible Dictionary. Edited by Katherine Doob Sakenfeld, Samuel E. Balantine, et al. (Nashville: Abingdon). The current standard for biblical reference. This multi-volume work has a series of wonderful, complete entries supplemented with exacting bibliographies.

Major scholarly journals

The frontline of biblical scholarship occurs in serial publications – most being published four times per year – that print "peer-reviewed" articles. Once submitted (and approved), all articles are then sent to other scholars who vet their contents. Peer-reviewed publications are the most carefully and most rigorously prepared work in scholarship.

Access to them, however, can be challenging to the non-specialist. Two major databases are highly useful. The first is the database of the American Theological Library Association (ATLAS). This database is now published electronically. A second major resource is the internet-based search engine JSTOR. Many journals now publish electronically; their tables of contents can be viewed for free via the web, and individual articles can be purchased for a nominal access fee. Major public and nearly all university libraries also offer "inter-library loan," where photocopies of articles can be exchanged, for an even lower fee. Most well-appointed university libraries where biblical studies courses are taught will have access to both JSTOR and ATLAS.

Bible and Critical Theory. A relatively new, internet-only journal, this focuses on essays that employ cutting-edge methodologies for biblical readings.

Biblical Interpretation. The focus is largely on essays that explore alternative methods of biblical interpretation.

Catholic Biblical Quarterly. As the title may suggest, the leading peer-review journal for Catholic biblical scholarship. This by no means suggests that all the authors or editors are Catholic.

Journal of Biblical Literature. The showpiece scholarly journal of the oldest modern professional association of Bible scholars.

New Testament Studies. An elite, peer-reviewed journal for New Testament studies.

Novum Testamentum. The companion to *Vetus Testamentum*. A standard peer-reviewed journal.

Zeitschrift für die Neutestamentliche Wissenschaft. Despite the German title (which translates as "Journal for New Testament Scholarship"), this journal is often held in English-speaking university libraries. Many of its articles are printed in English.

Miscellaneous

The following items, in some ways, didn't seem to fit the categories of "commentary." Not specifically themselves interpreting the

Bible, they are surveys or anthologies of the scholarship on the Bible. In other words, they could be said to be commentaries on commentaries.

Ancient Christian Commentary on Scripture. Edited by Thomas Oden. (Downer's Grove: Intervarsity). This series is a selected anthology of Christian commentary on biblical text. Note: it is *not* exhaustive.

Blackwell Bible Commentaries. Edited by John Sawyer, Christopher Rowland, Judith Kovacs, and David M. Gunn (New York: Wiley-Blackwell). A wonderful series that surveys the use of the biblical text through several centuries. This series focuses on both biblical scholarship and popular culture.

The Church's Bible. Edited by Robert Wilken (Grand Rapids: Eerdmans). Similar to the ACCS, this series concentrates on biblical commentaries and has longer excerpts.

The Queer Bible Commentary. Edited by Deryn Guest, Robert E. Gossa, Mona West, and Thomas Bohace (London: SCM Press, 2006). This commentary offers readings of biblical texts from the perspective of alternative sexualities. Given Paul's central location in contemporary debates on this subject, his work is treated in multiple places.

Women's Bible Commentary. Edited by Carol A. Newsome and Sharon Ringe (San Francisco: HarperSanFrancisco, 1998). A good resource for commentary on Paul from a feminist perspective.

II Some Recommended Reading

Aageson, James W. *Paul, the Pastoral Epistles, and the Early Church*. Peabody, MA: Hendrickson, 2008.

Agamben, Giorgio. *Homo Sacer: Sovereign Power and Bare Life*. Trans. Daniel Heller-Roazen. Stanford, CA: Stanford University Press, 1995.

Agamben, Giorgio. *The Time That Remains: A Commentary on the Letter to the Romans*. Trans. Patricia Dailey. Stanford, CA: Stanford University Press, 2005.

Auerbach, Erich. *Mimesis: The Representation of Reality in Western Literature*, 50th anniversary edn. Trans. Willard R. Trask with foreword by Edward W. Said. Princeton, NJ: Princeton University Press, 2003.

Augustine. *Augustine of Romans*. Atlanta, GA: Society of Biblical Literature, 1982.

Augustine. *City of God*. Penguin Classics. New York: Penguin, 1984.

Augustine. *Confessions*. Trans. Henry Chadwick. Oxford World Classics. New York: Oxford University Press, 1998.

Badiou, Alain. *St. Paul: The Foundation of Universalism*. Trans. Ray Brassier. Stanford, CA: Stanford University Press, 2003.

Barth, Karl. *The Epistle to the Romans*. Trans. E. C. Hoskyns. New York: Oxford University Press, 1968.

Bassler, Jouette. *Navigating Paul: An Introduction to Key Theological Concepts*. Louisville, KY: Westminster/John Knox, 2007.

Baur, Ferdinand C. *Paul the Apostle of Jesus Christ*. Trans. A. Menzies. London: Translation Fund Library, 1876. Contains the essay "Hebraists, Hellenists and Catholics."

Baur, Ferdinand C. *Paul: His Life and Works*, 2 vols. London: Williams & Norgate, 1875.

Beker, J. Christiaan. *Paul the Apostle: The Triumph of God in Life and Thought*. Philadelphia: Fortress Press, 1998.

Blackman, Edwin C. *Marcion and his Influences*. Eugene, OR: Wipf & Stock, 2004.

Boyarin, Daniel. *A Radical Jew: Paul and the Politics of Identity*. Berkeley: University of California Press, 1994.

Brooten, Bernadette. "Paul and the Law: How Complete Was the Departure?" *Princeton Seminary Bulletin*, supplement to issue 1 (1990), 71–89.

Bruce, F. F. *Paul: Apostle of the Heart Set Free*. Grand Rapids: Eerdmans, 1977.

Bultmann, Rudolf. *Kerygma and Myth*. San Francisco: Harpers, 1961.

Callahan, Allen D. *Embassy of Onesimus: The Letter of Paul to Philemon*. Valley Forge, PA: Trinity Press, International, 1997.

Campbell, Douglas A. *The Quest for Paul's Gospel: A Suggested Strategy*. Journal for the Study of the New Testament, supplement series 274. Sheffield: Sheffield Academic Press, 2005.

Campbell, William S., Peter S. Hawkins, and Brenda Deen Schildgen. *Medieval Readings of Romans*. Harrisburg: T. & T. Clark, 2007.

Castelli, Elizabeth A. *Imitating Paul: A Discourse of Power*. Louisville, KY: Westminster/John Knox, 1991.

Chilton, Bruce. *Rabbi Paul: An Intellectual Biography*. New York: Doubleday, 2004.

Conybeare, W. J., and J. S. Howson. *The Life and Epistles of St. Paul*. Grand Rapids: Eerdmans, n.d.

Crossan, John Dominic, and Jonathan L. Reed. *In Search of Paul*. San Francisco: HarperSanFrancisco, 2004.

Crossan, John Dominic. *The Historical Jesus: The Life of a Mediterranean Jewish Peasant*. Edinburgh: T. & T. Clark, 1991.

Davies, W. D. *Paul and Rabbinic Judaism: Some Rabbinic Elements in Pauline Theology*. Philadelphia: Fortress Press, 1980.

Deming, Wil. *Paul on Marriage and Celibacy: The Hellenistic Background of 1 Corinthians 7*, 2nd edn. Grand Rapids: Eerdmans, 2004.

Derrida, Jacques. "Circumfession." Pp. 3–315 in Geoffrey Bennington and Jacques Derrida, *Jacques Derrida: Religion and Postmodernism*. Trans. Geoffrey Bennington. Chicago: University of Chicago Press, 1993.

Donfried, Karl P. *Paul, Thessalonica, and Early Christianity*. New York: T. & T. Clark, 2002.

Donfried, Karl P. *The Romans Debate*. Minneapolis: Augsburg, 1977.

Dunn, James D. G. *The Theology of Paul the Apostle*. Grand Rapids: Eerdmans, 1998.

Ehrman, Bart D. *Peter, Paul and Mary Magdalene: The Followers of Jesus in History and Legend*. New York: Oxford, 2006.

Elliott, Neil. *The Arrogance of Nations: Reading Romans in the Shadow of the Empire*. Minneapolis: Fortress Press, 2008.

Engberg-Pedersen, Troels, ed. Troels. *Paul in his Hellenistic Context*. New York: T. & T. Clark, 2002.

Engberg-Pedersen, Troels. *Paul and the Stoics*. Louisville, KY: Westminster/John Knox, 2000.

Esler, Philip F. *Conflict and Identity in Romans*. Minneapolis: Fortress Press, 2003.

Fee, Gordon D. *Paul, the Spirit, and the People of God*. Peabody, MA: Hendrickson, 1996.

Fitzmeyer, Joseph A. *Pauline Theology: A Brief Sketch*. Engelwood, NJ: Prentice-Hall, 1968.

Fortna, R. T., and Beverly Gaventa, eds. *The Conversation Continues*. Nashville: Abingdon, 1990.

Fredriksen, Paula. "Allegory and Reading God's Book: Paul and Augustine on the Destiny of Israel." Pp. 124–65 in *Allegory and Cultural Change*. Edited by Jon Whitman (Leiden: Brill, 2000).

Fredriksen, Paula. "Paul and Augustine: Conversion Narratives, Orthodox Traditions and the Retrospective Self." *Journal of Theological Studies*, 37 (1983), 187–206.

Fredriksen, Paula. "*Secundum Carnem*: God, History and Israel in the Theology of Augustine." Pp. 187–206 in *The Limits of Ancient Christianity*. Edited by W. Klingshirn and Mark Vessey (Ann Arbor, MI: University of Michigan Press, 1999).

Furnish, Victor Paul. *The Moral Theology of St. Paul*. Nashville: Abingdon, 1985.

Gager, John G. *Reinventing Paul*. New York: Oxford, 2000.

Gaventa, Beverly Roberts. *Our Mother St. Paul*. Louisville, KY: Westminster/ John Knox, 2007.

Georgi, Dieter. *Remembering the Poor: The History of Paul's Collection for Jerusalem*. Trans. I. Racz. Nashville: Abingdon, 1992.

Glover, T. R. *Paul of Tarsus*. Peabody, MA: Hendrickson, 2002.

Goulder, Michael D. *Paul and the Competing Mission in Corinth*. Peabody, MA: Hendrickson, 2001.

Griffith-Jones, Robin. *The Gospel According to Paul: The Creative Genius who Brought Jesus to the World*. San Francisco: HarperSanFrancisco, 2004.

Hamerton-Kelly, Robert G. *Sacred Violence: Paul's Hermeneutic of the Cross*. Minneapolis: Fortress Press, 1992.

Hays, Richard B. *Echoes of Scripture in the Letters of Paul*. New Haven: Yale University Press, 1989.

Horsely, Richard A., ed. *Paul and Politics: Ekklesia, Israel, Imperium, Interpretation*. Harrisburg, PA: Trinity Press, 2000.

Horsely, Richard A., ed. *Paul and the Roman Imperial Order*. New York: Continuum, 2004.

Jennings, Theodore W. *Reading Derrida/Thinking Paul: On Justice*. Cultural Memory in the Present. Stanford: Stanford University Press, 2006.

Jervell, Jacob. *The Unknown Paul: Essays on Luke–Acts and Early Christian History*. Minneapolis, MN: Augsburg, 1984.

Jewett, Robert A. *A Chronology of Paul's Life*. Philadelphia: Fortress Press, 1979.

Johnson, Luke Timothy. *The First and Second Letters to Timothy: A New Translation, Introduction and Commentary*. Anchor Bible 35A. New York: Doubleday, 2001.

Johnson, Matthew, James Noel, and Demetrius K. Williams, eds. *Onesimus our Brother: Reading Religion, Race and Slavery in Philemon*. Minneapolis: Fortress Press, 2009.

Jones, Amos Jr.. *Paul's Message of Freedom: What Does It Mean to the Black Churches?* Valley Forge, PA: Judson, 1984.

Keck, Leander E. *Paul and his Letters*, 2nd, rev., edn. Proclamation Commentaries. Philadelphia: Fortress Press, 1988.

Knox, John. *Chapters in a Life of Paul*. Nashville: Abingdon, 1980.

Kraemer, Ross Shepherd *Her Share of the Blessings: Women's Religions among Pagans, Jews and Christians in the Greco-Roman World*. New York: Oxford University Press, 1992.

Kraemer, Ross Shepherd, ed.. *Maenads, Martyrs, Matrons, Monastics: A Sourcebook on Women's Religions in the Greco-Roman World*. Philadelphia: Fortress Press, 1988.

Kreitzer, Larry J. *Pauline Images in Fiction and Film*. Sheffield: Sheffield Academic Press, 1999.

Kreitzer, Larry J. *Philemon*. Sheffield: Sheffield Phoenix, 2008.

Lake, Kirsopp. *The Earlier Epistles of St. Paul*, 2nd edn. London: Rivingtons, 1965.

Layton, Bentley. *The Gnostic Scriptures: A New Translation with Annotation and Introductions* New York: Doubleday, 1995.

Levine, Amy-Jill, and Marianne Blickenstaff. *A Feminist Companion to Paul*. Cleveland: Pilgrim Press, 2004.

Lüdemann, Gerd. *Paul, Apostle to the Gentiles: Studies in Chronology*. Philadelphia: Fortress Press, 1984.

Luther, Martin. *Commentary on Romans*. Luther Classic Commentaries. New York: Kregel Classics, 2003.

Luther, Martin. *Galatians*. Crossway Classic Commentaries. New York: Crossway Books, 1998.

Luther, Martin. *The Jews and their Lies*. Philadelphia: Liberty Bell, 2004.

Lyall, Francis. *Slaves, Citizens, Sons: Legal Metaphors in the Epistles*. Grand Rapids, MI: Zondervan, 1984.

Lyotard, Jean-François. *The Postmodern Condition: A Report on Knowledge*. Trans. Geoff Bennington and Brian Massumi. Minneapolis: University of Minnesota Press, 1984.

Malina, Bruce J., and Jerome H. Neyrey. *Portraits of Paul: An Archaeology of Ancient Personality*. Louisville, KY: Westminster/John Knox, 1996.

Marchal, Joseph A. *Hierarchy, Unity and Imitation: A Feminist Rhetorical Analysis of Power Dynamics in Paul's Letters to the Philippians*. Atlanta: Society of Biblical Literature, 2006.

Marchal, Joseph A. *The Politics of Heaven: Women, Gender and Empire in the Study of Paul*. Minneapolis: Fortress Press, 2008.

Marshall, I. Howard. *A Critical and Exegetical Commentary on the Pastoral Epistles*. International Critical Commentary. Edinburgh: T. & T. Clark, 1999.

Martin, Dale B. *Sex and the Single Savior: Gender and Sexuality in Biblical Interpretation*. Louisville, KY: Westminster/John Knox, 2008.

Martin, Dale B. *The Corinthian Body*. New Haven: Yale University Press, 1995.

Meeks, Wayne A., and John Fitzgerald. *The First Urban Christians: The Social World of the Apostle Paul*, 2nd edn. New Haven: Yale University Press, 2003.

Meeks, Wayne A., and John Fitzgerald. *The Writings of St. Paul*, 2nd edn. New York: Norton, 2007.

Moore, Stephen D. *God's Beauty Parlor*. Stanford: Stanford University Press, 2001.

Mounce, William D. *Pastoral Epistles*. Word Biblical Commentary 46. Nashville: Nelson, 2000.

Murphy-O'Connor, Jerome. *St. Paul's Corinth: Texts and Archaeology*. Wilmington, DE: Glazier Press, 1983.

Origen. *Commentary on Romans*. Edited by Thomas Schenck. Fathers of the Church. New York: Catholic University Press of America, 2001.

Pagels, Elaine H. *The Gnostic Paul: Gnostic Exegesis of Paul's Letters*. Philadelphia: Fortress Press, 1975.

Pfitzner, Victor C. *Paul and the Agon Motif*. Leiden: Brill, 1963.

Pippin, Tina. *Apocalyptic Bodies: The Biblical End of the World in Text and Image*. New York:

Pseudo-Dionysius. *The Complete Works*. Classics of Western Spirituality. New York: Paulist Press, 1987.

Räisänen, Heikki. *Paul and the Law*. Philadelphia: Fortress Press, 1983.

Ramsay, William M. *Pauline and Other Studies in Early Christian History*. New York: Hodder & Stoughton, n.d.

Ramsay, William M. *St. Paul the Traveler and Roman Citizen*. Edited by Mark Wilson. Grand Rapids: Kregel, 2001.

Roetzel, Calvin J. *Paul: A Jew on the Margins*. Louisville, KY: Westminster/John Knox, 2003.

Roetzel, Calvin J. *Paul: The Man and the Myth*. Minneapolis, MN: Fortress Press, 1999.

Roetzel, Calvin J. *The Letters of Paul: Conversations in Context*, 4th edn. Louisville, KY: Westminster/John Knox, 1998.

Roetzel, Calvin J. Routledge, 1999.

Sanders, E. P. *Paul and Palestinian Judaism*. Minneapolis: Fortress Press, 1971.

Schmithals, Walter. *Paul and James*. Trans. D. M. Barton. London: SCM, 1965.

Schüssler Fiorenza, Elisabeth. *In Memory of Her: A Feminist Theological Reconstruction of Christian Origins*, 10th edn. New York: Crossroad, 1994.

Schweitzer, Albert. *The Quest of the Historical Jesus: A Critical Study of its Progress from Reimarus to Wrede*. 1915; London: SCM Press, 2000.

Segal, Alan F. *Paul the Convert: The Apostolate and Apostasy of Saul the Pharisee*. New Haven: Yale University Press, 1990.

Stanley, Christopher. *Arguing with Scripture: The Rhetoric of Quotations in the Letters of Paul*. New York: T. & T. Clark, 2004.

Stendahl, Krister. "The Apostle Paul and the Introspective Consciousness of the West." *Harvard Theological Review*, 56 (1963), 199–215.

Stendahl, Krister. *Paul Among the Jews and Gentiles, and Other Essays.* Philadelphia: Fortress Press, 1976.

Taubes, Jacob. *The Political Theology of Paul.* Trans. Dana Hollander. Cultural Memory in the Present. Stanford: Stanford University Press, 2004.

Theissen, Gerd. *The Social Setting of Pauline Christianity.* Philadelphia: Fortress Press, 1982.

Tucker, Ruth. *From Jerusalem to Irian Jaya: A Biographical History of Christian Missions.* Grand Rapids, MI: Zondervan, 2004.

Von Harnack, Adolf. *What Is Christianity?* Fortress Texts in Modern Theology. Philadelphia: Fortress Press, 1986.

Walsh, Richard. *Finding St. Paul in Film.* New York: T. & T. Clark, 2005.

Weaver, D. "From Paul to Augustine: Romans 5:12 in Early Christian Exegesis." *St. Vladimir's Theological Quarterly*, 3 (1983), 187–206.

Welborn, L. L. *Paul, the Fool of Christ: A Study of 1 Corinthians 1–4 in the Comic-Philosophic Tradition.* Early Christianity in Context 293. New York: T. & T. Clark, 2005.

Wimbush, Vincent L. *Paul the Worldly Ascetic.* Macon, GA: Mercer University Press, 1987.

Wire, Antoinette. *Corinthian Women Prophets.* Minneapolis: Fortress Press, 1990.

Witherington, Ben III. *Conflict and Community in Corinth: A Socio-Rhetorical Commentary on 1 and 2 Corinthians.* Grand Rapids: Eerdmans, 1995.

Witherington, Ben III. *The Paul Quest: The Renewed Search for the Jew of Tarsus.* Downer's Grove: Intervarsity Press, 2001.

Index of New Testament Citations

Index of Subjects and Proper Names

Ephesus, city of 31, 33
Ephraim, ancient Christian
    writer 92
Erasmus 155–6
Erastus, city treasurer at
    Corinth 22
eschatology, ancient Christian 64,
    112–13
ethnicity 207–8
Eucharist 132–4
Eusebius of Caesarea 86, 93,
    95–6, 100, 186
Eve, biblical character 116,
    131, 203
Exodus, biblical book 107, 177

Fee, Gordon 209
first missionary journey 30
Fitzgerald, John 210
Foucault, Michel 203
France 127
Francis, St. 145
Freud, Sigmund 212
Friedrickson, Paula 102

Galatia, Roman province/region
    2, 8, 23–4, 55, 62, 200
Galatians, epistle of 36, 47, 73, 82,
    87, 94, 103–5, 107, 120, 141,
    154, 159–60, 163, 172, 177,
    192, 194, 216, 219–20, 226
    Baur's view 2–3, 8
    synopsis of contents 54–6
Gallio, proconsul of Achaia 31
Gamaliel, teacher of Paul 19, 34
gender and sexual preference
    204–6
Genesis, biblical book 94, 110,
    115–16, 122, 131
gentile believers in Jesus 16
    conflicts with Jewish believers 55

Germany 127–8, 148, 185
Giuliani, Rudolph 215
Gnostic(s), Gnosticism 77–9, 87, 99
grace and law 106, 158, 189, 199
Gregory XIV, Pope 169
Groot, Hugo de 155

Hall of Tyrannus (Paul's
    school) 31
Hebrew Bible/scriptures 78, 81,
    82, 83, 102, 106–8, 121,
    127, 130, 152, 158, 160,
    163, 199
Hebrews, letter to the 93–4, 102,
    141, 192
    Pauline authorship of 72–3
Hegel, G. W. F. 189
hegemony 166
Heidegger, Martin 216
Helena (mother of Constantine I)
    144
heresy, defined 76
Hermas, author of "The
    Shepherd" (non-canonical
    book) 99, 100
higher critic(s), higher
    criticism 165
Hilduin 129
Hippo, African city 102–3
Hippolytus, ancient Christian
    writer 75, 81, 87
Hobbes, Thomas 216
homosexuality see gender and
    sexual preference
Horsley, Richard 210
Huckabee, Mike 215

Ialdabaoth, Gnostic deity 77–8
iconography 126–7
Irenaeus, ancient Christian
    writer 75, 81, 87, 96

MacDonald, Dennis Ronald 228
Macedonia (Greece), Roman
    province 31, 54
"Macedonian Man" 31
"man of lawlessness" 65
Manicheans 102–4
Marcion, marcionite 74–5, 77–8,
    87, 91, 99, 194
    anti-Judaism 79
    canon 81–3
    non-use of the pastorals 82–3
    significance of 83–4
    teachings of 78–83
Mark, Gospel of 69, 133, 140, 175
Mark *see* John Mark
Marshall, I. Howard 209
Martin, Dale 206
Mary Magdalene 84
Matthew, Gospel of 117, 133, 140
McCain, John 214
Meeks, Wayne 210
Mesopotamia 128
metanarrative(s) 185
Milton, John 146
missionary societies 165
modernism 184
Monad (Gnostic deity) 77
Monica (Augustine's mother) 102
Moore, George Foot 171
Moore, Stephen D. 206, 217
Mosaic Covenant 160–1
Moses, biblical character 107
Mounce, Edwin 209
mysticism 143–4

natural theology 132
Neoplatonism *see* Platonism
Nero, Roman emperor 60, 86
Nevi'im 81
"New Perspective" on Paul 4,
    199–201, 222

Nicaea, Nicene Creed 77, 92–3,
    96, 99, 100, 221
Nicholas of Cusa 146
Nicopolis, Roman city 36
Noah, biblical character 107

Obama, Barak 216
old and new covenants 126, 141
Old Testament 101, 127, 130,
    169
    see also Hebrew Bible/scriptures
Onesimus, associate of Paul 61–2,
    175–7, 178–81
ordinance 134
Origen, Christian exegete and
    scholar 72, 93–5, 101
orthodoxy 75–6, 96
Ostian Way 86

Pagels, Elaine 82, 87
Palin, Sarah 215
Passover 135
pastoral letters 47, 80, 101, 128,
    167, 186, 209, 226
    scholarly views on authorship
        of 49–50
    synopsis of contents 66–8
    see also Timothy; Titus
Paul
    asceticism of 119
    conflicts with Jewish leaders 31
    conflicts with pagan
        religions 31
    cultural context 209
    death of 60, 82
    first-century views on 44–6
    Greco-Roman cultural
        context 26–7
    historical problems 7–8
    illnesses 14
    imprisonment of 21–3

Paul (*cont'd*)
  intellectualism vs. mysticism 124, 128
  and Judaism 4, 219–23
  miracles of 32
  mission in Greece 31
  model for cloistered ascetics 139
  model for missionaries/ missions 166–7
  model for resistant ideology 83–4, 157–8, 161, 215, 223
  mystic journey to the third heaven 121–2
  Nazarite and other temple vows 34
  Pharisee background 19, 33
  physical description of 86, 126–7
  political views 197
  popular and historical views of 14, 20
  Roman citizenship of 32, 34
  views of women 36
  views on sex and marriage 90–1
  views on slavery 178
  as Weberian "type" 216
  "year of Paul" (2008–9) 9
  see also Corpus Paulinum
Pauline "school" 51
Pelagius 113–14, 116–18
Pennsylvania Bible Society 169
Peter, apostle 17, 33–4, 53, 70, 80, 85–7, 97, 99, 136–8, 140, 150, 152, 172–3, 189
  epistles of (canonical) 82
Philemon, biblical character 175–7, 178–81
  abolitionist views of 179–82
  letter to 23, 36, 47, 67, 174–82

synopsis of contents 61–2
Philippi, city of 1, 25, 31
  financial support of Paul 59
Philippians, letter to 36, 47, 67, 172
  synopsis of contents 61
Phoebe 177, 202
Pilate, biblical character 140
Pippin, Tina 64, 113
Plato 102, 110
Platonism, Neoplatonism, and early Christianity 64, 110, 112, 114, 120, 130
Pleroma (Gnostic deity) 77–8
Polycarp, ancient Christian bishop 68
Pontus, Roman province 74–5
post-colonialism 207–8
postmodern, postmodernism 184–6, 195, 211–13
Praetorian guard 23
primitivists, primitivism 156
Priscilla (also Prisca), associate of Paul 31, 202
prison epistles 47
  see also Colossians; Ephesians
pseudepigraphy
  ancient views of 91
  defined 88
Pseudo-Dionysius the Areopagite (St. Denis) 100, 120–4, 137, 146

Radbertus 135
Ramsay, William 3–4, 170–1
Ratramnus 135
Reed, Jonathan 1–2
regula fide 156
Religious Trust Society 168
Revelation 100
  see also Apocalypse of John

Titus, associate of Paul 34–6, 47, 226, 228
  letters to 36–7, 47, 59, 100, 137
tongue-speaking/ecstatic speech 52, 128
Torah 81
Trinity, Trinitarian 75–6, 96
Trophimus, associate of Paul 32
Tübingen, Tübingen school 171, 173–4
Tucker, Ruth 168
Turkey 54–5, 127–8
Turner, Nat 180
typology 93, 103, 108, 130

United Bible Societies 169

Valentinus, ancient Christian 77
Vincent of Lérins 75
von Harnack, Adolf 186–9, 191, 222–3

Weber, Max 215–16
Whitehead, Alfred 102
Wittenberg 148, 151
women in Pauline letters and communities 52–3, 201–4
Wyckoff, W. H. 170

Yahweh (Hebrew deity) 78

Zechariah, Hebrew prophet 16
Zwingli, Ulrich 156